LIFESHIFT

LIFESHIFT

Doing The Dream

PLUS Directory of 300 Holistic Resources

Andrew Ferguson

Author of 'Creating Abundance'

Cartoons by Barbara Lynne Price

Breakthrough Publications

First published in 1999 by Breakthrough Publications,
a division of Breakthrough Centre Ltd,
Wester Marchhead, Elgin, Moray, IV30 8XE

The moral right of the author has been asserted

A catalogue record for this book
is available from the British Library

ISBN 0 9536878 0 5

Cartoons, Design & Cover by Barbara Lynne Price

Layout and typesetting by Ex Libris Press
Bradford on Avon, Wiltshire

Typeset in Palatino and Lucida Sans

Printed in Britain by
Cromwell Press
Trowbridge, Wiltshire

Many of the cartoons in this book are also available as Postcards and T-shirts. Call 020 8347 7484 for details of these and other LifeShift services.

CONTENTS

In memory of Rosemary Evans, née Sich

ACKNOWLEDGMENTS

Many people contribute directly or indirectly to the production of a new book. Especially with a self-help book as this is, based on thousands of client interactions, it is often hard to acknowledge the source of ideas. They almost seem to float in the ether.

Several people and their ideas are however referred to in the text, and their contribution to the evolution of holistic enterprise is gratefully acknowledged here. In most cases the reference takes the form of a review, and wherever possible the material reviewed, or failing that a recent relevant text or address is included in the Resource Index. Some references have been collected verbatim, and over many years; the same principle applies here too.

In addition to acknowledging these antecedents and fellow travellers, I must acknowledge the support and encouragement of Barbara Lynne Price who has not only translated the text into such striking visual images, but read and constructively criticised the many rough, sometimes very rough, drafts of LifeShift.

I commend to you all those listed in the Resource Index, and I invite you to acknowledge yourself for LifeShifting.

Andrew Ferguson
Scotland 1999

CHAPTER 1

Living The Rhythm of Life

The rhythm of life changes every seven years or so, creating a series of life-phases. Each phase brings its own challenges to face, its own set of priorities and tasks. What has seemed important for the last seven years gradually pales into insignificance as a new phase of life beckons. These periods of "lifeshift" contain within them the confusion of lost clarity and security shaken. Letting go of what has become familiar can be painful and unsettling. We have invested heavily and formed attachments that structure our experience of life. And there are forces flowing through all our lives that require us to release the past so we can mature and engage with the future.

Watch the waves beating on the shore. There is an almost hypnotic rhythm, building to a climax with every seventh wave...just like our lives. Every seven years there is a cleansing that washes away the marks of earlier, smaller impacts and sets the scene for a whole new experience, something quite different. The music stops and we all change places.

The task for a 35 year old, changing or improving their life is qualitatively different to the task for a 42 or 28 year old. And the more of these changes you've missed come 42 or 49, the more of a challenge mid-life will pose. Old cycles that may have been suppressed or neglected at the time will have to be relived and genuinely faced now.

Every individual also has their own rhythm, arriving early or late for certain phases, lingering longer with some periods because they are comfortable or contain a major life challenge. And we all have personal cycles defined by some early perceived trauma. We also have an overall colouring to our lives, an element of say the age 49-56 cycle in our make-up which affects how we experience all the other phases.

Beneath the individual rhythm, the rhythm of life is ticking away. Life then is very fluid, not the rigid road map we often like to imagine it is. We like to lay down railway tracks and roads, having commonly had the first stage of our lives run by other people's railway tracks. We have a clear sense of some idealised progression through life, and even talk about a career "path". We will return to this in Chapter 2 and see what has happened to this quaint idea in the last 25 years. Meanwhile there is some advantage in pursuing the metaphor of a road map, because it can form a bridge from our present perception of how life works to a new, more flexible perception that will work better for us.

There seems to be this network of roads and lanes, weaving through a varied landscape, connecting up all the places we know. Some places along our path are familiar landmarks where we feel comfortable. Some have exciting connotations for us. Some are "roads less travelled". And some are painful spots we'd rather forget, but which still have an impact on us.

The path you are pursuing right now may have been a conscious choice at one time, or it may have been less thoughtfully taken, under pressure or to escape an even less attractive set of circumstances. Whether your path now seems to have been a mistake or just an experience you might now move on and away from, it can still exert a powerful tug on you. It represents income, security, investment, familiarity. "Better the devil you know than the devil you don't," says a voice somewhere inside.

"LifeShift" is about taking a new road, gratefully acknowledging the service of previous road-makers and asserting that your path now takes you elsewhere, maybe to build roads of your own or to head off the beaten track altogether.

The journey through life can be a headlong affair, not so much driving as driven along the road. As we swept along, there were often intriguing or barely visible alternatives we might have opted for. But we felt we had somewhere else to go, and were in a hurry to arrive there. So we had to take the motorway. Not infrequently we found ourselves almost mesmerised by the idea of going with the crowd, following the car in front, measuring our progress against others. The fast lane has had a certain appeal too, but as we sped along faster and faster to get ahead of ourselves and the rest, we missed some turnings and arrived somewhere that is so similar to the place we came from, with so many other people, that we may wonder why we ever thought "there" would be better than "here". At a gentler pace, and with less pressure to get somewhere, we might not have dashed past so many other exciting possibilities.

The further you drive on your road to somewhere, the more committed you become to it. Each turning you drive past closes a door to alternatives, and, yes, opens the door to others. Changing direction now can feel like a major U-turn, a waste of all the time and effort you spent racing to your original destination. Is it unthinkable to abandon your Moscow, or will you release your attachment to the past in order to secure your future? Which is it to be? Retreat or defeat? The difficulty you have in rediscovering the intriguing possibilities you once held dear has far more to do with releasing the headlong motorway than with finding your way there. That possibility was also part of a previous life-phase, so you and it will have moved on. You will almost certainly have to find a version of it which reflects the life-phase you are now in. There is no going back, but there are ways of recreating now the experience you denied yourself then. This starts with a decision to take a new direction which honours you.

A New Way Forward

Next you will need to recognise what distracts you from taking a new direction, even when you are totally convinced it is the right decision. "LifeShift" has been written to help you do this. It is not one of those frustrating books or articles that describes the situation, shrugs its shoulders and leaves you without any tools or guidelines for action in your own life. We'll be your guide to a new way forward for you, identifying the path that is right for you, supporting you in releasing your attachment to the route you're growing out of. Our main job is to loosen the ties and brush away the distractions, doubts and fears that make you reluctant to leave even when you're ready to go. This takes vision and courage. You're not just changing your brand of toothpaste, so you need more than helpful little practical tips and other people's success stories. You need a guide who can accompany you to the depths of yourself.

Life is not a destination. Destinations are conclusions, endings, generally a disappointing anti-climax, until you realise that each destination is just the start of something new. Life then becomes a series of new departures, until it is neither a destination nor a departure, but a series of places to be in and experience. Each place is a joy, and your journey and your life becomes joyful. Joy, happiness, is important because it has the power to create the abundance you need to support your life. No amount of money will do this, because the more money you accumulate the more fear of loss you generate. Wealth, and the pursuit of money as an objective, is a need that is never sated. It controls you. Only joy has the power to create the abundance of a free spirit. Regenerating joy usually involves unravelling huge killjoy swathes of your life: it can take time...and volumes of courage. But what price a joyless life?

Most of the pitfalls to avoid and distractions to be overcome in re-inventing your life emanate from commonly accepted strategies for survival through wealth generation. And the particular hold they have on you at each stage of life is subtly different. We will be naming the culprits and suggesting new strategies for releasing their power over you, dispelling the modern myths around what it is to be successful.

You define your own success now. Those who have been held up as successes for the last 100 years are telling us it's not worth it. The modern day Mephistopheles doesn't have to wait for the next world: it's hell here! So much of the pain and heart-ache of modern life is caused by people trying to achieve someone else's prescription for success, or rebelling against it and putting nothing in its place. Sadly even when you win through you lose, because you've arrived "successfully" at a place you never wanted to be in the first place. And you lose because almost every step of the way has been miserable. Only a tiny percentage ever make it to the top, yet we have allowed ourselves to be conned into believing this to be the only way, dismissing what might have been right for us. The result is that the so-called winners are disenchanted, and the rest of us feel we have failed, because we didn't achieve these joyless dizzy heights.

The whole thing is an aberration.

Real life is an entirely different sort of journey. It is a journey where our task is to discover, and continually rediscover and re-invent, what our task is. You never discover this finally, because no sooner do you achieve clarity than a new dimension of the task reveals itself. It is a constant process of unpeeling new layers, deepening, broadening, enhancing and revolutionising.

Life begins with vision

There are periods of rest, but these are not so much a collapse and escape from the rat-race as an integral part of the music of life. As in music a rest is a short period in which we breathe out and release the tension before rebuilding it again. Music without rests is tedious. Tension is good. Stress is good. It means you're alive and active. Distress (which is what modern society wrongly calls stress) is not good. Distress is caused by working on the wrong task and not moving onto the right one, or working too hard or resting too long, or being where we feel we should be rather than where we actually are.

Distress is caused by believing in road-maps. But that map of roads to get somewhere is an illusion. It has restricted your vision. Think of it as an overlay sheet printed on perspex. You can just lift it off to reveal the unmapped terrain underneath. Then you can simply enjoy being where you are. This book then is a guide to being where you are, that recognises several dimensions, more perspex overlays, each representing a different way of looking at your life from your perspective and each needing to be lifted off so you can look beneath it. As you explore you find out more about your experience, your task, your lesson. As you see more you develop the muscle to see even further. Because as we shall see in Chapter 3, there are lessons and experiences for each stage of life, and for each energy that you can work with. Each stage of life typifies a particular energetic way of being and has a rhythm to it. Once you understand this, much of the mystery of life is revealed and anything becomes possible.

So throw away the old maps and start creating your own. Start living your own life!

What will have kept you reading this far is the desire to change, so we'll take that as read. You may be happy with some areas of your life, or none. There may just be one or two bits of it you want to change at present, or you may feel everything needs a thorough overhaul. Either way something always holds you back: and as you'll see as you carry on reading, that something is different at each new phase of life.

Vision is the Key

It takes something pretty powerful to carry you through the changes, to overcome the resistance that interferes with your desire to change. There is one *principal* ingredient whose absence stops those who desire change taking action to achieve it. There are plenty of varied distractions that conspire to knock you off course once this core ingredient is in place, and without the fundamental motivation this ingredient gives you the distractions will usually win. But once you have it in place, you have a power that will take you through. This will enable you to shoot the rapids, and finding it is one of the two primary foci of this book.

So why might you desire change, think and talk about it all the time, and still not do anything about it? What is this vital ingredient? Vision. If you do not have a sense of yourself being that changed person, if you do not have a sense of yourself being free to be whatever you wish, you will find yourself constantly dragged back down into the thin soup of mediocrity. This sense of yourself is what is meant by personal vision. If that vision of who you might be is not very strong, you will always end up being defined by others' perceptions and judgments of you.

This book is dedicated to you and your discovery of your personal vision of who you are now becoming. That vision is the motivating force, the engine, for your discovery of your task. And like your task, the discovery of your vision is a life-time's undertaking.

Life begins with vision. The possibility of you living the fullest life you might, discovering more and more layers of your extra-ordinary self, and being joyful begins when you make a contract with yourself to name and live your vision.

Far too much emphasis is given elsewhere to the "how" of living with vision, without enough attention being given to the discovery of a vision powerful enough to motor you *through* the how. The result is that most people either never start on the how or become futilely bogged down in it.

I have worked with thousands of people now over a period of nearly 20 years, and I have worked on myself too with growing awareness of what helps and what hinders. As a result I have no doubt that the principle reason for lack of fulfilment is the absence of a vision sufficiently realistic and powerfully desired to be worth seeing through to fulfilment. Time and again people have come to me with a muddle (or an idea they have not yet embraced and owned), sorted out for themselves the central core, the golden promise that makes their heart sing and astounded themselves and everyone else by the clarity, commitment and self-confidence with which they suddenly take charge of their lives. Often the breakthrough comes not during but after the session proving that nobody can do it for them. Nobody can tell them what it is. But there are those who can hold a space in which others can find their own power. The benefit for me has been seeing, thousands of times, what the blocks and pitfalls are at each phase of life. And that is the research on which this book is based.

Your life begins with you seeing, visualising, envisioning yourself differently. Not just talking about it, and certainly not whinging about why you personally can't, but allowing a clear picture of yourself to appear and come to life. Whatever life has given you thus far is what you have to work with first. Making it an excuse for inaction, wallowing in self-pity is not just self-defeating, it totally misses the point of how you take control of life.

What is it you most want to have happen in your life? Take a moment to jot down 10 different things to answer this question for you, without judgment or censorship. Better still do the exercise with a couple of friends, so one can prompt you to keep coming up with something else and the other can write it down for you.

The first answers you come up with are likely to be superficialities, but as you get nearer the bottom of the list, what you *really* want to have happen emerges. Put a circle round the answer that most truly expresses your deepest desire for life. Maybe it's not there yet and you need to let your subconscious mull it over for a bit. That's fine. This is not an exercise you do once and forget. It's a self-questioning you spend the rest of your life doing. It keeps evolving, shifting, deepening, changing as you grow, learn and understand yourself better.

Even so, see if for now you can encapsulate what you most want to have happen into a three-word phrase...which includes a verb. *Having* something happen implies that you will be taking some active part in this eventuality (verb), not just sitting back in a meditative (or morose) stew waiting for the universe to do you a favour (noun). Having something happen requires both action on your part, and allowing it into your life: doing and being open. You are *doing* this exercise, aren't you? Just reading about it isn't going to change anything. Engage! Get involved! Scare yourself!

Your three-word phrase might be something like 'Having fun, writing', 'Joyfully transforming work', 'Integrating Russian 'n' gardening', 'Fearlessly expressing musically'. The words suggest and build into a rich picture which is important for evolving vision. Vision means literally *seeing,* and what we see are pictures, not words or rational concepts. When we see more deeply we enter the realm of imagination. Here we have an image of ourselves as we might be, but much more than this we tap the wise insight of the magi, the true magicians who have the power to achieve change through the application of their will. The way you imagine yourself sets the parameters for what you may become. We are all magicians now.

Limiting your imagination limits what you may become. Unlimiting it opens up possibility, and above all else it opens you up to your next lesson or task. If you face this and press on, there will be more tasks. If not, check whether you have yet owned your vision. Are you telling yourself the truth, or are you applying conditions, saying in effect "This is what I want, as long as...it doesn't hurt, it doesn't cost, it doesn't require any effort on my part." When your stated vision does not happen, you just discover there is something else you were not aware of that is more important to you, something else you *actually* most want to have happen. If that's the truth and you like what you get, fine. Give the rest of your life to it. If not, if your energy is all being applied to something that increasingly depresses you, LifeShift! Either way this book will structure it for you.

Unwrapping the Vision

Your initial attempt at expressing your vision probably produces no more than a context in which something else can happen. Dedicating your life to ballet-dancing for instance only creates a context. *What* you do is context. *Why* you do it is what matters. *Why* you are a ballet-dancer - to express beauty, to face the ultimate challenge for you, to pioneer new possibility.

Each why in turn becomes a context for another deeper level of why. Why do you need expression, beauty or challenge? Clearly these things matter more to you than anything else, but why? Why do you care about them...more than anything else? Your life's task is to discover this, uncovering as the years go by more and more of yourself and your core why for being here. The clearer you are now and from here on why you wish what you wish, the more revealing and fulfilling your journey will be. You will understand the changes of context better, and why you are drawn to new pastures when you are. Doing your why is the route to fulfilment. It doesn't matter how apparently mundane or socially insignificant your context is: all that matters is how you work with it to manifest your why and reveal new levels of it.

It can be uncomfortable to recognise how much, or how little, of what you actually do is directly in pursuit of your stated vision; and how much, or how little, of the time you are happy. Life intervenes.

We'll be mapping and heightening your awareness of how that happens, how you distract yourself from living the life you *say* you want, and what you can do about it, in the pages that follow.

Uncovering your vision is a process that takes time. But that should be OK, because it is the most important thing you ever do. Even those who know from an early age what they want to be and even why, discover new dimensions as they grow through it. That learning is success. A day at the end of which you can say "I learnt something new today, and it helps me develop my vision" is a day well spent. Failure is blocking that learning, allowing oneself to be distracted by the glamour of the context or financial inducements. Even failure becomes an essential step towards success though, when you learn from it, or catch yourself getting bogged down in context instead of engaging with the why that makes sense of it. At any age, the why you perceive is right, as long as you are open to a deeper why, which may be even more challenging and uncomfortable.

Daily review of your life helps keeps things in perspective, so you see the lesson in everything, grow from it and learn how to handle yourself better in future. And you need to be open to new insight, to new and deeper interpretations of your life that take you through the layers of why. Each new layer is likely to be less comfortable and more challenging than the last, as you keep questioning assumptions and received ways of doing things. This is not to say that the previous steps were all wrong. In order to get from A to Z, it may be necessary to spend time with B, C, X and Y. Without B, you may not have the capacity to cope with C. So B, both the context and the why of it, is right, so long as you stay open and always alert to the possibility of moving on.

Every context is a learning experience, and one lesson that keeps cropping up is that we deserve better. The problem and challenge is just that each new phase of life has such efficient distractions from learning the truth about how incredible we could be! What helps enormously is that a critical mass of people have now seen the light, and it is almost fashionable to adopt a way of life and an approach to work, business and life that is more whole, wholesome and balanced. The presence of and continual search for vision is the primary ingredient in this new, "holistic" approach.

Welcome to Real Holism

"Holistic" is a familiar word in complementary medicine, where it means that instead of just treating, and trying to suppress, the symptom, you consider the whole person and what this symptom might be saying about them and their lifestyle. In much the same way holistic enterprise concerns itself with not just the context of life - being an accountant, mother, teacher, MD or road-sweeper - but also with the why behind it. Holistic enterprise applies to all forms of employment and work - employed or self-employed, part-time or portfolio person. 'Holistic' simply means that you're approaching your work from a different perspective, "coming from a different space, marching to a different drum." There is a deeper sense of personal vision and a more fulfilling concept of life and the place of work in it.

You decide what matters to you, what you care about, what life is about for you and where you can derive the greatest joy and growth; and you bring all that to your work and every part of your life. The sceptical may object that everyone can't have this much fun. Oh yes they can! The way you view and approach your work, whatever it is, makes all the difference. It can be a drudge to make a pile of money or it can be both a source of income *and* a context for learning and growth, joyful and soul-enhancing, a constant succession of rewarding challenges. You choose.

People with vision are inspiring. There is something inspired that lights up their lives and rubs off on others, especially if they are open to positive change. With the quality of vision in your life, there is also a passion for life, an excitement about possibilities which makes you determined to succeed, to be all that you might be. Visionaries, for that is what they, and you, become are resilient. There may be awful difficulties and disasters, but they pick themselves up and get straight back in there. They learn from the hard knocks, and they shrug off the scepticism and negativity that are the main blocks to allowing vision to flower. As you read this book, allow and trust your vision to appear as we name and release each of the negative states that block the way forward.

Each chapter in this book proposes one particular lesson to learn, one key distracting influence to be aware of, one classic pitfall to avoid and one apparently desirable attachment to release and let go.

The First Lesson

The overall **lesson** of this chapter has largely been covered. It is that the **power of vision** alone makes a life worth living, and that the whole of life is worth dedicating to its discovery, because it is the principal task of life and designed to take a whole lifetime. Only when we envision our own personal definition of success can we have something that will lead to fulfilment.

What primarily **distracts** us from finding our vision is our busy preoccupation with an exaggerated fear of survival. We overdo it. We are so wrapped up in the stresses and **busy-ness** of human existence that we simply cannot relax and be. We forget that we are human beings, not human doings. As Paul Hawken put it in The Ecology of Commerce, "We are speeding up our lives and working harder in a futile attempt to buy the time to slow down and enjoy it all". And the longer we've been doing this, obsessed with the aberration of industrial life, the more we have to let go and the more dangerous it looks to do that. But do it we must if we are not to condemn ourselves to a life of increasing desperation and unhappiness. There is no new growth without judicious pruning.

No growth without judicious pruning

What stops us Doing the Dream?

Chapter 2 has more to say about the way this distracts us and how to release its hold on you. In general, the distractions this book will parade before you are the contexts you work with at each new phase of life. So your task is to see through them, to do them but with awareness and not to the exclusion of all else. This is not some flaky New Age escapism: I'm not recommending that you opt out of the reality of human existence. Far from it. Work is *the* context in which we learn most of our lessons, a challenging place where we "make our love visible" as Kahlil Gibran has it. What I am strongly recommending though is that you live your life with awareness, and balance all the outer application of will with a healthy inner development.

To cope with the overall distractions of busy-ness, make a point of asking why more often, questioning assumptions, both your own and others', inviting the opposite of busy-ness to find a place in your life.

Coping with **pitfalls** is different. They are to be avoided and removed, even though you can learn useful lessons from falling prey to them. Distractions, if engaged in without awareness are a bad enough waste of time. Pitfalls destroy your life. You can thrash around in them for ever and waste your entire life on them. And the first one to look at and dissolve is **negativity**. It is what stops most people even picking up a book like this, because "it wouldn't work for me: it's all very well for those people with all the advantages of birth, money, education, looks etc but I don't have that luxury." With that mindset you don't even start to live. The first step is to stop giving up on you.

The sceptical, cynical, defeatist who-do-you-think-you-are, logical mind-set kills everything stone dead. It is dead itself and threatened by anything that is alive, so it has to kill it. It destroys commitment and is incapable of vision. Negativity is the province of people whose own lives are still off-track and who don't want you to get on-track and show them up. Any negativity you have yourself is fuelled by the climate of negativity that surrounds you. What then can you do about it? Well, the rest of this book will be revealing the various forms it takes. But in general you first have to acknowledge it is there and name it. Then you have to listen to it all, the bile, the futility, the ill-concealed envy and spite of it. Once it has done its worst and put its case in full, you decide whether to buy it or not. There is no need to explain, defend or counter it. You are dealing with the future and there can be no proof that your future or negativity's subdued version of it is the true picture - except that negativity limits the future to only negative possibility, whereas a positive outlook at least allows the possibility of a positive outcome. Nothing is guaranteed. You have taken the "best" negativity can come up with, and you remain unconvinced.

Funnily enough negativity thinks it's helping you. It has looked at the predicament of life, and your life in particular, and come up with a strategy for you. Its overcautiousness may have kept you safe while you hadn't evolved a more positive possibility for yourself, so we shouldn't be too hard on it. That's negative! But negativity doesn't listen, so you don't waste your precious time responding to it. It won't hear you. Listen to it; ask it what it's afraid of if you like; ask it what is the worst thing that could happen and what it thinks might help; but don't be too surprised if this is unproductive. A closed mind has little to offer. However an open mind can use even negativity to derive positive benefit. "A wise man can learn from a fool, but a fool cannot learn even from a wise man." The value negatives have is that they define who and what we don't want to be. So whenever negativity presents itself, see it as a way of homing in on what is positive, defining it just as the dark defines the light.

Negativity is described here as an 'it', because there are no negative people, and you are not negative. But there is a 'quality' of negativity just as there is a quality of positivity that we can embrace. Just as with children, you decry the behaviour you want to discourage not the child, so with the mindsets that are not serving you.

Others' negativity only affects us if it feeds our own negativity. And the busy-ness with which we fill our lives also flows from a fear of inadequacy which is often our inner reality. Both represent the darker side of what we see when we look inside ourselves. And this **shadow** self is very comfortable and compelling, in an uncomfortable sort of way. We know where we are with it and we know we're not going anywhere with it, so we can happily vegetate.

The idea that they might be perfect and omnipotent is one that most people cannot contemplate, while they will fight to the death to hold onto the idea that they are not good enough, especially when life seems to confirm this. This then is the core **attachment to release**. Throughout this book you will find that what blocks your way forward is what you are most reluctant to let go, because you are attached to it, limpet-like. As long as this shadow is in charge, you can't improve because you don't believe you deserve any better.

Dare to Let Go

Letting go your attachments happens instantaneously. The resistance to let go can take forever. It takes trust, self-belief and a lot of negotiation. Each chapter in the book reveals another dimension of it, so you will have the opportunity to release it in stages. For now it is enough just to acknowledge that the shadow is there and notice how much of your life it runs, and how much of your energy it uses.

A generally excellent book by Susan Jeffers suggests that you "feel the fear and do it anyway". The phrase has become part of common vocabulary. The idea that fear is not a good enough reason not to do something is valuable. The idea that fear is the principal reason why we don't do anything is less helpful. It is often silly little things we have become over-attached to, places we've got ourselves by listening too much to received wisdom (ie non-sense). The similarity is that just as most fear is only in our imagination and can be overcome once it is faced and felt, so most other excuses for not living our own lives are figments we can release once we've identified them.

A woman in her mid-thirties was induced to eat mustard for the first time in her life by a market research exercise. Her evaluation was "I never thought anything my mother told me I wouldn't like could be so good." And a professional friend of mine, Michael, phoned me while I was writing this. "I think I've just done what you keep recommending," he said. "I'm 50 now, and I've decided not to flog myself to death any more trying to earn £15,000 a year to pay private school fees. For the first time in years I'm sleeping properly. I feel 30 years younger." Letting go of old assumptions is incredibly empowering, when you finally get around to it.

SUMMARY

● Tear up the old maps. They don't go anywhere.
● Learn to enjoy where you are and change what diminishes you.
● Define success for yourself and take responsibility for it.
● Life begins with vision, that capacity to see clearly how one could be, in relation to everything else. Vision is the quality that answers the question *why?* for each of us.
● Discovering your vision is a life-time's work.
● The holistic visionary approach applies to all work and all life.

LESSON to LEARN:
The power of **Vision** alone creates a life worth living.

DISTRACTION to TRANSFORM:
Busy-ness, being preoccupied with the superficial and futile business of survival and temporary advantage.

PITFALL to AVOID:
Your own and others' **Negativity**.

ATTACHMENT to RELEASE:
Your **Shadow**, the belief that you're not good enough.

EXERCISE

● Suppose for a moment you could re-invent yourself. What would you change? How would this make a difference?
● Focus on that desired difference. What could you do *to-day* to bring more of that different quality into your life?
● What does this tell you about your purpose in life, your 'why'?

Reinvent Yourself

Make a brief note here before you read on.

At the back of the book you will find your own Personal Priorities Pages. Use these to highlight the key steps you're resolving to make and to ensure you remember to take them.

CHAPTER 2

Change Is The Only Constant

An undercurrent of change has come to a head in these decades surrounding the millenium, which has made it both possible and essential for each of us to clarify a powerful vision for ourselves.

Issues that used to belong in protest and campaigning movements or to the left of politics have moved centre-stage as individuals have taken back their power, demanding the right to live their own lives.

In particular, two significant shifts have occurred in Western developed economies - disillusionment among those who were thought of as "winners" under the old industrial system, and what the Royal Society of Arts Tomorrow's Company Report has called the "death of deference".

Throughout the C20th the possibility of defining one's own life, and the context in which it is lived, has become less and less the province of a small privileged minority. The power of the collective has gradually caved in to the rising tide of individualism as free thinking and the freedom of the human spirit has become more acceptable. Not everywhere yet, but especially in the super-power countries of the last two centuries, the stranglehold has loosened, and even where this has not yet happened, the battle for individual freedom does now have several international precedents.

Change often happens imperceptibly with many false starts and setbacks, sometimes taking quite aberrant forms that re-empower those who fear the loss of influence that change brings. This has certainly been true of the power-shift away from the collective.

At the beginning of the 20th century an oligarchy controlled the collective culture and imposed severe sanctions on those who stepped out of line. These controllers were the dictators, political leaders, their executive/civil services and military enforcers, supported by the captains of industry, banks, religion and the press, and they exerted their influence not just over their own populations, but often over whole other countries as well.

Commonly, those who overcame an old collective power-base created new collectives which in turn became oppressors. It has been a long march, slowly freeing ourselves from a succession of tyrants. Now, standing on the shoulders of the campaigners, radical writers and protesters of the C20th, who in turn built on C19th breakthroughs such as the abolition of slavery, now we stand at the start of the Freedom Century, where millions of individuals are creating the C21st by defining their own lives.

The Freedom Century starts here

For centuries we tended to accept that the collective's view of success was real and worth achieving. But in the '90s it emerged that a significant percentage of the workforce were actively questioning this assumption. It seems we finally ran out of excuses for not recognising our power. In the '40s the World War took precedence: and the '50s brought stifling austerity and convention in its wake. In the '60s convention turned into a materialist drive to leave austerity behind: however the seeds of the post-industrial revolution were sown then too. The booms and busts of the '70s, as materialism went haywire, preoccupied rich and poor alike, and degenerated in the '80s into the rampant avarice which mortgaged most of the next century to satisfy the false hopes it raised. We tried to buy happiness and had to discover the hard way that the lady was not for sale.

The '90s brought realism and realisation, but with it the heavy cost of the previous 50 years' madness. However instead of concentrating on beating the escalating costs, more and more people now question the whole crazy ball-game. And the status of these people is even more significant than their numbers. The very people who have been winning the rewards, such as they are, of what is affectionately known as the rat-race, are telling us it's not worth it. The sacrifices are too great. These people have opted to exchange some of their quantity of income for an enhanced quality of life.

The Irresistible Attraction of LifeShift

Research in Britain (mostly by Henley Research Centre) reveals that by 1996 6% of the workforce had opted for this rebalancing LifeShift, with a further 6% planning to follow by the end of 1998. Research experience in the United States is very similar.

Bearing in mind that only 5% of the UK workforce are paid enough for even a modestly comfortable lifestyle, 6% opting out is pretty significant. 35% earn above the average wage (of around £19,500 in Britain) so 12% lifeshifting represents a huge level of disillusionment. And those who want to follow their example when they can accounts for a further 42%! If you've had enough of the old system, you're in the majority! We have stopped deferring to those who set the targets for us, and we have stopped deferring happiness.

Money may create comfort, and the lack of it can seriously undermine our ability to be joyful and open-hearted, especially at the bottom of the pile, but it cannot actually create joy or happiness. As I put it in my earlier book (Creating Abundance 1992), "there is no amount of money you can accumulate that will create prosperity, let alone happiness."

Most of the commentary on this trend focused on high-fliers

taking to the hills, and on the financial and lifestyle implications involved. "Stuff the Porsche: I'd rather have a life". The *real* pioneers of LifeShifting however, who've lived with this for 20 years, know that while finances are the excuse for not taking the plunge, no amount of tinkering with the financial machinery can create the motivation or energy to see it through. For that you need powerful vision.

The first barrier all but the wealthiest LifeShifters face is however probably financial: "Nice idea, but how do we pay the mortgage?" This does need facing, but it is only a knee-jerk reaction, not the real barrier to your life working for you. If you wait till you can afford it, you'll probably never do it. But as you develop your own LifeShift vision, and gradually let go the attachments and distractions that are the real obstacle, the money will start to take care of itself and seem less important. In fact as long as money is not working, it challenges you to connect with the vision, integrate it fully into your life and actually implement it. We return to this in the following chapters.

Even though poor cashflow slows down the LifeShift trend, those in the middle ground, not poor but not affluent either, are coming into a new relationship with money. Instead of feeling they are failures for not making it to the top of the heap, they are realising they were right all along. Quality of life *does* matter more than "success" defined in purely quantitative or material terms.

This desire for greater individual freedom, and the growing self-confidence that feeds it, is a trend which has run parallel with changes in organisations' attitudes to employment. By and large the drive has been to down-size the workforce and "empower" the survivors to do three jobs instead of just two. This is seen as more efficient, but the rewards are not shared with the workforce that creates the savings. Henley calls this "decoupling" - separating wealth creation from wealth distribution. This is because employers cannot afford to pay people the salaries that would support their unrealistic expectations. Even the few they retain and work harder cannot earn enough to compensate for the sacrifices they make.

At the same time that fewer workers are being needed, the population has been growing - by a third in Britain since 1945. The economy has not grown to accommodate this and attempts to do so have proved unsustainable. The career path is proving to be a cul-de-sac. 80% of respondents in a 1996 Mintel poll recognised that the job for life was a mirage, and 7 out of 10 said they actually *wanted* more flexible working hours. This wish may be granted, as a survey by Management Today/WFD concluded in June 1998 that flexibility was the answer to both employers and employees getting what they want.

Although many want this to happen, there is still a degree of panic, as some resist and try to pretend it is not happening. There is still (and probably always will be) a hard core of "conspicuous consumers", very visible and heavily targeted by status-symbol marketing departments. This group has been declining since the 1970s. Research (mostly by Taylor-Nelson and Applied Futures) has tracked the growth of a group in society known as "Inner Directeds" since 1974. The prediction in 1984 was that this group which by then represented 34% of the population would grow to 55% by 2020. Inner Directeds are people who are not phased or impressed by the outer material rewards, which define life for Outer Directeds. They make their own minds up about what is important, and judge their progress against their own measures of success.

LifeShift is a major trend now because conspicuous consumerism has been seen only to work for a small minority (who are now saying it's not working even for them!), and because the appeal of Inner Directed values has been growing. Consumerism has us screaming along in second gear, but now we're discovering some less stressful options in our gearbox. We're "coasting" in top.

Doing the Sums
Because money is such an apparently imponderable obstacle to the real work of defining a new vision for ourselves, we need to consider a strategy for dealing with it, at least temporarily.

The winners are disenchanted. The aspirers are caught between the rock of escalating costs and the hard place of insecure income. The difficulty of rising above the financial non-equation has become an impossibility, so the sums on which the equation is based have to be reappraised. Whether you're starting from scratch or have already reached first base makes a big difference to what is immediately possible but not to the general principles of "coasting". The key is to get out of the "energy system" you're stuck in and move on up a level. But first you have to cure the wheelspin.

The **lesson to learn**, in the light of this undercurrent becoming mainstream, is that we must **re-evaluate** our financial aspirations and values. The whole thrust of our lives has changed. As well as clarifying vision, we also need to review the practicalities of financial life now, and look at how we can severely prune costs and long-term commitments. Then we can put this to one side and return to the main thrust of this book.

In Britain, the problem revolves around the cost of housing which more than doubled *as a percentage of income* in the 30 years 1961 to 1991: it is now slightly lower at 16%, against 9% in 1960.

This heavy housing burden combines with inflated energy, heat and travel costs to leave the rest of the home budget tight or worse. The most crucial area to re-evaluate therefore is your housing situation, not least because a large mortgage or heavy rental commitment is the main reason given for not shifting to the lifestyle we want.

Two people can live (and work) very comfortably in 50 sq metres (500 sq ft) simply organised. A bedroom doesn't really need to be more than 5 sq metres (50 sq ft), and there is a limit to how many reception rooms you can sit in at any one time! Costs can be reduced by sharing space with others, property sitting, or renting a room or two in a house that is too large for its occupants, who can then live free. Smaller homes cost less to run so the savings are exponential. You might even be able to reduce your net housing cost to less than £10 per person per week, if not now then within the next 10 years.

Sorting out how you can get a free roof over your head before you have children has become crucial because the presence of children has a major impact on how possible it is to balance income and expenditure. Having children has the effect of halving the income of the parents, whether one has to give up paid work, or both scale down or extra help is bought in. Two DINKYS (Double Income No Kid Yuppies) earning the UK national average of £375 a week each can by sharing costs achieve the same modest level of comfort enjoyed by the top 4% of earners...until they yield to the temptation to become ORCHIDS (One Recent Child, Heavily In Debt)!

85% earn £10,000 or more, so most couples can achieve the average *household* income of £420 a week; but if there are children, the family is reduced to subsistence level. If you already have children, you know this, but may not have recognised that all other needs, plans and luxuries must be foregone for the next 20 years - cars, holidays, entertaining, fancy trainers and CD players, anything non-essential. Children are a choice, and delightfully rewarding given proper care, but we must understand the consequences.

Having children is no longer obligatory. And as long as the tax burden on each adult is as high as it is, £7,500pa in the UK, few can afford to. The few who can don't have time to do the job justice. 20% of young people are now looking at the consequences and choosing to be childless, 25% of graduates. The UK birthrate in 1997 was the lowest for 150 years.

Given the loss of quality involved in generating the high incomes needed to support children (and give *them* any sort of quality), this trend can be expected to grow. Traditionally there has been great social pressure to have children. But many are now questioning whether they really are the only essential for a full life, or the only acceptable excuse for leaving the parental home.

25% of the UK workforce experienced unemployment between 1992 and 1996 (The Independent March 19, 1996), and 31% feel insecure about their jobs (The Telegraph Work in Life Survey, October 1996). The combination of job insecurity with *pension* insecurity as well now has most people worried about their future and careful about what they spend. This has completely traumatised the marketplace and further aggravated the economic difficulties most people face, and the insecurity also affects whether any of us can see far enough ahead to enter the very long-term commitment to children.

To start making sense of the expenditure which stops you having a life, compare your costs now against the figures for the average household of 2.4 people, which are set out below. These Average Household figures are taken from "Family Spending: The 1997/8 Family Expenditure Survey", published by The Office of National Statistics (ONS).

Weekly Expenditure Guide

Item	£ per average household
Mortgage / Rent / Council Tax	£ 51.50
Fuel & Power	£ 12.70
Food & Drink	£ 69.20
Other Living Expenses	£ 72.00
Motoring	£ 46.60
Other Travel	£ 8.10
Personal, Holiday & Leisure	£ 67.60
Pension / Life Assurance	£ 19.30
Income Tax	£ 56.70
NI Contributions	£ 16.50
TOTAL EXPENDITURE	**£420.20**

Question every item of expenditure and identify what is core, basic essential, and what is desirable but deferrable. Motoring like housing is a cost that has got totally out of hand, as our expectations lost touch with reality. Opt for the smallest possible and do without a car if you can. £2400, the average motoring spend and rising at 13%pa, buys an awful lot of taxis, trains and buses. Discover the joys of eating, entertaining and partying at home. Holiday at home or take a paid holiday. Once you lifeshift, you won't need holidays; there'll be nothing to get away from!

The next priority is to clear debts and mortgages, starting with those that carry the highest interest rate; or if you must borrow, keep it to a minimum and do it while you're still earning high. Up all your credit card limits to cover occasional cashflow hiccups.

The main *extra* costs to allow in your budget are a proper pension or wealth scheme so you can continue to coast for the 25 years you can expect to live after so-called "retirement age". Set up your wealth fund good and early. A worker on average income setting aside 10% of their income from age 20 and investing it wisely stands a good chance of arriving at age 60 a millionaire! As the first priority is to ensure a small roof over your head by age 35, the fund might be a little smaller but still adequate even at 55. The emphasis is on *small* roof: go for the absolute minimum. (If you're now a parent and in a position to make a gift to your twenty something children, a small roof is hard to beat, transferred as a "potentially tax-free gift" over 7 years. For details of how to build up a wealth fund - it's not complicated or even very risky - see Personal Finance Education Services [Jean Hicks] in the Resources Section).

The final message on balancing the books is "Make do!" You need very little when your life is full of a vision that enthrals you. Company cars become totally irrelevant. When you can invest, and want to, invest in the best and in developing what you love in tandem with the skills you need to keep developing.

Economic Aberration

Economic reality is telling us what we should have realised long ago - that our planet is grossly overpopulated. The human race has now assumed plague proportions (in the West, never mind the rest of the world). Nature has been raped in the attempt to provide for an unsustainable system that is out of control and working for nobody.

Nature however has a wonderful knack of restoring the balance. She seems to be using economics to force us to get our house in order (which is what economics means). We have to think very carefully what commitments we can afford to make and what expenditures are realistic, including children. Families and children are contracts without break-clauses, so unless you are absolutely certain they are the highest priority for you for the next 30 years, it's best to defer this until age 35. Chapter 6 may give you further pause for thought too!

We've been looking here at the financial implications of making a LifeShift, because these are the first obstacle most people hit, but also because these are the **distractions** to beware of - the **smokescreen** of unquestioned assumptions about what makes a life and what we need all this money for. The practicalities need our attention, but it is only an inspiring vision based on the desire for quality and new values that will motivate you to make these practical changes.

The **aberration** of Industrial Age thinking is what got us into this mess. Einstein said "No problem is soluble at the level of consciousness at which it was created". **Let** it **go.**

Responsibility for Excellence

LifeShift demands a major **re-evaluation** of your values too, what you live by, what you care about, what matters to you deep down. New values form the basis for new choices. This is the next **lesson.**

In a way it is difficult to define the new values for this new Freedom Century, because values now are individually formed, not imposed by social pressure. What is valued by those taking charge of their own lives and refusing to be disempowered any longer is whatever leads to a more fulfilling life for the individual concerned. The first principle of LifeShift is individual responsibility.

In "Creating Abundance" I invented the word "self-ful" to describe this approach to life. The self-ful person takes responsibility for their own life and is not a burden to others. They value freedom, but recognise that their freedom must not interfere significantly with anybody else's. We are all born with it, and only forfeit it if we interfere with others' freedom. Self-ful people believe in the golden mean, eschewing both greedy, anti-social selfishness and selfless martyrdom. These then are neither yobs nor slobs, sharks nor flakes, but people who take care of themselves and are therefore well-placed to take care of others. What's good for the individual is good for the community. We revisit self-ful people especially in Chapter 4.

Those who try to control other people's lives will not agree with this, and as you LifeShift they will be your principal antagonists. They will call you selfish, in the best "Pot calling kettle black" tradition. They will ask "Who do you think you are …(releasing yourself from my control?)" and complain that if everyone did this, the system would collapse. Great! It's almost collapsed already, so let's give it one last push. "I" am the system now.

One of the disabling tricks busy-bodies use to stop you being true to yourself is to rubbish your plan by describing an extreme version of it. So you're not a caring, responsible socialist, you're a Stalinist! You're not opting for a more sustainable lifestyle, you're a hairshirt ascetic or a hippie drop-out. You get the picture. Any response you make is then branded defensive, over-sensitive or over-reacting. It's a petty game, another feature of a farcical society now fading away. Don't waste your time playing. Instead thank them for their concern and ask how they would like to help. If they can't, leave them behind. Making a new life for yourself may involve leaving behind those who can't cope with you being you. Independence has its price.

There are now many precedents for LifeShifting. In addition to the 12% who are exchanging their quantity of income for a better quality of life, there are many more who have for years put quality first and eschewed the seduction of the elusive big salary. Self-employment in Britain doubled between 1978 and 1990, and has hovered around the 12/13% mark since (officially!) Many of these people are motivated by the desire for more personal freedom, even if income especially early on suffers.

Self-employment is central to this discussion. Given the uncertainties of employment, most workers are having to think of themselves as self-employed, managing their own careers, planning their own training and development. Work increasingly consists of a hardcore of full-time staff around whom revolves a variegated array of ad hoc project groups, contract/portfolio/tele-workers, part-timers and specialist suppliers. By 2020 90% of the workforce will be self-employed, and the typical worker will be a freelance woman. The organisation's reluctance to be tied to employee contracts and the individual's desire for freedom and self-dependency combine to make self-employment the best working structure for the future.

Futurework
This flexible work- and life-style has a natural, organic flow to it which feeds us, physically and spiritually. Jack Welch of General Electric has said, "Employees need to feel rewarded in both the pocketbook and the soul."

An American futurist with a good track record for accurate predictions, Faith Popcorn, has defined 'spiritual entrepreneurship' as a significant trend for the future. And reference has already been made to the 25 year old research by Christine and William Kirk MacNulty of Applied Futures who identified the growth of "Inner Directeds". The predictions of other futurists are also coming true.

Charles Handy coined the term Portfolio Careers and proposed that ad hoc project groups would take over from solid state organisations. Francis Kinsman mapped Teleworking years ago, and James Robertson did the same for New Work. We are already living Alvin Toffler's Third Age and will soon be living ICI ex-Chairman John Harvey-Jones' prediction that by 2020 multinationals like ICI "will employ about 3000 core staff and a helluva lot of networkers".

LifeShifters then are the pioneers of a new rebalancing of work and life, where work no longer totally dominates. Instead you connect with yourself and then build what you do on who you are.

Quality takes over from quantity as the principal objective of life. The lack of quality in the acquisitive drive for quantity is now widely recognised. It used to be assumed that if you generate quantity (of income) you can buy quality (of life), but it is now seen that the two are mutually exclusive. Quantity rules out quality, and quality is now preferred, even if it requires concessions on quantity.

The Quality Life starts with a clear why. Every day, every moment, you are being your why and it lights up your existence. This also lights up the lives of everyone with whom you have contact (if they are not completely closed to it): your example ripples out, no matter how apparently mundane your choice of life container.

Instead of pretending to be something social pressure demands of you, that serves no-one in the end, you put honesty and authenticity first. This is the genuine article! From deeply real being, dedicated doing flows.

Care and love are new words on the employment scene, good examples of the way the old head-oriented, analytical approach is being balanced by emotion, intuition and spirituality. We all need to draw on both dimensions in a holistic way.

LifeShifters seek to deepen their experience of life. They want to come into a deeper, more wholesome, caring, loving relationship with themselves. High on their list of objectives are personal growth and learning. Life becomes a journey towards wholeness, constantly noticing where one is out of balance. There is then a holistic rebalancing of head with heart, structure with spontaneity, action with reflection, spirit with matter. The LifeShifter becomes more and more present at all levels of their being.

This becomes the central purpose of life, but not in any dull, stodgy, academic sense. When life is in balance it is joyful - tough, challenging, unacknowledged maybe, but joyful. You may have to look pretty hard for the joy sometimes, but the absence of joy and fun challenges us to go looking for it, to question all the aspects of life that deny it and bring ourselves back in balance. Abundance is a sense of joy that manifests the resources we need. No amount of misery or money will achieve this.

LifeShift goes deep. It involves and requires a major shift, like turning a diamond to find an entirely new and more brilliant facet. If all you change is the outer context - merchant bank to goat farm for instance - very little actually changes. You take yourself with you, all your old doubts, insecurities, aberrations and distortions. To make a LifeShift that will make any difference requires that you go deep, through a transforming personal journey.

For most, the outer change is however a good first step in taking individual responsibility. There somehow needs to be dis-illusionment, the loss of illusion, often in the wake of some crisis. Having taken this first step, the personal journey opens up. If this is not pursued, the outer change turns sour. But usually the LifeShifter is hooked by then and presses on with the deeper journey.

When you discover the thrill of taking personal responsibility, when you strive for quality and excellence, and engage enthusiastically with life, you start to experience personal fulfilment. You find yourself committed to your chosen task in life in an extraordinary new way. No longer is your commitment conditional on any return for yourself. Nor does it have the quality of attachment, limited to a particular result that will flatter your ego. You are committed to your process, because it is the only way for you to be, regardless whether the result brings you reward, fame, recognition or advancement. The process is the price and the reward.

Valuing Relationship
Taking responsibility for your own individual vision involves connecting with yourself at a deep level. Once you have this deep, excellent relationship with your whole self, meeting your own needs from your own resources, you become more desirable as a friend, co-worker, supplier, human being generally. You arrive in a place where you can effect transformation of outer reality. And your heart is open for external relationships. Your capacity to love and care for others, to extend your acceptance of responsibility and capacity for relationship to the world around you can come into play. You have done what you need to on the inner, often through your relationship with the outer. Now you can effect change on the outer too.

Being less dysfunctional and wrapped up in yourself you can "be there for" friends, family and other intimates. Your open personality invites others into your network of associates, and your constant willingness to give unconditionally sets up a positive flow of energy, contacts and resources in your direction too.

Your being has a positive impact on your community too, whether you join in or not. And beyond this local influence, your life is a positive contribution to humanity. Just being you transforms humanity. And on this solid base you build what you do.

LifeShifters have a lot in common with environmentalists, valuing the natural world, sustainability, the "minimal footprint" philosophy. This is a "SWELL" new value system, replacing the STALE old industrial age culture. **SWELL** is Sufficiency With Elegance Living Lightly. **STALE** stands for Struggle To Attain Luxury Excess. It has taken 10 years, but the SWELL culture has arrived and is even fashionable with much of the media. It was not always so.

What then are your values? As above? Or expressing creativity, peace and silence, forgiveness and compassion, "mens sana in corpore sano" as Juvenal recommended in his satire on the vanity of human wishes 2000 years ago? Perhaps your vision and values are coming into sharper focus. And perhaps the immediate practicalities are nagging away. "Yes but...a bit more dosh is what I need first". As St Augustine pleaded, "God make me chaste, but not yet"!

It may well take more than an hour's reading to transform the patterns of behaviour which have left you not only short of cash but sad. The demands of making a living and the whole **smokescreen** of social pressure around generating some cash are the principal **distractions** from making change at all stages of life. It has different dimensions and shapes at different ages, but it runs through life, tempting us not to risk being true to ourselves. The longer you put it off, the more ground there is to catch up and the stronger your attachment to the precarious structure you have built up to protect you from all this. But in the end being authentic is the only way forward to a fulfilling result.

What is this extra money you think you need actually for? This is the real objective, so focus on that rather than how to make the money which is just the means you currently see to achieve your end. Is more money indeed the way to get where you want to, and is "there", where you think you want to arrive, really so appealing?

Look back to the earlier section on "Doing the Sums", re-evaluating and reducing costs, and see if you really need to stuff more stuff into your home. And check that you're not being someone you don't want to be, trying to get somewhere that isn't worth arriving.

Chapter 4 takes a longer look at what you have to offer that you could turn into income. For now recognise that the route to income and fulfilment starts with a clear vision of who you are and values you care about. Give yourself time, a phased plan, gently building up and don't worry if you seem unable to get started. There may well be resistances to identify and clear before vision can happen.

Building the Muscle

We have already seen how the first two steps we need to take interfere with each other. The fundamental barrier to LifeShift is the absence of a clear, inspiring vision, so the first task is to start homing in on this, but hot on its heels comes the objection that tomorrow's vision is not going to pay today's bills. These two primary tasks conflict. Time spent on envisioning can seem to be a waste of income-generating time, and the mortgage imperative rules out the vision quest.

It can seem an impossible task to handle, but the great **pitfall** is **procrastination**. Most people are too busy making a living to have a life or make their unique contribution. We get embroiled in something and in supporting ourselves in some sort of comfort, and there is never time for the grand project.

The solution to this apparent conflict is to allocate some time to envisioning and make it the *first* priority each day. Ideally allocate one hour every morning when you will take a step however small. If you promise you will do this after you've done the income-generating bit you will find you have no time or energy left over to fulfil your promise. Whereas if you do it first, you start the day with heightened energy and will be subconsciously working on it all day. In fact working on tomorrow's vision *does* in a way start paying today's bills, because the extra energy you take into your everyday life raises your profile and motivates you to do better!

If an hour is really too much of an imposition, try 10 or even 5 minutes. There are more than 1000 10 minute slots in a week, so you can surely spare 7 to transform your life! 10 minutes would be a good start, and thoroughly worthwhile. It is like starting any new exercise. The first walk you take, for instance, might only be once round the block. Then you build up to twice and so on. Before you know it, you're walking a couple of miles.

The next cause of procrastination is not knowing where to start, what to do in this 10 or 60 minutes. Anything that reduces the embroilment in busy-ness is better than nothing. Your first step into a new LifeShifted you might be to pause and reflect, with a notebook; it might be to take a short walk, noticing what you notice; or you might sit quietly and breathe, or listen to some music that moves you. Any of these starts you on a more meditative, self-aware approach to your life.

To the over-busy mind this can all seem a supreme waste of time, a sort of procrastination, but it is more a change of gear, the beginning of a LifeShift. You've probably been "running on empty", putting yourself under stress in order to create a daily adrenalin surge to keep you going. When you stop and take time to be still and nurture yourself, the absence of stress can feel flat and set up the panic that you're about to grind to a halt. Treat this as a holiday, if that helps. But this time, when you come home, you're going to get your adrenalin from working your vision which recharges your batteries, not from "hurry sickness", which runs them flat.

As your new journey progresses, you will have a steady stream of resistances and distractions to overcome, emotions to face. These are all material to take into this quiet time you start each day with. To start working on vision you first have to get to it, to lift off all the layers of doubt and negative self-talk that cover it. This is easier said than done! How do you release something, the absence of which you cannot imagine and have never experienced? The dilemma is that financial pressure reinforces sadness, undermines joy and closes your heart, when the very thing you need to do is open you heart, find your inner joy and let go of the sadness; doing this relieves worry and makes you magnetic to people, money and life-force; it relieves financial pressure. You have to break the loop somehow.

The same applies to envisioning. You need to *build the muscle* and get the flow going. The best way to do this is slowly at first, gently, not overdoing it. Do too much and it will put you off; you won't feel like doing it again tomorrow. Always do less than you can. Michael Caine says, "If you're knocking yourself out, you're doing it wrong!"

This process starts when you recognise that life is not working for you in some way; and that more of what you have been doing -

worrying, busy-ness, striving - is not going to solve it.

With the help of this book, keep identifying the obstacles - the distractions, pitfalls and attachments - that undermine your hopes and dreams, and focus on releasing them. You will know what they are and can spot them when they put in an appearance, so you can resolve to do less of them. Their total absence from your life may be unimaginable, but less is something you can manage. As you gradually reduce the obstacles, you gradually have more time and energy, and perhaps feel safer about facing the next layers of resistance. Gradually you allow joy and heartfulness out to fill the empty space.

The key word is "gradually". You start where you're at, the only place you *can* start, with what is familiar, and work your way in from there. Climb the ladder one rung at a time. If you try and leap up 8 steps at once, you will likely fall off and break your neck; which would be an excellent way to prove to yourself that this was a bad idea. Now which bit of you wants to do that?!

Remember the eventual aim is to have your vision happen. So don't disappear into the negativity. You're focusing on it so you can release it, and also because along the way there will be some important learning - about trust, about tolerance of ambiguity and about the new relationship you're forming with life and your inner self. If all else fails in these initial steps, sit quietly with it, count your blessings and listen to what something inside you has to say about it.

That is not procrastination; that is where LifeShift starts.

Sloughing off an old skin

Have you ever watched a snake sloughing off its old skin? It looks intensely uncomfortable. Some bits seem to stick while others have clearly parted company. And it's a wriggling, awkward performance that seems to demand huge amounts of energy. It must seem very strange, something so far removed from the daily routine it has to be relearnt and remembered each time it happens. You feel the poor snake must feel quite raw and prickly, as though it's suffering a nasty case of sunburn. And yet beauty emerges. Startling bright colours, fresh and shining, without a blemish on its pristine new skin.

This is a perfect image of the transformation people are having to perform these days. The old familiar process of gradual development, improvement and consideration still goes on, but frequently a more radical shift is called for - the complete letting go of an old, though once brilliant, presentation and its replacement with something that has been preparing itself under the surface.

Don't assume from this that only a massive shift will suffice; that's the workaholic's response. Preparation is the process too. Sitting quietly for 5 minutes might prove to be the biggest leap of your life.

The Breakthrough Experience

This happened to me 10 years ago when The Breakthrough Centre emerged as a unique new pioneering venture, born out of an old patchwork quilt of a training business. Its new colours merged training with networking and on-going counselling in £140,000 worth of dedicated building and equipment. And jolly bright and fresh-smelling it was too.

It was incredibly difficult and painful 7 years later to let go of all this and go through the whole transformation process all over again. But 7 years is a good innings and a classic time for an old cycle to give way to something new.

If you're in a hole, stop digging

So what I'm suggesting here is not some nice theory I've never put into practice. I have lived this. I am familiar with all the fear, hurt pride and hopelessness that accompanies these transformational crises. I know how messy and confusing it all seems, while the shift has not yet happened and you can't see what's needed and there's nothing to show for the sacrifices you've already made. The preparations I've encouraged you to make can I know seem fatuously trivial and pointless. Sit quietly indeed! But you see, if you're in a hole, you don't get out by digging it deeper. When shouting stops working, you have to try listening.

My personal learning is that the only way forward is to let go. We may never quite manage it! And to be honest I often feel I've barely started the letting go process myself. There are no quick fixes, and we're never done. Even so I've managed to reduce my costs by 65%, and create a more satisfying and rewarding business. I actually have time for people and myself, which makes my business much more useful than the empire I once felt I had to build! Now I'm working on putting the rest in place. I wonder if 7 more years will complete the preparations! It hardly matters because meanwhile the journey is joyful.

When your world is in turmoil, the only rock is your vision, your values and a healthy relationship with a deeper dimension of yourself. So keep returning to them. And when it's all too hard, offer up the problem to that wise old bird that lives inside you...and listen.

SUMMARY

- The Industrial Age has disillusioned even its "winners".
- Individual freedom is beating collective oppression, the culmination of a century of change.
- All assumptions about costs and aspirations must be reviewed.
- Quality and quantity are mutually exclusive.
- The new values are individual responsibility, rebalancing work and life, deepening the experience of life, the personal

journey, excellence and relationship with self and other.

● No amount of money can create prosperity, let alone happiness. Only vision and joy in service to values can do that.

● The strangeness of the new and the insistent call of the old conspire to halt your progress. Preparing, sitting still, taking time with yourself may be where you start.

LESSON to LEARN:
LifeShift requires a deep **Re-evaluation** of assumptions, values and aspirations.

DISTRACTION to TRANSFORM:
The **Smoke-screen** of cultural pressure and cash generation.

PITFALL to AVOID:
Procrastination

ATTACHMENT to RELEASE:
The **Aberration** of Industrial Age Materialism.

EXERCISE

● Close your eyes for at least 2 minutes, allowing yourself to become still. Then ask yourself...
● What do I care about most? And why?
● What have I done in the last 7 days to move it forward?
● What will I do in the next 7 days to move it forward?

Make some notes here and transfer any actions to the *top* of your To Do List, and to your Personal Priorities Pages at the back of the book.

CHAPTER 3

The Grounding Years (0-21): Catching Up With Yourself

Who invented you first time round? How did you become the person you are today? And is that the person you want to proceed with?

Whether natural evolution, re-invention or some more root and branch demolition seems right for you, read on. This chapter outlines what needs doing to ensure the foundations are solid.

Who invented you first time round?

There are those who believe it's all in the genes, that our essential nature, skills and abilities are all predetermined. And others reckon the way we are has more to do with our education and upbringing.

Nature or nurture. The debate continues and the jury is out.

The answer probably lies somewhere between the two. Whether we are born with it or as tabula rasa, the blank sheet on which the impact of life leaves its mark, may not make that much difference. It is what we *do* with it, how we develop and respond that defines our individual uniqueness.

Our nature can stagnate or evolve into its full potential. The nurture we receive can be rejected or selectively integrated, to create who we are today. Nurture cannot perhaps change what we are naturally born with completely, and nature does not deliver us into the world fully and finally formed. Either way we arrive as a complex potentiality, and our task in life is to unwrap that potential and make the most of it.

Some things will be easier than others, and some things will always attract us more than others, depending on what is natural to us, how we have been brought up and how very early on we explained the mystery of life to ourselves . As we grow up, we gradually "colonise" one dimension of ourselves after another. We are all always active at all levels of ourselves, but at different times our focus is most fixed on one or two dimensions at a time. Frequently we get stuck, either unable to cope with new learning about ourselves or so absorbed in a particular way of being that we stop moving on.

At various points we may feel we have found ourselves and can stop looking for more. You see the fallacy of this argument when an old industry closes down, and the people who used to identify themselves as workers in that context refuse to redefine their roles.

Continuous professional development is obligatory for everyone now, and the same applies to our personal evolution. If we ever try and stop, life gives us a salutory kick up the backside to move us on.

It is a good idea occasionally to go back over the stages of life you have already completed and fill in the gaps. There may be whole dimensions of yourself that for all sorts of reasons you never found, and your development of some other dimensions could have been decidedly lop-sided. If you're going to build an extension or replace the old structure, the foundations had better be solid. So our next task is to check out what should have happened and whether it did!

Phases of Life

Imagine if you will that we arrive as a seed, which first needs to put down roots and can then grow into a plant, which will in time produce flowers or fruit. Up to age 40 or so life is about grounding and establishing this seed. Then the inner journey of growth takes over. We flower and more or less gracefully wither away.

In the first half of life, a series of *separations* takes place - from the physical focus of childhood around 10, from received wisdom around 20, from all that life was grounded in around 30. By 40 we have prepared the soil, the outer growth medium, and it is time for the inner self to flower and escape from matter.

From here on, a series of *connections* takes place. Around 50, following the warnings of mid-life crisis, the fight to control the outer is mercifully over and inner life demands our attention.

Whereas up to 35 or 40, your inner self will humour the ego's demands for progress and rooting, at 50/55 she increasingly insists on the focus shifting to the acquiring of wisdom and understanding. This analysis makes some sense of the way many careers seem to end around this time. There really is something different about being a "Third-Ager." Quite simply the feedback life gives us at this point is "Change your priorities. Stop fighting. Go within."

The timing is not rigid. Both inner and outer processes are happening simultaneously, and we each travel at different speeds. At *any* time, if the ego's direction is out of synch with where the inner you needs to end up, difficulties often mystifying and illogical will block the way. Once the time comes to pursue more personal inner priorities, no amount of pushing and shoving on the outer will help!

What works is an awareness of the route we are on through life, a willingness to listen, react courageously and trust the inner sense. We have all experienced those moments of bliss, of feeling the absolute rightness of some action or relationship. This is what inner work feels like when you are in touch with it. Quiet space, retreat, gentle creativity, breathing and meditation are all good places to listen and be and hear the inner connection resonating. It is a place of intense unknowing and inexplicable knowing. When huffing and puffing on the outer fails, try listening and breathing on the inner.

Decades are a nice simple way of dividing life up into segments, but the big shifts in life focus seem to be a little shorter, around 7 years, with a year or two for transition around these milestones. You will have your own cycles too, interwoven into the overall trend, and will sometimes arrive early, sometimes late (and if you're not careful there are some places you will never reach!)

You will also have your own preferences for ways of being which "colour" your approach to everything. So for instance even when it might be time to focus on mental development, you might take a rather more physical or emotional line on it. The process is universal, your path through it is your own. Any stage you skip first time will have to be attended to later, and this can seem to interfere with the neatly incremental life programme presented here.

What tends to happen is that in addition to handling the content of the phase you're in, you may simultaneously be dealing with some previously neglected area. That's when it gets most confusing!

Many traditions tell us that the human condition has four main dimensions to it. There is the physical dimension, which we share with all living creatures; an emotional and a mental dimension which we seem to have developed more than most other species; and we have a fourth dimension, a deeper self variously known as soul, spirit or higher self.

The Grounding Years

As we grow up we discover each of these dimensions and the various combinations of them, what I call "colonising". And it does seem that the span of time we allocate to each of these discoveries is roughly 7 years. To re-invent yourself or just catch up, you need to revisit the journey so far, starting with the first 21 years, when we acquire the basic materials for life. Notice what gaps there may be for you to fill in, and where you seem to have done well first time around. The patterns that define our later lives are set in this first 21 years, many of them well before age 7, so if we want to change things now, we need to go back to these formative years.

We start at the simplest, most basic level, focusing for the first 7 years on discovering the physical body. This is when we arrive. Some of the most difficult things we will ever learn come up in this phase. Walking, balancing, interpreting what our eyes are giving us are all tasks we get little if any help mastering very early on. By the age of 7, we have established our relationship with our own physical reality, the foundations on which our lives will be built.

This physical dimension can and does change of course as life proceeds and our focus shifts elsewhere, but up to age 7 the *primary* focus is on things physical.

We frequently embarrass our elders by the fascination bodies and bodily functions have for us. It takes most of the first year for us to work out where "I" stops and "other" begins, what noises and expressions get us what we want, how to make sense of the images around us and calculate how to interact with our physical environment and for instance catch a ball. Then we speed up, from a crawl to a run, and handle more complex coordinations like using tools, riding a bike or playing sports.

Evolution of physical energy does not come to a halt at age 7, any more than our other energies are on ice before that age. The body keeps growing and changing shape after this, but our attention moves on to emotional and then mental states.

Some people identify so strongly with their physical selves that all through life they remain essentially paragons of this energy. These people have a solid physical presence, and often engage in body-building and other very physical pursuits. They become very efficient physically, capable of sustained physical effort that others find exhausting just to watch. While the focus is on this physical energy, the person is quite single-minded. The thing to do is what's in front of them right now, and the time to do it is now.

For all of us this first 7 years is the physical foundation on which everything else stands. Without it, the danger is that we float away, ungrounded, blissfully separated from reality. We need to keep taking care of the physical.

Reflect for a moment on yourself. Did you give yourself time to arrive? Or did you skip this, and make do with being a bit weedy? What was your health like at this age? Did you listen to what your body was trying to tell you, and take the appropriate action? Or did you ignore the warning signs? And what effect or implications does this have for you now? You might recognise from this why your physical energy is as high or low as it is.

Patterns are set in motion at this very early age which run until we change them. You can get a sense of what your pattern is by appraising how much you've been doing physically of late, your health and diet, how much exercise you take, how good a custodian of your environment you are. If your relationship with your body is abusive, don't be surprised if it lets you down. It's the essential container for implementation of your visions and inspirations.

Taking a walk or a run between chapters is highly recommended ...anything physical to hold you in connection with the ground. Select some activity you will enjoy that gets you breathing deeply and feeling tired, but not exhausted afterwards. The temptation is to overdo it in a splurge of unaccustomed activity, a guilty response to the couch potato years. This is counter-productive. Never do quite as much as you can: then you are far more likely to do it again next time. Gradually your capacity will increase, and you will be able to do more.   Diet needs attention too, the main aim being to get your digestive system in good shape, so it can assimilate what you give it instead of dysfunctionally storing fat and starving you. Reduce the things that destroy the friendly bacteria in the gut (coffee, alcohol, antibiotics, denatured food etc) and consult a nutritionist or at least the health food shop. All of this will help your physical energy to rise and you will probably sleep better.

Never do quite as much as you can

The "unfair advantage" you get from arousing your physical energy is the stamina to keep going, which means you get to see things through to completion and get a result. A word of warning: just because you have all this extra energy doesn't mean you have to use it all up! Pace yourself. The main way to reduce stress to acceptable levels is to increase your physical activity, so this attention to your body is really helping you in several ways to catch up with yourself and lay the foundations for growth.

Getting emotional

As this first 7 year phase draws to a close, the focus gradually shifts from the physical to the emotional. This is the time for belonging. Before this there is of course an emotional life, in an embryonic form, just as there is an embryo before physical birth. There are tears at being crossed, and temper tantrums, both often set off by physical frustrations. And emotional ties form especially with those who provide succour and security. From age 4 to 7, through nursery and first school, we start to develop relationships with others and the community beyond the family. Self-consciousness grows and if this sensitivity is not treated compassionately, chronic shyness can manifest as a protective strategy, which stays with you for life.

In most cases well before the age of 7, it has been borne in upon us what we should and should not do, what we may not feel and when we may not express it, what we are to think and what is unthinkable. To the child it is natural to ask a parent dying of cancer "when are you leaving?" Yet socialised adults find this difficult, even callous.

Our feeling selves develop stuntedly within these rigid guidelines of acceptability, especially from about age 7 to 14. How emotionally repressed we are depends largely on the amount of freedom we had to express the full range of emotions in those turbulent years.

As I chewed on my pencil (sorry, hovered over my laptop) waiting for inspiration for the next paragraph, a 6 year old sitting opposite me on the train emptied a cup of hot tea into my lap...just so I could remember how grown-ups don't organise the world properly and always blame us kids for how we seek to navigate and re-organise it.

The child now wants to experiment with the wider range of possible feelings, just as it earlier experimented with what its body (and the bodies of any hapless pets or humans it might chance upon!) could do. From about age 4 or 5, how my body *feels* becomes more important than how it is or how it works. The need now is for affection, rather than just the relief of hunger and discomfort.

Family is important now not just for the physical protection it provides, but as a context for exploring relationship with otherness. From there socialisation with other families and at school follows. First girl/boyfriend relationships are experimented with. Best friends are important now, and whether or not you are accepted into the gang. It's terribly important to be popular and appreciated.

Children who "get it wrong" and become petty criminals, drug addicts, football hooligans or bigots, form a dysfunctional relationship with society which is like an imprint or tattoo, hellishly difficult to remove. By age 14, social values are fixed, creating a major challenge later when those values no longer serve us.

Some children are rushed on to academic achievement up to age 14, and others are deprived of emotional experience at this time, through absent parents, abuse or poor role models. Emotional education is poor, with the result that many of us find communication and relationship a complete mystery later on. We try to substitute physical assertiveness or clever strategies for emotion, but it's a rotten exchange. The main problem we have is that we lack a relationship with ourselves and therefore with each other. We need to rediscover our emotional selves.

Those who stay with this emotional energy and take it into their later life are readily recognisable as the lovely, bubbly types who exude warmth and love chatting for hours. They are the communicators who breathe life into stodgy offices and dead communities. They feel, they cry, they experience the whole gamut of emotional life, and we experience emotion through them. Diana's death opened up emotions that mystified cynical head types.

Their lack of structure may drive us crazy, but without them life is drearier. Happiness is their touchstone for what is worth doing, and they teach us about happiness, enthusiasm, vitality and joy. Given that joy creates a life that works...and work that lives...arousing this energy is a high priority. Without it we take too little pride in ourselves and feel isolated, rejected or excluded.

To what extent does emotional joy light up your life? What feelings have been uppermost for you over the last 2 or 3 months? What ups and downs have there been, and what triggers them? What have you enjoyed or felt really good about from your earlier life? And which of your relationships have ever helped you empower yourself? What does any of this suggest you need to do to reinvent yourself on the emotional front?

While you're taking that walk between chapters, make certain you take yourself somewhere you will really *enjoy*. While you walk, reflect on what you have most enjoyed in your life. When did you last do any of these things? Make a list of your top 5 enjoyments, and allocate time to do all of them for at least an hour before the end of the month, starting with the first one today.

Practise doing things just because they feel right, and because they have a positive impact on your community, and include these actions in your priority joy list. Join associations and networks that give you a context for connecting with others, and make a point of giving of yourself in these communities.

But as with your renewed physical activity, pace yourself. The tendency if this socialising is unaccustomed is to feel gauche and inadequate, to take any small reversal as a major rejection. Gradually the shyness and self-consciousness gives way to a warmer self-awareness. Find a role model, someone who typifies this emotional energy. Take time around them and learn from them. This reduces the problem of becoming something you can't imagine.

Going Mental

All this time the mind has been ticking away. Some whose lives will be more defined by their heads than by their hearts will already have been quite busy on this front. Early signs of this will have been for instance learning to read and write, to do sums and engage in intelligent discussion. The teenage years are focused on intellectual development, but emotional development still continues into the excitement, pain and confusion of first love. This in turn is also an early engagement with the opening of the heart which follows this phase of mental development. It's an explosive time as we start to get our own ideas, and rebel against received wisdom, without having gained any certainty for our emerging beliefs. But it is time for maturing as we try to integrate all these dimensions of ourselves - think, feel, do and love.

The theme to all this is questioning. All the beliefs, mindsets, concepts and prejudices we acquired from parents and other authority figures are called into question, even those we eventually accept and make our own. We treat everything as illusion for now and turn our experience of life up to this point into a coconut shy.

This can take the form of earnest study or delinquency. It all depends on how sure of ourselves we feel. The uncontrollable, violent youth is one whose early life has not equipped him or her with any self-esteem, who has not been valued nor given intelligible boundaries. There is no basis for respect, not for themselves nor for others, because during the emotional focus years they have been treated too harshly or too coldly. They have no sense of relationship or community, and what passes for thought is rarely more than the most simplistic prejudice enforced by thugs and bullies. When teenagers are denied their own thoughts, you create the empty faces and disillusioned minds that were supposed to have been processed into fodder for industry, but have just been turned to mush.

The studious ones are those who have for one reason or another retired into themselves to process their thoughts and find something they can rely on. The school system is designed for them, the 10% of academic achievers who will use their heads to get ahead in life. School doesn't always honour the talents of the rest, so they form a jaundiced view of intellectual life and a poor opinion of themselves.

The lucky ones are those whose imagination has been awakened or at least not suppressed in primary school and allowed to flourish into creativity. Come the mental development years, their right and left brains evolve in tandem, balancing fantasy with rationality, learning with personality. They probably excel on the artistic side of things, not much appreciated by society and "the system", but emerge as people rather than puddings, our guides to the unseen depths of the human spirit.

How we use our minds to sort out both who we are and what we have experienced already in these crucial years sets the scene for the rest of our lives. To change direction later, we must return to these formative years and re-parent ourselves, putting back what we missed then - physical, emotional or mental.

Those who stay with this intellectual energy through life are the thinkers, commentators and researchers, fascinated by new ideas or delving deep into their own chosen field of study.

Did you emerge from this time with a mind that helps you make sense of life, or were you turned off by heartless intellectualising? Few survive to 21 with their own thoughts intact or with any basis for thinking things through. Does your mind support you or has it only learnt how to sabotage you? Could you make a deal with it..."you (mind) help me make sense of my life, and I'll listen to you and help you get what you want"?

This walk you're taking between chapters is really important, because the best way to sort things out mentally is to take them for a walk. If you give your mind a chance it can make a lot of sense. It's only when a mind has been told constantly it's stupid, wrong or inadequate that it reacts negatively. Treat it right and it will pour out positive, creative ideas for your enrichment.

These thoughts need to be balanced with feeling if there is to be humanity there. Keep it in balance, and keep noticing where you lean too much one way or another. If you're going to reinvent yourself and make a LifeShift, you need to be able to think, feel and do. Mens Sana in Corpore Sano is all very well, and very wise, but without Cor Sanum (healthy heartfulness) it's too mechanical.

A Turbulent Transition

We arrive at the end of these grounding years with a somewhat tenuous hold on reality. Our development of the basic physical, emotional and mental building bricks is as we have seen sketchy, but worse than that it is probably based on false assumptions and other people's ideas and prejudices.

There is intense pressure in these first 21 years to achieve a result in terms of skills and exams. There is obviously merit in honing your talents, but not to the exclusion of all else. Many of the distractions we'll be looking at here are not bad things; but when they assume a disproportionate impact, they can shut out all other considerations. Exams have this effect. The student is not unreasonably led to believe that a good grade is important. Anything that then competes with studying to get the grade is discouraged. And this is where it gets out of balance. Always a bad thing.

The principal **distraction** for this phase then is everything that leads to a good **exam** result. To maintain this exclusive focus on exams, some absolutely crucial information is withheld. In the headlong drive to exam success, nobody mentions that while a highly developed head may help you get a job and the comfort that brings, heart is what gets you a life. What really matters in the end is relationship. Am I actually in relationship with myself, with other and with the planet? Because when I am, I probably have enough positive self-regard to cope with life, whatever my economic state. Without that relationship, I am probably miserable, however high paid the job or brilliant the exam result.

Renewing your relationship with your emotional self probably involves reducing your reliance on the head or the body, and you may experience great reluctance to do this. Take it gently and give yourself time. Remember 7 years was allocated to developing this first time round: it make take a couple of weeks to catch up now! Or a couple of years!! In general it is wise to think of this as a fairly long-term exercise and evolve a plan for a number of years. Often the place you want to get to and the place you want to get away from require time to elapse. Rushing it just leads to disillusionment and hopelessness, which is the opposite of fulfilment.

It _is_ your life!

It is a well kept secret too that it *is* your life! And that all the things that are presented to you as incontrovertible are choices. You can choose what you study or focus on. You can choose how hard you work at it, and what else you fit around your work. You can even choose what work you fit around your life! Settling down, having children, climbing the career ladder (usually someone else's), saddling yourself with a big mortgage and loads of other status symbols are all choices. You don't have to do any of them to be a respectable human being.

Whatever you choose, there is a cost. And not acquiring any skills to sell has a very high cost. But so does throwing your life away in pursuit of some expensive cul-de-sac.

There are more secrets which lead us to make more false assumptions. A widespread assumption is that other people will be as committed, reliable, dedicated and compassionate as you are. Now while it would be nice to take the positive view that everyone is there to help, it is safer not to assume that everybody can be relied on to do it for you. By the same token you are not responsible for anyone else either, just yourself. You get in a mess, that's your problem, no-one else's. If you buy the idea that "we all help each other", you may find that you're always digging others out of a hole, while they just dig your hole deeper. It may pay them to keep you in the dark, serving their needs. Positive thinking helps you set things up for yourself, but be realistic about how much it will impact on others' negativity.

The Non-Vanishing Act

You not only can have a dream of your own, you must! It's the only basis for a life, and not one defined by others' prejudices. Really check out whether the key principles you think you believe are yours at all, or whether you just bought the party line years ago and have been defending it without thought or question ever since. When you spout one of your pet philosophies, is it really one of yours, or is it a home-spun one taken down off the shelf along with all the other family argot? We get so used to saying some things we actually come to believe them.

One of the biggest secrets, the main thing they don't tell you in school is that life has these phases, and that you, and everybody else changes their focus roughly every 7 years. The person you meet and whose outlook on life fascinates you at age 21 will have become somebody else by 28 and by 35 will be barely recognisable. Bear this in mind before you make any long-term commitments.

The battering you receive from this introduction to life, the bigoted and demeaning stuff that's rammed down your throat, the constant suppression of your uniqueness, creativity, dignity and authenticity can leave the tender adolescent pretty disparaged. The intellectual flattening is piled on top of the emotional damage (and physical abuse) to leave you disillusioned, diminished and wounded. This all shows in the body as dis-ease. What the disease is doing to your body is what these first 21 years did to you.

One way or another the great danger is that you disappear. You have been so bullied by the system that you've gone. All we have left of you is a pale impression covered with a garish mask. If you don't disappear by giving in, you disappear by rebelling. All your energy goes into fighting the system and there's none left for you to develop you. You are defined by what you rebel against, quite as much as by what you buy into.

It's too late to change the past. But it's not too late to stop the past running or rather ruining the future. Nor is it too late to change your relationship to what's past, to see it in a new light, to see the glorious things you got from it. You can re-invent yourself using all that past sh*t as fertiliser for new growth. However well or badly you've got on thus far, there is every morning, every minute, a straight choice - growth or atrophy. Stop growing, stop learning and soon you stop living. Our souls stick around for a bit waiting to see if we'll get the message and step back into life, but then if we make it clear we're not up for any more we go. It's time to give up your seat to someone who needs it and will make better use of it.

Why do we make such a meal of filling the old gaps? Partly it is the distractions we're lost in at that stage of our lives, eg exams while we're teenagers. But it is also fear. Here I am, dimly aware that I need to make some big change in how I am or how I cope with reality. I've no idea what it would be like to have made that change, and cannot imagine it. And I have no guarantee that it will do the trick.

I may also fear that if I allow this new stuff in, I will lose my old way of holding life together and generating an income.

Catching up with yourself does mean juggling these four contrary balls. You are reducing the amount of time and energy you have been giving to an old faithful, which also generates income. And you are introducing more focus on something unfamiliar which you missed out on earlier. You are fearful that swapping these two things will jeopardise your financial viability. And you have the additional deterrent of the "early stage distress" we commonly experience when we start to colonise unfamiliar territory.

At the same time, we are only doing all this because something about our life no longer satisfies nor fulfils, and our values and vision for ourselves have shifted. It is very disconcerting. All the more reason to take it slowly, one step at a time. If your physical state is not desperately deficient, there's no need to give yourself a hard time over it. Focus more on developing other energies. And if you get by pretty well intellectually, leave it at that. We don't need to be Einstein...or Schwarzenegger! Then there's the emotional and relationships, probably the energy you most need to arouse. Our pressure cooker society with its distorted appreciation of intellectual gifts and excellence over everything else suppresses the influence of heart, which makes life heartless.

A further reason for being gentle with yourself is that after 21 both body and mind are in decline. From 19 on brain cells are dying faster than you can replace them, and few sports heroes last much beyond 28. Emotional development continues evolving however through exploration of heart energy into the spiritual realm. This lift-off into spirit coincides with the most marked decline of the body from age 40 on. So if the work you now need to do to catch up with yourself seems hard, this is why. Go gently!

From all this you must select what if anything is a priority for you. You don't need to make work for yourself! There's plenty to do without that. It's also worth checking back to your vision to see what you need to have on board for its fulfilment. What does your vision tell you you need more of in your life and what do you need less of? Is it still as important as it seemed at 21 to become Top Dog in the Kennels, or is Personal Fulfilment (and a more heartful life) now crying out for attention? Are you still trying to do your bit for economic growth or have you realised that Personal Growth is your job...and your principal contribution? Act accordingly.

Suppose for a moment you could re-invent yourself, what would you change? Smaller ears, straight nose and green eyes perhaps? Drop dead gorgeous blonde or stunning Eastern beauty? Who would you be with? What parents would you have chosen? And what job? What do you regret - those foot in mouth moments you die over daily? How would life have been with more children or less, sooner or later? With more or less goodies accumulated? What would matter most if you had your time over? Would you still value and believe in the same things?

This is how one 85 year old summed up how she'd reinvent herself. You don't have to be 85 to be wise but it helps.

PICKING MORE DAISIES

"If I had my life over, I'd dare to make more mistakes next time. I'd relax. I'd limber up. I would be sillier than I have been this time. I would take fewer things seriously. I would take more chances. I would take more trips. I would climb more mountains and swim more rivers. I would eat more ice cream and less beans. I would perhaps have more actual troubles but I'd have fewer imaginary ones...

You see, I am one of those people who live sensibly hour after hour, day after day. Oh, I've had my moments and if I had it to do over again, I'd have more of them. In fact I'd try to have nothing else. Just moments, one after another instead of living so many years ahead of each day.

I've been one of those persons who never goes anywhere without a thermometer, a hot water bottle, a raincoat and a parachute. If I had it to do again I would travel lighter than I have. If I had my life to live over I would start barefoot earlier in the spring and I would stay that way later in the fall. I would go to more dances. I would ride more merry-grounds. I would pick more daisies."

Nadine Stair, Louisville, Kentucky

So what would it take to reinvent you? What would actually need to change? Picture this new pretend you. Balanced, congruent, whole, integrated, self-empowered, genuine, authentic, open-hearted, free, aligned, attuned, connected, joyful, happy, living a quality life, learning and communicating your own truth. Pick your own description. All that needs to change is your image of yourself and your willingness to change it. The main thing we're **attached to** from this era is the **self-image** and all that baggage we entered adulthood with. If we're going to move on we need to reframe this, construct a healthy adolescence for ourselves, let go the attachment to this outmoded self-image and allow the ideal self to crystallise.

The **pitfall** of this phase then is that we **disappear**, and create a false self-image to which we become obsessively attached. If the socialising flac gets to us, we can emerge with a damaged, low self-image, to which we are strangely attached. If we reacted to the propaganda with the classic adolescent rebellion, our self-image becomes defined as defensively assertive. Even if we came through reasonably unscathed, we still have a self-image which is probably now obsolete. Choices we made then are not choices we'd make now. We may feel trapped in old decisions and their ramifications. Now is the time to choose/decide again. The world and everything around us has changed since then, so why shouldn't you? In fact why on earth haven't you? You must be mad to think you can stay "Good Ol' Jo" when the market for Good Ol' Jos is closed. All these self-images are distortions and we need to let them go. Drag it to Trash. How difficult this is depends how long you've been locked up, and how much parole you've managed along the way.

SUMMARY

● Nurture your nature.
● We keep learning and growing through all of life's 7 year phases, starting with physical development, emotional discovery and intellectual awakening.
● Question all assumptions.
● Take it gently.
● Pick more daisies!

LESSON to LEARN:
Moving your life forward into the future requires a **Re-invention** of your past.

DISTRACTION to TRANSFORM:
Exams while important need to be put into perspective.

PITFALL to AVOID:
Disappearing, losing your personal visibility.

ATTACHMENT to RELEASE:
Low or otherwise unhelpful **Self-Image.**

EXERCISE

● What did you miss out on during your grounding years?
    physically
    emotionally
    intellectually
● What do you need to do as an absolute priority, in order to plug this gap?
● What strengths do you have that will help you with this?

Make some notes here and transfer any actions to your To Do List and the Personal Priorities Pages at the back of the book.

CHAPTER 4

The Breakout Years (21-28): Stepping into Your Vision

The conventional route through the twenties drives us to embark on an urgent search for the well-paid job. There is also massive pressure to enter into life-long commitments. This is jumping the gun. At 21 we are still run by old received wisdom, prejudiced belief systems and self-sabotaging mind-sets. We have not properly checked any of this out or discovered who we really want to be. It is therefore madness to set our lives in concrete, and yet all the pressures of society force us into premature decisions that can trap us for decades. People burden us with their unsolicited worries about our futures and insist that we "be responsible" and conform.

The *real* twenties task is to open our hearts to ourselves. It's the time to become someone you could like; someone who is genuine, authentic, caring, respectful, compassionate, reverent of self and of all life. This is someone who reacts joyfully and enthusiastically to whatever happens, who sees what *is* working and is grateful for it. This is also someone who is practising love, giving, coming from the heart with clear intention. This involves surrendering the need for external validation, fame, recognition, security, line-shooting and control dramas. Rage, pride, judgment, attachment, rule books and negative beliefs all must be let go, but not the righteous anger against injustice.

You have the opportunity at this age to set yourself on a path which is congruent, happy and healthy, as a free agent unencumbered by demoralising low energy work and people who drain your energy. Instead you take time for yourself and others you gather round you to use your talents constructively, joyfully and wisely, and to have fun.

This phase of life should be a time of experiment, broadening our experience, trying out options, unearthing a direction we value that also values and honours us. It is a most precious time to gather our energies while we get clear what is *worth* committing to before we actually commit. Focusing on our own personal growth at this time does paradoxically aid income generation because a growthful approach to life is what removes the blocks to that income generation. By being holistic, we work towards our needs being met.

This has the makings of quite a battleground - learning to love and value ourselves while we lay down the foundations for a life that adds up financially. Both love and money are ways in which we seek to assert ourselves. Love is an act of will, willing the good and personal growth of oneself and other, the ultimate expression of our personal human potential, whereas money is society's supreme symbol of successful self-assertion.

Income generation is actually one of the main arenas for personal growth and learning. Opting out is not an option. There needs to be a good balance between the inner personal growth and the outer practical relationship with the economy. Anything else is flaky and insupportable.

Balance is a terribly important component of LifeShift and the holistic approach to enterprise. There is no place for dogmatism or hierarchy of one element of life over another. Initially as one discovers a new dimension to life, there is a tendency to land heavily on it and feel it has some supreme significance. This is out of balance and lacks the compassion, acceptance, wholeness and relationship that is necessary for forward movement. The danger otherwise is a sort of spiritual fascism which is as destructive and unproductive as rampant consumerism.

When we engage in the spiritual as well as the material dimension, we have a more healthy lifestyle. But when work is overdone, the rest of life gets squeezed out. We lose touch with our true selves, and the context takes over from the content. Go to the other extreme and we lose touch with anything solid to relate to, and thus with relationship itself.

Self-Assertion Time

The first 21 years give us some building bricks for our personal development. After this we should sort out what we want to do with them as preparation for firming up the structure and shape of life. Much of the general principle of how you go about doing this has already been covered. Now we can add some specifics.

Defining your own clear inspiring vision of success is still the start point, and how we respond to new circumstances is still more important than the circumstances themselves. You are still encouraged to notice what distracts you and gets in the way of the task before you. The process still involves not being deflected as you fill in the gaps and build one layer on top of another.

LifeShift invites you to relive your life, phase by phase. Age 21, which give or take 3 years is the threshold to adulthood, is the moment when classically we step out into the world, away from previous influences, parents and education. The focus for The Breakout Years (21-28) is particularly on the energies of love, will, responsibility and provisional commitment.

If you're actually in this 21-28 age range, this self-assertive phase is what's up for you right now. This, and renovating the physical, emotional, mental foundations is your immediate task. Before you climb into the clouds, it would be wise to fix your ladder firmly on the ground.

So get physical. Roll your sleeves up. Put yourself about. Whingeing pathetically about how tough it is out there will get you nowhere. You need your body in fighting trim, so take care of it: exercise regularly and eat healthily. Your body is a temple, not a dustbin.

Emotionally, it is important to reconnect with your feelings after so much focus at school or college on mental gymnastics. Practise noticing what you feel moment to moment and express more of this. Giving is a very good way to connect emotionally, and giving is good for you. When it's done unconditionally, and that's the only way to do it, what you give comes back to you traditionally tenfold, if you're open to it.

Intimacy and community involvement is the very stuff of emotional development. When you combine this with the physical business of work, you discover the intensely satisfying experience of "getting sweaty together".

Balance this emotional expression with mental competence. Get your head in gear, serving you, not just keeping old unhelpful mindsets in place. Don't get stuck in the head. Getting a first and not growing up is not success, nor is it exactly failure just a rather tragic misunderstanding. Head trips don't lead to fulfilment. Sanity is fine, Vanity is another matter. There is a strong interaction between the mind and feelings. The more negative feelings we have about ourselves emanate from the mind and its capacity for worry and judgment. Positive feelings give us a positive perspective on life. Let your head and your feelings talk to each other as equal partners. Let the head sort out all the nitty-gritty details of the tasks your feelings take you into.

For the twenty somethings future chapters provide a sneak preview of what's coming shortly: this is vital information which often seems to evade school and college leavers, and consigns them to one mistaken cul-de-sac after another.

If you're older than 28, this chapter describes the energy you next need to find or rediscover in yourself. If the twenties was not a particularly empowering time for you, you will need to relive them and put the heart back into your life.

In our twenties we should be experiencing some of the power that has been accumulating as we laid the foundations. It may be worth stressing that if you don't experience yourself as very powerful, this almost certainly indicates that you need to return to the energies you should have been building in those first 21 years as well, whatever your present age.

This phase is the test of how much self-esteem the rigours of life have left us. We take many hard knocks in the early years: now is the time to face this and take action to shrug them off. It is time to fall in love with you, because otherwise your lovelessness motivates you to compensate all the time. The desperate search for piles of money is often a reaction to feelings of low self-esteem: if we don't feel we exist we have to surround ourselves with things to prove we do. The widespread dissatisfaction with this money-obsessed way of life is amongst other things an indication that we are reclaiming our self-esteem - discovering "self-fulness".

Some people retain this "self-ful" twenties quality throughout their lives. They seem to have a good relationship with themselves, not selfish, arrogant or defensively aggressive, not selfless, shrinking violets either, but realistically convinced of their talents in an enlightened way. Their aim throughout life is to contribute what they came here to do and be, and they have a good sense of what that is, as it evolves. They are often unreasonable, pioneering, rebellious, sometimes difficult people especially for those who have not yet owned their own power.

Without this self-ful quality, life is endlessly unrewarding and motivation is a problem. Nothing matters enough to be worth taking a risk on. Without this solid sense of self, one is constantly looking to others to prop one up and supply the love one denies oneself. Sadly this is doomed to failure.

Climb your own ladder

A Passion for Life

The **lesson** for this phase is to discover your **passion** for life, to take the risk to feel deeply into your heart and apply your will to activate your vision. Many seem to be embarrassed by others' passion and emotionally charged determination to live a whole life. We have to rise above this squeamishness and face squarely the personal and inter-relational issues it brings up for us. In a society dedicated to character assassination, we have to risk standing out.

All this may well seem to be in stark contrast to what actually happens in the twenties! Commonly we're not sure what we want to do so we do whatever comes along. It's not ideal but it's on offer and seems to promise a financial return on all the preparation we've been doing. There may even be some good prospects. Once installed in this we get better and better at delivering something that was not very enthusiastically, wisely or thoughtfully embraced. We develop a track record that takes us further and further away from who we really want to be, if we only knew what that was. The distance between these two selves gradually separates us from who we might be.

Moreover we may have fallen into the classic blunder of climbing someone else's ladder without ever asking "why climb? why ladder? and why someone else's?!" The problem is you end up relying on the organisation to train and develop you, and what they do is help you become what *they* want. A large part of the catching up you then need to do is to remember to train you for what *you* want.

We are entering a world of work which looks very different from what culminated in the '80s. Now we have interlocking networks where individuals come together in temporary arrangements and then disperse into something else; teleworking villages; portfolio careerists cobbling a job together out of several diverse strands; multi-nationals contracting out so they become split into thousands of autonomous units; whole institutions being declared redundant; the normalisation of zero and negative growth economies. This scenario (which some of us have predicted since 1994) is coming ever closer, as everyone realises they need to be Managing Director of their own lives.

In the new holistic enterprise economy, service comes before profit and trust in that yields the profit; enlightened self-fulness replaces greed and acquisitiveness and networking takes over from bloody-minded competitiveness. Your skills, constantly upgraded and expanded are all you have to rely on for survival. No longer can you abdicate from running your own life. Each of us needs to deal with the practicalities as we draw up the highest potential from within us, uncover our vision and grow into it. But external validation becomes less important as our own authority and self-directing ability takes over. As MD of our lives we create our own work and facilitate work for others in our network, and each job is an apprenticeship for the next. All of it is our apprenticeship to life, the energy we need to learn to work with at this phase of life.

What are the commitments you made around this age (or what are you planning if this is yet to come for you)? And are they still working for you? The ones that work are the commitments you make to yourself and to what makes your heart sing.

The idea that life arrives in a series of phases is not a new one, but previous presentations have tended to emphasise the phases as a series of problems, preordained and inevitable. There is a lack of vita (life in Latin). I hope I am making it clear that each phase has its tremendously positive possibilities as well as pitfalls and problems that distract us from the task in hand and the lessons we need to learn. Other versions leave you with a sense that you cannot be you until you're 50 or 70 or never! My emphasis is on what you can do NOW to be you. And this is what I want to move onto now.

Calculated Choices

This is where you ask "Whose life is it anyway?" and shout "Mine!" Trade in your old life and the debilitating values it was based on and commit to your own life and values. This is a much better plan, and this process has already started. We have already been looking at what you (could) offer, and it is now time to pull this all together.

For those of you still in your twenties this is absolutely what's in front of you. For those beyond this age, this is an opportunity to review where you've been and make a new start. We all need to keep doing this throughout our lives. Nothing stands still and yesterday's plan will not suffice for tomorrow. If life is a project in discovering our vision as I believe it is, every new phase will of course require us to rethink our direction and what we now need to leave behind us.

Use the format on the next page to "map" your options.

Summarise right in the middle of the Options & Opportunities Map where you are now. What are the skills and resources that you currently rely on for income? These go in the middle circle, around the word NOW.

Next use the boxes to note the options you currently see for yourself. Place options that draw on old skills and interests in the top row, sideways moves in the middle row, and newer, riskier options that take you into fresh territory, in the bottom row.

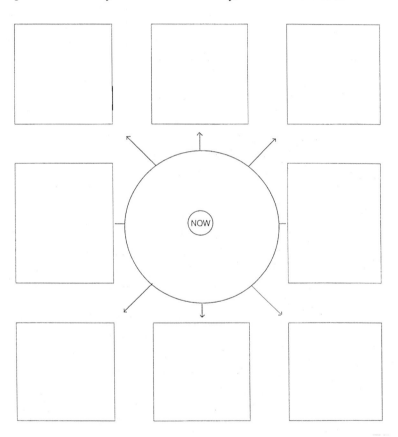

OPTIONS & OPPORTUNITIES MAP

What's Your Trip?

If you're working through this book with someone else (which is a great way to do it) take 5 minutes each to talk through what you came up with. Or just sit with it for a moment. Stillness and sharing are fundamental to LifeShift. Where have you come from? Where are you now? And what is your desired outcome? What looks most exciting at this stage? As you proceed through this exercise keep returning to the map and adding more options. What sort of person is emerging from this exercise so far? OK so nobody's perfect, but everybody's good at something. The trouble is we don't always recognise it. We don't know our own strengths! People are much too good at telling us what we're hopeless at, less fluent when it comes to telling us our good points. And when someone does compliment us, we probably stammer "That's easy", and underrate ourselves. It's high time you valued the sort of person you are.

As you've been introduced to each life phase, you've been told that some people retain the "colouring" of a particular phase/energy throughout life. Here those personality types are summarised, so you can get a sense of which one(s) are you. And each is allocated a colour code for easy reference. "Colouring" was not just a turn of phrase. This colour code is not arbitrary either; some readers will recognise it as the colouring commonly given to the "chakras", the energy centres we all have spinning inside us. This classification is based on a tradition which goes back at least 6000 years, and still has volumes to tell us about human life.

So, are you an **active** person, with lots of get-up-and-go? Are you physically fit, keen on sports or body-building? Your stamina will be a real asset in getting things to happen. This is the **RED** physical energy associated with the first 7 grounding, arrival years.

Or are you more of a **sociable** person? Do you have lots of friends and a great network of contacts? Do you join clubs and groups and enjoy doing things with other people? Is it you that worries about work colleagues when they're off sick, or deals with leaving presents and parties? What a wonderful strength to have, since life is so much about relationships. Your vitality and enthusiasm will be infectious. This is the **ORANGE** emotional energy of the interactive years 7-14.

Perhaps you're less emotional than that, but easy going and

73

flexible with a keen eye for detail and getting things just right? Others may wilt under the strain but you have the concentration to crack it. You enjoy and adapt quickly to new situations. And you're probably good with drawings, technical specs and prototypes, research, learning and anything intellectual. You're a **YELLOW**, skilled in the autonomising, individualistic energy of the teenage study years (14-21).

Does all that clever stuff and attention to detail drive you up the wall? Were your teenage years heavier on freeing yourself than on the nitpicky mental application? Sounds like you're more of a **go-getter**, determined to get ahead. That drive, determination and willingness to take risks will come in very handy especially to generate an income, win against the competition and persuade people to do what you want...like buy from you! You probably recognise this as the energy we're describing in this chapter, the **GREEN** energy of the self-assertive twenties (21-28).

Yet another strength (linked to a phase we have yet to come to) is the ability to get things **organised** and see the overview. If you've had some management experience or had to supervise people, you probably have this strength. It can save so much time and wasted effort, enabling you to be good at thinking things through in a practical way. You draw on others for advice without relying on it too much. Many will appreciate your calm, clear, decisive, efficient approach. They feel you can actually deliver. This is the **BLUE** energy associated with the assured, consolidation years from 28 to 35 (Chapter 5).

Some people always seem to be in the right place at the right time. These are lucky people, because they see the lucky breaks others miss, because they're so much more **aware**. They're sensitive to what's going on around them. They tend to see the way things are going and catch on to new trends almost before they happen. This often goes with being rather artistic, designing neat new ways of doing things. They draw on intuition rather than mere logic. This energy is colour-coded **INDIGO** and inspires the search for meaning and balance which typically absorbs us in our forties (42-49: Chapter 7).

What happened to the 35-42 phase?!! Chapter 6 will explain how these years draw on BLUE *and* INDIGO as we take stock in the lead up to mid-life crisis and spiritual awakening.

Most people have a combination of these six strengths though one will tend to be "most like me". The more you can draw on all these different qualities the more **creative** you will be. This is what life is working towards, and your work or business is the best place to do it.

As your enterprise grows you grow with it, acquiring more confidence and a wide range of abilities. This releases your creative spark and you can make a very considerable impact on your community and even further afield. Its colour is **VIOLET**, and we'll return to its creative, visionary quality in Chapter 8, when we look at the years 49-56 when wisdom matures into the deeper wholeness of the later years.

The way you are (and how you fill that out and keep learning and growing) is the first and foremost of your **Talents**. You have to do it, whatever it is, your way. This is a large part of your uniqueness, and this, the way in which you are "the only" something, has other dimensions. Your Talents are all your skills, knowledge, experience and competences. When you pause to think about it, you will be amazed to discover what you do know, what you do well and what you have experienced that makes you different. Think about talents you never had call to deploy in your work, and things you *used* to be good at or familiar with. Remember not to discount what people keep telling you you're good at or find easy. Languages, selling skills, the gift of the gab, all could be invaluable Talents. Finally consider what you admire in others: there is a very good chance that you're not bad at that yourself and just need to train up a bit.

Money or rather the lack of it is usually quoted as the reason for not shifting or going self-employed. And yet in my experience the one group of people who will never start a business are the ones who have all the money they need. They have too much to lose. Most entrepreneurs do not have immediate access to funds and start small. It's the best way, as there's a lot to learn and you stay streetwise.

Money takes many forms though. It can take the form of a good customer list, a keen supplier or influential contacts. Perhaps you know people with money or connection to it. And there are other **Resources** you can convert into readies - the information you have, premises to work from or lease out, a particular piece of equipment...and all the Talents you have now listed. Has this suggested any new options? Add them to your map.

We most of us spend most of our lives putting off what we really want to be doing, because we're not clear exactly what that is and because we keep getting distracted. Being clear what your **Intentions** are for how you will put your Talents and Resources to work is fundamental...and the underlying purpose of this book. Your Intentions stem from your motivations - making your mark in some way, being of service, freedom, independence, fun and togetherness, solving a problem. What do you most keenly intend to create in your life and why? What would be worth making money for? What do you want from your present job box and what do you want to have achieved 10 years from now, or if you won the lottery? Why delay? If ever now! Talents and Resources lie idle until you harness them to Intention...And **Passion**. Passion is the spark and the lesson to learn in this phase of life. What are you passionate about? What matters? What gets you angry? What do you really enjoy? Integrate your 10 favourite pleasures into your plan: it's your energy base.

Talents, Resources, Intentions, Passions. That's your TRIP! TRIP represents a logical approach to finding a career or business idea that fits you and your situation. It helps you give shape to what you already know. It helps you see how much more you have to offer than you might at first have thought. From all of this extract a list of your strengths and another of the possible directions you might take. Include as well as the sensible ones that draw on your strengths, skills and values; the crazy, impractical, unrealistic ones; the basic, fun money-earners and the goose-pimply ones that inspire you and give meaning to your life. Trust your feelings and allow new, exciting possibilities as you clarify what you really want to be doing. We all need, want and deserve to work. Without work we experience ourselves as useless. Work creates the context in which we challenge ourselves, learn, grow and make our contribution.

"To love life through labour is to be intimate with life's inmost secret...Work is love made visible." (Kahlil Gibran: The Prophet)

Scoring Your Potential

You might choose to return to these 3 grid exercises later if you're keen to read on for now. But at least cast an eye over them, because they will bring your direction into much sharper focus.

Grid 1: List the Strengths you now realise you have down the left-hand side of the Grid, and the Possible Life Directions you could pursue across the top. To what extent does each Strength boost the power of each Possibility? Score out of 10 how well each Strength in turn helps you deliver each Possibility.

ITEM							TOTAL
TOTAL							

Now add up the columns in Grid 1 (both across and down) to find out which Strengths serve you most widely, and which Possibilities you are best equipped to realise. From this select the best 7-10 possibilities and list them on the left-hand side of Grid 2.

ITEM							TOTAL
TOTAL							

How valuable are your best Possibilities?   Score each Possibility in Grid 2 out of 10 for how well it performs against the 6 criteria lined up across the top of the Grid. These 6 criteria are:

How much does it use your strengths?
How important is it to you?
How easy is it to access the market for this?
How much potential for growth/development?
How financially rewarding NOW?
How financially rewarding in the future?

Add up all the scores again to find your Best Possibility.

Grid 3: Reflect on what you might do, eg training, work experience, research, writing a book(!), obtaining a qualification, that would significantly improve your scores and redo Grid 2 on the assumption this action has been taken. This creates your Learning Contract.

ITEM							TOTAL
TOTAL							

Your Learning Contract with Yourself

Lifelong Learning is not an optional extra: you stagnate at your peril. So keep developing and combining these strengths to find new options that are special and unique to you. This probably involves simultaneously adding the new as you let go the old, and the old is also probably what you rely on for income, so it may take some courage.

Take the transformation gently. Many people experience panic around money when they try to make too major a shift all in one go. Panic is immobilising. We all need a bread and butter job, a money-tree to provide comfort money. Build on the skills in which you've already invested 10 or 20 years of your life. Don't give up your day job just yet, and don't jettison your track-record until you can replace it with something more exciting. Upgrade your existing skills. Specialise in a niche market and get equipped to operate superbly at the cutting edge of your trade.

Recognise too that it can take time to find a market for your new vision. There can be many false starts and wrong turns. It can be tough even finding where to start, sell yourself and get organised. It is *normal* after 22 months to feel utterly frazzled and dejected. *Normal.* Most people hopelessly underestimate the time it can take to get going. Having a basic, undemanding source of income while you get established takes the pressure off. If you are totally reliant on your new vision for money and it's not yet working, it hurts twice - once because there's no money, and once because what you're passionate about is being rejected.

It is __normal__ to feel frazzled

A Portfolio Career with 3 strands is recommended. Your old skills and your new vision give you two strands. The third strand might be a connection with a reliable larger venture where you don't have to do everything. This could be contract work or some other connection to a structure, a proven product range, a supportive team and in time an income. But select carefully and only join up if you can be passionate about the product or service.

See how your 3 possibilities compare with your costs and your Weekly Income Target. £250? How many "units of sale" does this represent? (A unit of sale might be an hour of your time, a window cleaned, a 45 minute service, what you make on an average sale.) If your Portfolio includes at least one skill that can earn £25 an hour, you only need to sell 10 hours a week to make that £250 target. Ideally the skill is "travellable" so you can go anywhere and find clients fairly quickly. Learning another language obviously helps.

Here are some possibilities to get you started:

Tutoring, private tuition
Teaching English as a Foreign Language (TEFL)
Teaching TEFL, swimming, windsurfing, backgammon etc
Training, eg computers, the Internet, writing web pages
Translation, interpreting, tourguide
Hairdresser, beauty therapist, make-up artist
Aerobics, dancer, modelling, escort
Journalism, writing, PR, word-processing, bookkeeper
Graphic/computer design, artwork, photography
Art/antique dealer
Musician, singer, busker
Chef, caterer, croupier, bartender
Massage, other natural medicine practice, freelance nursing
Counselling, mentoring, consultancy
Astrology, tarot-reading
Taxi/mini-cab service, Man with a Van
Plasterer, plumber, electrician, TV repairs, window-cleaning
Rubbish disposal, car-wash, glazier, construction site work
Emergency call-out (any trade), but specialise
Network marketing.

Marketing Your Portfolio
Now list 30 people you can sell to regularly - 10 for your old skill, 10 for the new, 10 for the third strand. These people must be either large organisations, or the people who work for them: they're the

only ones with the time and the money to buy your services. Beware of creating a list of people like you, self-employed and cutting down on expenses! Make yourself visible, desirable and indispensable to the resource-rich 5-10% of the economy.

LifeShifters think self-employed. Full-time jobs do not offer the flexibility, income or even the security they need, and are a dying breed anyway. But part-time especially contract work is a good option.

Ironically the downsizing and employee empowerment programmes, which have whacked up the pressure, stress and time/ energy demand of organisation work and thereby boosted the appeal of the LifeShift life, have also created work for LifeShifters too. Organisations are now so lean, there is no slack to take on new projects, solve problems, expand or even monitor and improve progress.

Contract work now appeals to larger organisations. Their commitment is limited and short term. They always get the people and skills they need, rather than having to make do with what they happen to have in-house. There are no pensions, tax, NI, SSP, pregnancy leave, redundancy, industrial tribunal or other expensive bureaucratic nuisances. And there are no company cars, telephone bills, office space, secretaries, empire building, perks, training, career development or learning curves to invest in. It's like a dream!

And the people who are best placed and keenest to fill these contract jobs are the experienced ex-company men and women who have opted for LifeShift. They have the necessary corporate track-record to reassure nervous buyers, and they manage themselves.

Love is...

The 20's then is the time to first connect with and assert your own power and potential. You need to emerge from this phase with a broad experience of life and a bank of talents selected from intense experimentation with possibility. And you need to have practised coming into relation with love, will, power, commitment, determination, enterprise and money, without feeling the need to make irrevocable commitments just yet. These are all the key qualities and contexts for experiencing the essential energy of this phase of life.

Whenever you are reviewing your direction and contemplating another LifeShift you also need to re-experience this "green" energy in order to find the will and powerful intention to see it through. And simultaneously you will also need to be working with the energy of whatever age phase you are in chronologically. Indeed this is what is happening throughout our lives: we are always bringing all the earlier phase energies to bear on working the phase we're in; and we are always trying to do this without the benefit of having yet experienced the phases yet to come. It can feel as if you're walking backwards through life, gradually seeing the sense of it revealed behind you like a wake! We live in a rear-view mirror!

In this chapter we've been looking at the tasks and energies especially associated with the age range 21 - 28, a most crucial time for you to get in touch with your true self and gather around you qualities and skills you enjoy, that also honour you.

When you value your talents and the contribution you can make to the grand scheme of things, when you commit to be and do whatever it takes to exhibit these talents and share your power with the world, when you grasp the inter-connectedness of yourself and the cosmos, you rise, rather than negatively fall, in love with YOU.

This is where love starts, loving yourself unconditionally. You can only give others what you have first given yourself. And if you want to receive love from others you must first give it to yourself, because no-one can give you what you refuse to give yourself, any more than you can give someone what they haven't given themselves.

Love is not the slushy, mutually abusive co-dependency of romantic love. That is, to be sure, the propaganda of pop songs and other dysfunctional groups, but it is no basis for a fulfilled life.

Equally a love that goes no further than self-love is narcissistic and egotistical. To love is to will the good and the growth of oneself and another, and the greatest love is to will the good and the growth of all. And that includes you. It starts like everything else in the universe with you.

Love is an investment in that deeper dimension of you where you connect with a universal, cosmic quality and recognise that you are incredibly significant because you are indistinguishable from pan, the all that there is. When you act in love, the whole universe is beneficially affected. And when anything in the universe acts with love, you benefit. Because you and the universe are one and the same. Sir George Trevelyan explained it by saying "we are all droplets of divinity". In other words, we each have a unique identity, and we are all subsumed in a larger whole. If we forget our individuality and fail to act with personal responsibility, we let down the whole side, and someone else has to work harder to make up for our state of ignorance.

The more emphasis we give to the accumulation of money, the less energy we have left over to apply to love. But the opposite is not necessarily true. Putting love first and bravely facing the personal challenges implicit in learning to love engenders a sense of joy and abundance which may, if it is required, take the form of money. Loving yourself with passion is the task for the twenties.

Disempowerment, allowing others to interfere with your pursuit of passion, devaluing yourself even without others' help, is the principal **pitfall** to avoid at this time. This is a major component in the overall pitfall of negativity raised in Chapter 1. Disempowerment feeds on all the negative beliefs, restrictive personal practices, emotional blocks and control dramas lurking in your shadow.

Owning your Power

How do you sabotage yourself? What threatens you? What is your worst, deepest fear? All this needs to be faced at some time. It's your life challenge. Gradually, as your life unfolds, you step out of what disempowers you and into unconditional love with yourself. But overdoing the self-love, **ego** distortion, is the dangerous **attachment** you need to release.

There are tremendous temptations and pressures on us to give our power away. Queues of people line up to tell us what's good for us. They bully and manipulate us into making stupid decisions that leave us powerless for decades, and they batter us into submission with sophistry and humiliating power games. If you play their game you lose. But if you play your own game and hold your own power you win. And the prize is your life.

Money talks! When you gonna listen?

To most twenty year olds the King of the Castle Game seems to be the only game in town. It holds all the cards and promises the only route to all the rewards. Top jobs, big money, fast cars and faster women! Women are increasingly joining this game and for them the latter reward is replaced by the delights of ball-breaking. It is only later that you realise you can only "have it all" if you're prepared to give up everything.

The danger of engaging with your power is that you overdo it and get above yourself. This distortion of personal power is an unhealthy form of ego, which can get very absorbed in the glitter and glamour of status symbols and superficiality. Once hooked you can find yourself unable to let go, but let go you must. Otherwise ego colludes with the distraction of money to stunt the growth of your power. We'll be returning to what this looks like and how you escape in Chapters 5 to 7 especially.

For now the lesson is not to allow anyone to disempower you, least of all yourself, and not to get an over-inflated sense of your own power either. Come into a healthy relationship with your own power, not over- or under-playing it. Don't give your power away to people who try to minimalise you or to commitments that trap and enslave you, so you can never be free to flex your real power. Instead give your commitment to developing your self and your vision, and to growing all the skills and qualities you need to activate that vision. This is how you create a personality which honours and serves you, rather than a pompous facade that keeps you in the advanced stress of fear that you are about to be found out. Spare yourself the appaling waste of energy propping up that mask.

The tendency in the early stages of working on this is to be acutely aware of the power others have over you. This can take several forms. You may feel all the disempowerment of a victim, with no power of your own to effect a result. You can easily be guilty of oversensitivity and taking offence. Your worst fear will be humiliation or losing the battle. And rather than injecting energy into your surroundings you may react by sucking energy out of everyone around you.

All this is just a stage. It is what puts most people off and stops them ever stepping into their power. Like all the phases of life and the energies associated with them, there is always this difficult entry. It is like learning to play a musical instrument. At first it sounds awful and you fear you'll never make it, but gradually as you practise the sound improves and you keep amazing yourself with what you can do. Hang on in there! And don't give up at the first hurdle.

One of the great pressures to resist at this time is the pressure to get married and "settle down" with a "proper job". The twenties is a time to explore and experiment, not a time to "cement" anything permanent. Relationships entered into now have a rough ride through the separation that occurs around age 29. This is when we commonly release ourselves from the railway tracks on which we ran our lives up to that point. To get stuck with these old tracks when you're ready psychologically to move on is a severe prison sentence. It's committal, not commitment!

You don't need to even think about marriage or children until you're 35 and have a roof over your head that one way or another is not costing you anything. Society wants you married and mortgaged because that makes you meek and malleable. You do have a choice.

You don't have to get married to leave home and you don't have to get pregnant to give yourself value. But those are two of the main reasons for premature parenthood. Low self-esteem is a disempowering reason for doing anything. And when you enter into commitments, attached to some end result, conditionally or with someone whose commitment to themselves and the project is not equal to yours, you diminish your power.

Far better to use your twenties to take up your power, acquire a sense of yourself, build talents to support you and then consider sharing your powerful personality with someone equally powerful and committed. Committing to yourself builds healthy self-esteem. Then and only then, committed to yourself and your vision, and unencumbered by the chains of misguided commitment can you commit to others and to life.

A hard task when you are revisiting this phase is to unload all the commitments you made in ignorance all those years ago, which now trap you and deny you a growthful existence. This may take time but the sooner you start the sooner you will be free.

Realistic Commitment

Embracing the twenties energy means embracing personal responsibility, so you will need to release these commitments responsibly. You can't always just dump commitments and responsibilities, but you can express where you are now and enter into a dialogue. This in itself will be a good exercise in self-assertion without controlling, and you may need to work through that early-stage distress of colonising a new dimension of yourself.

When you do make commitments, commit only to those who have like you committed to themselves and their vision, are self-sufficient and equal to your commitment. Be sure the contract is really clear, preferably in writing. There are many people who will tell you they understand the contract and then change it unilaterally. Next they attack you because you don't subscribe to this new contract even though you didn't sign it or even know about it!

In every relationship there is a lover and a loved. When you notice which you are, change roles! Otherwise you get stuck and stale, and resentment builds up, whichever role you overstay. The lover resents the loved one's complacency. And the loved one resents the lover's clinging and constant pressure to give more. Other inequalities in the division of duties and responsibilities can also develop. In an earlier generation this was clearer and more clearly contracted. Now it has become a constant source of mutual disempowerment.

To summarise, get some experience of how commitment works in real life before you make any commitments. Then commit big time to you and your vision. Have impossible ambitions ... and start small. Avoid impenetrable, insuperable barriers and keep initial financial targets realistically low. Ask the impossible of others, but be satisfied with what you get. Commitment is a rare commodity and you don't want to be constantly disappointed.

There is another strategy you can adopt. It's called positive thinking. By expecting the best you create the best. All your wishes come true, everyone is as good as or better than you expected and you achieve that perfect balance of life and work we all eventually realise we want. There is absolutely nothing wrong with this strategy and no inconsistency with what has been said in this chapter...as long as you also apply yourself and avoid stupid decisions! Positive thinking is as dependent on you making intelligent commitments as any other approach.

Money is Feedback

One of the best places to practise commitment is the world of enterprise and money. As we have seen, **money** and the pressure all round to start making some is the principal **distraction** in the twenties that takes you away from the real job of learning about passion. Yet the reality for virtually all of us, at least between age 20 and 50, is that we need to work and generate an income. Work is where the human being is grounded in reality, and without it we are in danger of floating away. Money is also the arena where we learn about commitment. And it is a powerful feedback mechanism. Money really does talk! It tells us when we're out of touch with our heart, our passion, our capacity for loving.

Sometimes it floods us with cash: its message then is "How much do you need before you realise a) there is never enough and b) other things are far more important." "You've won this game," it says,

"Why keep playing it? Try something else. Try the *main* game, LIFE!"

Sometimes it leaves us short: then its message is "There's something crucial you've failed to realise. Listen to your heart and trust it will all work out." When what you're doing isn't generating an income, you might as well change. You've nothing to lose. If things do get worse, you've just made the wrong choice. Lack of money has a galvanising effect on even the laziest of us, but it may not galvanise us in the right direction. Eventually you realise there's an inner shift you need to make.

When the flow is just right, money says "That's it. You're in the flow, in balance. Well done...for now." So if you're loving what you do, *and* still learning lessons, you'll probably find money supports you. As soon as it's time to move on, money will tell you. Always money is saying, "You've a job to do and new lessons to learn (and teach). When are you going to start?" It's one of the principal ways we've invented for life/the universe to give us feedback. In many different ways it encourages us to go deeper.

The lessons are all in how you react to what life and money throw at you. Sometimes the lesson is to persevere more, sometimes less, to let go or hang on in there, to do more or to do less and be more. Always you're invited to make a choice and use freewill. There's always a choice in how you react, with worry, fear or anger, with guilt, pride or denial. And the lesson is in witnessing the reaction.

Money has many other variations to offer. "You're wasting your talents - change direction." "Count your blessings." "Is all this doing fulfilling you? Do you really need all this? Slow down. Enjoy it." "You want me? You gotta stop wanting me! Then you can have me." In the end, the key is to value yourself inside and get realistic; then your needs are met. Money talks! When you gonna listen?!

While you're experimenting and developing excellence in your 3 travellable skills, there's no harm in earning your living too. In fact it's one of the best places to learn some skills and see how not to do some other things. Employers are often keen to take on youthful people who inject some bubbly effervessence and breathe some creative life into the organisation. They also hope you will make fortunes for them. They are looking primarily for "gumption" backed by the proven ability to knuckle down and achieve results. If you didn't get around to this in your teens, that's your job now. If you did, exploit it.

Large employers hold the purse strings, so if you want access to the purse, you have to engage with them. But treat your time there as an apprenticeship while you develop your own business. You are there to acquire skills and credibility with their world, so you can hold your own there and secure contracts for self-employed, freelance or supply work. Use the mainstream to accumulate what you need. They have no long-term commitment to you, so you need have no compunctions. Your task as soon as possible is to become independent of the establishment, and the freer you are the better chance you stand of achieving this.

At 21 you have the opportunity to take full responsibility for your life. Up to this point others have had control over what you can or must do. But now you join the merry band of the economically active. You have your own money, derived from your own efforts. This new relationship with money reflects what is going on inside. Money is a symbol of investment and return. And the twenties are the time for you to make personal investments and even the first tentative commitments, to assert yourself and develop some self-confidence. So engage with **money** but keep it in perspective, so it does not become a **distraction** from the principal "green" task of allowing your power to materialise.

All in all the key is a flexible approach - taking a job, while advancing your skills, making useful contacts all the time, and keeping yourself free of burdensome encumbrances.

SUMMARY

- Resist the pressure to conform.
- Open your heart, learn to love and experience your power.
- Practise applying your will and responsibility to you.
- Review, value and build the strengths you've acquired into a TRIP worth committing to - your true self.
- Develop excellence in 3 strengths and start constructing a portfolio career. Meanwhile stay free and unencumbered.

● To love is to will the good of yourself and recognise your intimate relationship with the all.
● Only commit to those who're also committed to themselves.
● Money talks.

LESSON to LEARN:
Passion for life.

DISTRACTION to TRANSFORM:
Money - it's only of value if you value nothing else.

PITFALL to AVOID:
Disempowerment - and premature commitments.

ATTACHMENT to RELEASE:
All the seductions **Ego** is prey to.

EXERCISE

● Review the exercises in this chapter.
● What do you most love about you?
● How will you integrate this into your portfolio?
● Who or what's stopping you?

Here's the usual space to make some notes for Action This Day! What feelings, reactions and plans need recording on the Personal Priorities Pages at the back of the book?

Chapter 5

The Song-Bird Years (28-35): Creating a Life that Works

As we move into our thirties most of us are defining who we are for now. "I'm a manager, carer, operative, father, scientist, hopeless case, drug addict." Whatever our experience has been thus far defines what we see ahead of us. For many whose first 28 years have been less than satisfactory the priority is re-education, and yet the pressures may well be building to cover the costs and commitments.

There are two main ways we arrive at this next phase. The norm is sadly that we have taken a leap in the dark in response to external pressure. We have settled for whatever came along first and become good at what we don't now want to be doing and being. Or we may just have a sense of discontent whose cause we have not yet identified. This original career choice will possibly have given us some self-assurance, often quite strong. But this sort of self-assurance is shaky, because it is based on a narrow understanding of life: we are strong as long as we don't make any changes. The twenties have been spent becoming an expert in someone else's structure, a person who "knows more and more about less and less!" Knuckling down to retraining can be not just a challenge but a blow to the ego that thought it was beyond all that.

The other main way of arriving here is as described in the previous four chapters. You will have been practising the notes of your song and developing your own unique theme. The twenties will have been a time of self-discovery and experimentation, of varied experience sorting out who you are, your priorities and what life might look like. Meanwhile your gumption will have enabled you to pave and pay your own way. This creates a broader, more rounded relationship with life together with some justified self-assurance having researched the possibilities properly. Such a person will have made several provisional commitments and discovered what fulfils and what produces an equal reward for effort. They will have spent their twenties learning personal responsibility rather than relying on their position within an organisation for their self-respect.

The dangers for such people lie in the individuality which is also their great strength. To carry on hanging loose, ducking from one commitment or responsibility to another will be too dilettante for this next phase, which calls for firm decisions, stickability, applying all you have learnt up to now. It is time to "fire the pot" you've been working on and sing your song loud and clear. The individualist gets a life together on their own terms. Their priority is activating their personal vision, not least because this is the only way to discover and define it. The person who has retained their teenage enthusiasm for learning through the developmental twenties automatically grasps the thirties re-education challenge in a way that the narrow wage slave finds oppressive. The facility to always keep learning a new song is crucial because getting over-attached to any one thing limits your growth and the possibility of new fulfilling experience.

The key quality for these years and also for this stage of your development is **determination**, applied as much to learning as to the evolution of one's vision.

Just when you feel like being determined and settling into something, the suggestion that you go back to the classroom may come as a shock. But if you're following the recommended route, giving shape to a well-researched vision, this is when you realise what you know and what gaps you need to fill. Activating your learning produces a result and feedback from the universe which defines the re-appraisal and re-education that this very result makes necessary. As you firm up your thinking and specialise in the field you've chosen the learning needs to go deeper.

If you have gone the route of specialising too early, you now have an altogether too narrow experience which needs to be broadened to make you less vulnerable to the slings and arrows of outrageous Fortune 500 companies. Real security comes from staying at the cutting edge of ideas, trends, knowledge, skills and best practice, and from managing your own training development. Whichever route you have taken, and whether you are now broadening and escaping or specialising and deepening, only excellence will do.

Those without an established position, "a proper job", can feel pretty inadequate in politely dismissive society. But those with conventional success under their belts can feel defined by the job box and ignored for themselves. Being a cog in someone else's machine is no compensation for personal vision. Society seems to divide us up into those who are valuable because they have a job, and those who are inadequate because they don't. So we feel under pressure either to stick with a job we may well have grown out of, or to get a job whether it takes us anywhere or not.

You are not your job!

Contrary to popular belief, you have an existence, a value and an identity separate from your job title. This however is no charter for the feckless and workshy. You need a job, but not as an alternative to being a human being with intrinsic value. You need a job, or rather a work context, because work is one of two principal places where you do your personal growth and learning. And of course it is how you generate a living and relieve others of the burden of having to pay for your reluctance to take charge of your own life.

You are not your job

You're the Managing Director of your life and you decide where you're going to direct your resources, where you're going to work. Now with all the experience and adaptive capacity you've acquired so far (or realise you tried to skip and are returning to as your next priority), you reach the moment of decision. It's not of course the last or only time you'll take this decision, but at around 28, you're on schedule if you're firming up on a work context for the next 5 to 7 years. Where it goes from there is unknowable. If you feel it *is* knowable, do it now: stop wasting time and deferring happiness. Don't end up on your death bed saying "Well it was all good preparation!"

What you're looking for is a context in which you can apply your unique blend of skills, talents and excellence and continue to grow and develop yourself. You're looking for a structure that works for you, is enjoyable and leaves you with a constant succession of fulfilling experiences. This creates a life that works and work that is alive. Instead of limiting your experience of yourself to your job spec, you build what you do on who you are. You integrate all your previous learning into creating a new fulfilling relationship with work and life. When you're doing the work you love, you tend to make a better job of it: so this strategy is also a strategy for secure income generation.

The range of work contexts to choose from is widening, as explained in an earlier chapter. The job for life is long gone, replaced by a more flexible workplace. At the more conservative end of the spectrum, there are full-time serial positions, where you move within the same function or industry. More likely these days you change function/career as you move around. Short-term contracts are becoming more popular, led by the computer industry: the trick here is to keep the next job lined up for a seamless shift. Full-time contracts are more difficult to thread together, especially when the the contract is open-ended, because you often cannot give the next contractor a start date, so it is advisable to maintain a reasonably undemanding secondary activity that can be turned on and off (or up and down). This might also be a stop-gap placement you keep on a back-burner, where there is always work to be done, but little commitment required.

The typical worker in the 21st century will be a portfolio careerist with 2 to 4 part-time activities, and typically she will be a woman. Part-time can mean part-day, part-week, part-month or seasonal. It's a mix 'n' match lifestyle, and has at least as much security as the old job for life. If one part of the portfolio comes to an end, there are other parts that can expand to fill the gap. By working at several different functions and in a range of different environments, you reduce the risk of getting stuck in a declining industry. Actors have been doing it for years: now it's as common for the rest of us. Casual work, moon-lighting, property sitting can all act as bedrock for a portfolio.

There will always be a hard core of full-time staff maintaining an overview of the operation, providing a central focus around which all the freelancers, networkers and contract suppliers revolve. Just as the hub of a bicycle wheel supports the outer rim in a ratio of 10:1, we will see 10% of the workforce employed full-time and 90% involved in a variety of self-employed functions. As now there will be directors with their own limited companies, loose associations of complementary workers, sole traders including freelancers, teleworkers and independent suppliers. This group is set to grow from around 20% (officially) in 1998 to at least 70% by 2020 (UK).

At different ages we will have different relationships with this complex "solar system" workplace. In our twenties we will be flitting from one sun to another like roving satellites. In our thirties we might be more settled, like planets revolving regularly around these central sun energy sources. Or we could be moons attached to several planets depending which from time to time has the greatest gravitational pull! And some of us will be suns at some stage in our evolutions.

All this will also apply to the voluntary sector, where more of us might choose to spend part of our time. There is a less rigid barrier now between the various workplaces. We no longer need to make such a total commitment to one way of living and being as before.

Opting to live in a "Diggers and Dreamers" type community has involved a bit of a desertion of commercial viability, but it will be increasingly possible to live in such a community and contribute significantly to it, while also teleworking your services around the world and doing 20 hours a week for the local planning office for instance. This has been happening at The Findhorn Foundation in Scotland and The Redfield Centre in England for many years now.

As conspicuous consumption becomes a less popular obsession and maybe even socially undesirable, we can expect to see many more of working age who no longer need to work or work very much. They will be adequately self-funding, and will be able to spread their resources around to reduce others' need to work. Work can become more something we choose to do for its own merit and for our personal learning. This will include the good life, self-sufficient grow your own, wilderness seekers, but the popular representation of LifeShift as hordes of merchant bankers becoming goat farmers in Wales is a journalistic fantasy.

America already has its senior citizen travellers, their trailers adorned with bumper stickers proclaiming "Get your own back. Spend their inheritance now!" And as our needs diminish, we might see more tramps, squatters, buskers and beggars happily eaking out an excellent sufficiency. The New Age Traveller may have started something. And even those who do not go to quite such extremes will be looking for a very much more rewarding balance of work with the rest of life. The decisions we take at this time go way beyond just fiddling with the mechanics of work.

The underlying complaint of most workers now is that they have the balance of their lives wrong. Home, family, relationships, lifestyle, hobbies and other personal fascinations have had to take a back seat, and as we saw in an earlier chapter even the winners, perhaps especially the winners, are saying the sacrifices are not worth it. So as well as taking decisions about where you will work, you can if you have not lost control of your life already take decisions about where you will live, what sort of home you will have, what your priorities for spending will be. Or take back control.

Break Out of Convention

There still need be no pressure to make life-long commitments to others. Who else and what else you invite into your life is up to you. But the more commitments (and people) you allow in, the higher the costs will be and the less options you will have. Leave plenty of scope for self-determination and insist that everyone involved has a clear, sensible plan for which they are prepared to take full responsibility.

As women colonise 50 and then 60 or 70% of the jobs and work to be done, men have a special quandary. They will need to sort out what they have to offer that will make them desirable to a female earner! Continuous Professional Development might include practical, home-making skills and even a more sophisticated approach to love-making! But dependency is another old tradition which has breathed its last. Only the self-sufficient, determined and indispensable are in the running. The casualties in this new world will be the passengers.

So will you be someone else's something or your own somebody? Can you love yourself enough to be *you*? Can you allow the universe to reorganise itself in your favour by allowing the best of you out into the open? Or will you make life impossible by setting unrealistically high targets and burdening yourself with harsh judgment? Which of these two scenarios is closest to your truth will depend on how much of the groundwork you've covered from the previous phases and the chapters dedicated to each of them. How strongly the distractions of this phase drag you off course will also depend on decisions taken earlier and on your determination to make the LifeShift that puts you back in charge. And it is self-love, self-assurance and clarity in your path and its rightness that gives you the determination to see it through.

It has been impossible to start describing this phase of life without immediately raising the issue of what distracts us from life as the 30's approach. The **distraction** we all have to work with is **convention.** This is no minor aggravation. Convention is a major distraction to be fought off. The form it took in the twenties was financial. Now it becomes the constraint of everything a job means. Status, keeping up appearances, having got somewhere, being a responsible citizen. And it still has financial implications of course. But whereas being unconventional is acceptable if you have money in your twenties, still not towing the line in your thirties with or without money is highly dubious.

The challenge then is to be yourself and still cater to the power and sometimes small-mindedness of convention. Whatever we do we have to have a foot in the mainstream camp, because the challenge for this phase of life is to learn what work and organisation alone can teach us. Convention is the game and we have to treat it as a context for applying ourselves without getting caught or overtaken by it.

The strategy should be clear from the foregoing. You take a self-managing approach to any job you take, and you take it tactically. You create a self-employed portfolio career with several intertwining strands in which you attain excellence. And this structural container is enlivened by the deeply felt personal vision you bring to it. And you network like crazy to keep in with the mainstream without selling out to it. 28-35 is the time to consolidate this and create work that is not a distraction from your vision, but an enhancement. Skip learning this and the rest of your life can degenerate into a chaotic shambles.

The principal failing of conventional organisations as much as of people is their lack of vision. They try to replace vision with other enticements like money and status, and political in-fighting and gamesmanship. They create a chess game of a structure and make you a pawn even if you're the queen. A structure however brilliantly put together and richly endowed is cold and lifeless without a deep spiritual purpose. What we're proposing here for you is a container that will enable the vision to shine out and not restrict you.

At each phase of life and with each energy you bring to bear on the vision there are things to deflect you from it. As I explained at the outset, there are distractions within whatever context you're working in. They go with the territory. Exams are the context you work with in the teenage years; money is it in the twenties; and as the thirties approach the context is convention. You don't get out of it by ignoring or avoiding it; you engage with it because that's where life happens, but you don't allow it to enchant you. There are pitfalls too which are not the same as distractions because they are not necessary as a context for progress, but are more of an aberrational way of reacting to the context and all its distractions.

And then there are the attachments to let go of. These are what we get hung up on as time goes by. Over-indulgence in the contextual distraction may well be connected. In any event attachments are the great challenges of each phase. They are the qualities and things we rely on most heavily in the belief we cannot do without them and would be unable to sustain life if we did not give them all our attention.

Letting go is a rite of passage

Yet these attachments are in fact the aspects of ourselves that most interfere with the authenticity of our lives. We have already seen how ego and self-image undermine us and allow the external aberration and the internal shadow to separate us from our truth; and how we fight not to give them up. Letting go of whatever we are most reluctant to let go and are most attached to is like a rite of passage into the next phase of life.

Rattle the Cage

As the thirties approach, the hold that convention has over us is the fear of losing the security convention promises. What controls us at this age is security. The great **attachment** to release now is the oversignificance we literally attach to **security**. Nothing we feel must be done to threaten it, and we weigh every decision against the fear that we might lose this precious security. So at the same time that discontent with old decisions is exercising us, fear of loss of security holds us back from changing those decisions. If we let security win, there is no moving forward. We stay stuck in structure - cagebirds not songbirds. And the journey into meaning and deeper purpose we enter in Chapter 6 and beyond is a closed book. Carl Rogers said "The only way to find security is to embrace insecurity." If you are weighed down with responsibilities and an expensive lifestyle, you are less likely to take risks with your security. But if you have followed Mr Micawber's advice and kept costs low and well covered by income, security may have less of a hold on you.

What this phase of life calls for, whether for the individual or any project they are advancing, is a clear head. This is where the "blue" energy first described in Chapter 4 comes into its own. It is where you apply your mind to practicalities and manage the overview.

As with all these phases there is a personal blueprint that typifies the energy required. The typical "blue" person is decisive, concerned with form, structure and planning, experienced by others as authoritative. They invented "Management by Objectives" and like sound, solid, achievable (preferably guaranteed) objectives. With the business plans and strategies for organising the future this part of you delivers in place, your energy is focused and you feel in control. This is the energy that organises both career and home and makes things happen, and is most at home with organisational life.

Whichever energy you primarily work with, its blue component is the implementation of role, creating the appropriate vehicle in which your energy can flourish. The green might opt for an entrepreneurial role, the orange for the emotional interconnectedness of networking and a vehicle that thrives on word of mouth referrals. You need some of this energy to organise a context in which your will can be expressed. Without it you are vulnerable to constant nasty surprises. "Failing to plan is planning to fail."

However there is such a thing as overdoing this energy and being so strait-jacketed by future plans that present reality is never experienced or valued. "Life is what happens while you're making other plans!"

If this does not come naturally to you, you will tend as with all new experience to land heavily when you start to practise blueness.

The tyro blue is obsessed with rules and regulations, trying to force structure in an over-rigid way. They rely heavily on sarcasm to control others. And the obsession extends to frustration with chaos, waste, irresponsible behaviour and shows of emotion which threaten their narrow, controlling view of the world. There is a desperate need for status and respect for their authority, which however matures into greater self-acceptance and a more natural commanding rather than demanding of respect.

At its most positive blue energy gives you clarity, clear purpose and the determination to see things through without heavy-handedness. In your blue period you also get clear what you value, what matters to you. The new surge in your intellectual powers means that everything is subjected to rigorous analysis. There is on every front a firming up of purpose, values, beliefs and opinions - not always for the best. And if the circumstances you have created for yourself do not allow you to implement these criteria, discontent can build. The mature outer facade commonly reflecting an inner assurance, can conceal uncertainty occasioned by a different kind of rigorous analysis.

Gail Sheahy (in her books Pathfinders and Passages) sees this as a generally depressing time, right through to 45. For her, discontent is the prevailing feeling and it is only this that inspires the thirty year old to intensify activity and extend themselves. Discontent can certainly be the motivator, but if you have spurned the cheap enticements of the conventional world, you will engage with the expansiveness and learning of this phase with greater enthusiasm and authenticity.

Balancing the mental rigour of planning and evaluating with a sense of fun and enjoyment will stop Jack being a dull clod. Notice when you are most happy and enjoying yourself and bring more of that into your life.

Risk Change

What might stop you living life to the full? It's a question for every age, because there are always distractions to block the way and pitfalls and attachments to wallow around in. But it's a question especially to address at this point for two reasons. Firstly this is the time when ways of being and believing become entrenched and if not shifted now increasingly difficult to remove later. It's crucial therefore to square up to what gets in your way. It's been forming for 30 years and is in danger of becoming permanent. Secondly the blue energy of the early thirties is what you need to deploy to create a context in which your will can be applied.

I experienced a curious reluctance to get into writing this section! The 'one more coffee, cigarette, stare out of the window meaningfully' syndrome was as firmly entrenched as any blocking mechanism can be! Do you find yourself ever clear as mud what your next priority is, how mankind will benefit, your dander fully erect, unquestionably inspired...and totally immobilised?!

A dose of highly motivated will is clearly called for, but will requires the determination that comes from having clearly worked out the how. You may have really powerful will to do X, but if you can't find a way into doing X, or haven't the faintest idea how to go about it, X is unlikely to happen. X quite probably involves starting out on a course of action which feels like it will take as long to complete as the role you have already taken your whole life to compile. No wonder there is some reticence about engaging with it! You need a really strong plan and barrel-loads of will.

How do you go about mobilising yourself in these circumstances? How do you break the "blank piece of paper syndrome"? Any or all of the following might apply. Beating yourself up or trying to force the pace will not work, or will at best produce a very unsatisfactory result. The first thing to do is notice that you are scrupulously avoiding your stated vision priority. This in itself would be a major achievement, a sign of the mature watchfulness which usually comes with later years (See Chapter 7). Acknowledging and allowing what is going on is the first step to unblocking what stops you. Push it and it will just dig its heels in. It's not all of you, just one hurt little bit that would like to be heard just once in its life. So listen to it, even encouraging it to expand on its theme. Then acknowledge it as OK. At last it feels listened to and becomes much less fractious. It can start to become more positive, transforming into a higher and higher quality of being. Persevere as resistance raises its head again, perhaps from another part of you you usually manage to ignore.

Here come the Judge!

What keeps the blocks most firmly in place is **judgment** which is the **pitfall** to avoid in this 28 - 35 phase. Judging yourself and your self-sabotaging mechanisms just reinforces them. It is a denial of you which is as dangerous as the denial that anything is wrong when you're busy avoiding life.

This harsh inflexibility is a strong component of what you go through in learning to apply the blue energy of structure. It crops up in the early stages when we all mistake bossiness for authority, and it typifies what happens when we go overboard on structuring our reality.

The bottom line belief just about all of us have is that we are not good enough. We have had years of training in this, from school, elders and other authority figures, commonly exhibiting blue energy at its most distorted. Part of the job at this time is to review these old belief systems and decide whether we choose to continue with them or give them the boot. More will be said in Chapter 7 about how to work with negative belief systems. For now suffice it to say that noticing, acknowledging and allowing them to be there is at least half the battle. The other half, as with all the pitfalls, is to make a choice to let them go and persevere through the reaction you're likely to experience.

Most success stories, when you delve a little, emanate from the release and letting go of some unhelpful behaviour or belief system. In the holistic mode, being well-organised, assertive, sharp-witted and energetic combines with inner congruence, emotional authenticity and connection to a transformative soul purpose. Success comes when we align with some inner force and face the challenges this presents.

If you feel anger with some recalcitrant supplier, this aspect of your shadow has to be faced, expanded and released before the supplier will deliver. If you feel anxious or in awe of someone, that must be resolved, not suppressed, before a more positive relationship can ensue.

Whatever you need to look at as you pursue your path of wholeness and personal development, you can be sure your work will create it for you - addictive ego, self-demeaning victim subpersonality, dysfunctional child patterns, conflict of vision, whatever: it's all going to present itself.

When you face the inner lesson and courageously break through the resistance, you free yourself up to be fully present, open to receive and communicate. Don't hang on for grim death. Be clear what you most resist releasing, let it go and be prepared to be amazed what comes in to fill the empty space. An unemotional journey is not guaranteed: gut-wrenching is much more likely, but the sense of release and relief is immense.

It does also help if you take responsibility for everything that is happening in your life. You can change you, and your reactions to what is going on. And if you don't like something someone is doing to you, you could at least tell them the problem this creates for you. If you don't tell them how will they know? Telepathy? Don't bank on it! This exercise will help you sort out who stays in your life. Those who don't believe you have a life beyond fitting in with theirs are for the high-jump!

Be aware though what judgmental control dramas you're using and which are being used to control you. Are you a whinger, a bully, a martyr or a stuck-up so-and-so? Do you interfere in other people's lives by interrogating them or giving unsolicited advice? Is life always happening to you or do you busy yourself living other people's lives for them? And do you know anyone who does this to you? If it bugs you, you probably do it yourself...in spades! Once again the answer is to notice it happening, come to centre and express what's up for you calmly but firmly. This is responsibility in action and frees you up to structure your life the way you want it, instead of allowing all these forms of judgment to limit you.

In creating a contextual vehicle in which your life can progress towards greater fulfilment, and as you face up to the things that block that progress, there are some useful blue skills of which you can avail yourself.

Time management is at the core of how you organise your life so it works for you, removing the blocks and giving your will a chance. Time management is usually presented in an exclusively blue way, as something only efficient managers know about, and indeed discovering how to manage your time is a fundamental part of coming to terms with the "blue" energy of organisation. But there are several approaches, to suit each type of person, and you are here invited to use what follows to create your own time management system now.

Mastery of time

Reflect for a moment, when you are most nearly a master of your time. Then list the ways in which you feel you waste time. What you will probably find is that there are four primary categories of time-wasting ... and four keys to time mastery.

TIME-WASTERS	TIME-MASTERS
Lack of Purpose	1 Do Your Why
Lack of Support	2 Create a Supportive Environment
Lack of Structure	3 Structure Your Experience
Lack of Commitment	4 Open Your Heart

Within each category there are approaches you can try. Any one approach could increase your time effectiveness by between 10 and 100%. The overall rule is to connect with life. Most time management systems are a fight against life - trying to accommodate all the distractions, compromises, irksome duties and unimportant tasks we allow to clutter up our lives. What follows is an attempt to integrate you and your way and your values into a time management system that works for you, without evading the necessity of learning the discipline of "blue" energy.

Having identified which category of time mastery is your priority (as above), there are four pairs of approaches for you to apply:

If Category 1 (above) is your issue, focus on Violet & Red (below)

If Category 2   focus on Indigo & Orange(below)

If Category 3   focus on Blue & Yellow (below)

If Category 4   focus on Green & Magenta (below)

But if say Category 3 is your problem, you should also work on Category 2 (Indigo & Orange) approaches, because the category above your priority category in the list will feed energy into you.

Flipping between say Violet & Red approaches (or any of the pairs of approaches that is relevant to you) is also restful and relaxing.

This in itself is a prime overall approach to adopt since stress and time are so closely interrelated.

Stop now and close your eyes for 5 minutes. Focus on your breathing. Notice what comes into your mind and then release it. Now read on.

VIOLET APPROACHES
● Clarify your Vision - what inspires you, your why, your soul purpose, what gives you bliss, the major thrust of this book.
● Meditate - on sub personalities that undermine you; on your Higher Self; on priorities and vision itself.
● Creative visualisation.

INDIGO APPROACHES
● Create different environments for different tasks, some away from 'work', some in nature, some busy but uncluttered.
● Investigate Feng Shui, colour therapy, crystals, aromatherapy.
● Connect with your inner sense of what feels right, what you feel excitedly drawn to, rather than forcing the pace to bludgeon your way through stuckness.
● Potter!
● Respect your pace, your cycles, your methods, what works.
● Allow natural rhythms into each day, week, month and season. Winter is naturally a time to be more contemplative and introspective: spring is the time to burst into new life: work towards an extended time-off or different location at a regular time in each cycle.
● Expand time by tapping the energy of space.

BLUE APPROACHES
● Prioritise. Your vision is the touchstone for assessing priorities:
> - what activities if you do them will take you the biggest step towards your vision - long, medium and short term?
> - allocate at least 20% of your time to important, non-urgent tasks.
● Group similar tasks, especially the block-clearance, statutory -duty ones, and break huge tasks into bite-size chunks.

● Delegate/'Syndicate', but only delegate what's worth doing and yet is routine.

● Take time and space at least once a month to reflect and review how your goals and priorities are changing, and where there is conflict. Clarify what you want now and where the conflicting goals come from - internally, from past conditioning or externally. Note where your vision is not yet integrated with the plan. Once you are clear where the conflict arises you can resolve to let it go or use creative visualisation to see it changed.

● Integrate your goals with those of the organisation and your boss, and beware unpopular attachments. Stay flexible, ready to unload unsuccessful liaisons. Politics is a blue skill.

GREEN APPROACHES
● Peel off the layers of negativity and open your heart.
● Make commitments and let go all attachment to results.
● Question all your goals and drop all external validation (status, money accumulation, desire for things and success). *What you most resist letting go is your major obstacle.*
● Keep learning. Invest in your own growth. Value yourself unconditionally.
● Celebrate successes and completions.

YELLOW APPROACHES
● Change your attitude. Reframe your mind.
● Exchange all negative mindsets for a positive mental attitude.
● Clear the clutter, the distractions, the hidden saboteurs.
● Draw up a detailed plan of action and implement immediately.

ORANGE APPROACHES
● Prioritise joy and fun. Plan them in first.
● Engage with others. Communicate, especially with those who disrupt and unbalance your plans. Break through conflicts.
● Give in relationships (or extricate yourself from them - there are no half measures). Offer others the commitment you seek yourself and give of yourself.
● Express your feelings, especially when stuck.

RED APPROACHES
● Don't rush into things, but do start ... slowly!
● Give it 5 or 10 minutes. You will be astonished what can be achieved with even the biggest tasks in just 10 minutes. And there are more than 1000 x 10 minuteses in a week!
● Do your Why *first*, your A1 long-term, non-urgent priority.
Give it 10 minutes to an hour, but don't try and do it all at once. Also pick one top priority task and finish it.
● Pace yourself.

MAGENTA APPROACHES
● Become a wise observer of yourself. This is the way of the Sage.
● Balance action with rest and relaxation of various kinds:
    -Red: Physical activity
    -Orange: Fun/social time
    -Yellow: Reading and travel
    -Green: Personal growth
    -Blue: Review time
    -Indigo:Music and nature
    -Violet: Meditation and creative activities
This improves your sleep patterns and re-energises you.

So what now will you change? Remembering that if you always do what you've always done, you'll always get what you've always got. So do something different. Write down three action priorities that are *new,* and three priorities for new ways of being.
The master of time is the master of destiny.

Structuring Space
Every month I personally spend about 2 weeks in the North of Scotland and the same in London. In Scotland I'm computer-based, but energised by closeness to nature and creative solitude. In London I meet people, clients for 121s, network members at gatherings, new contacts and old friends at LifeShift workshops. These meetings are the laboratory for the ideas in this book, which was mostly written on the train between London and Scotland, and tidied up on the

Scotland computer.

For 48 hours before leaving each place I am incredibly efficient. The enforced break means I don't just plough on without thinking. Twice a month I have to decide what is worth doing and what I will bin. Place is how I manage my time. And if I cannot work in one place, I take myself to another.

How will you structure your time and space - hourly, daily, weekly, monthly. How will you do it? How will you build in times of intense being as well as places of intense doing? If you're already overdoing, being may not come easy, but the more being time you give yourself, the more you will almost automatically get done. What rest and relaxation time will you integrate - physical activity, time with people, reading and review time, creative artistic pursuits, time in nature, reflective meditation? What emotional and practical coping mechanisms will you install? And what time management structures would help you - an admin. afternoon, a half-day to promote you, your potterring day and your Top Priority time (first thing every day)?

A whole new string of skills is required, for instance self-management. You will need to motivate yourself, setting yourself goals that matter to you and reviewing them sensitively with yourself. You will need to embrace insecurity and become resilient. You will need to be clear what is giving you a problem and develop awareness. If you try to do this all on your own, you will sink.

Isolation is the biggest problem you now face. Getting support from a mentor, counsellor or network is a sign of strength, realism and self-valuing.

People skills also assume a much greater importance. Suddenly you're responsible for selling yourself. It's like going for a job interview every day, and rejection is a daily fact. It's a free personal growth workshop that runs 365 days a year! And any niggling self-esteem issues you have will come right to the fore.

Learning is for life.

SUMMARY

● 28 - 35 is the time to consolidate all the learning to date into a flexible portfolio of excellence.
● This and the self-assurance that comes from being authentic make for far greater security than grimly hanging on to a job you've outgrown.
● You are not your job. The job is dead. Dependency is dead.
● Cultivate the "blue" energy of organisation to mould a vehicle your will can drive. Time management and self-discipline are key tools for clearing the blocks.

Rattling the cage of security

LESSON to LEARN:
Determination to keep on learning, changing and growing as you consolidate your role.

DISTRACTION to TRANSFORM:
Convention.

PITFALL to AVOID:
Judgment, the ultimate Denial.

ATTACHMENT to RELEASE:
The reinforced concrete cage of **Security.**

EXERCISE

What stops you rattling the cage of security?

What needs to change now so your mid-life crisis is not terminal?

What 10 hours a week will you stop wasting so you have time to implement your vision structure?

Finally make some notes here to slosh around in your subconscious, changing your life from the inside out.

Use the Personal Priorities Pages at the back of the book to rough out a plan for future happiness (and present joy!)

CHAPTER 6

The Crucial Years (35-42): Positive Mid-Life

A t 35 it's time to own up to the truth. There is a great deal of assurance and clarity that comes with the previous phase, 28-35, but this doesn't necessarily mean that what assures you also inspires you. You do have a great asset now, the knowledge you have acquired of a particular sphere or spheres, and this phase, 35-42, revolves around what you do with this asset.

Ideas, practical wisdom, innovative ability, know-how are now recognised as a company's principal assets, and they are yours too. The way you have applied your insight and intuition, your life-processing skills, are an asset springboard for the next half of your working life.

What you also have is clarity about what you have become, and enough self-assurance to make the most of it or make a major shift. This phase of life invites you to acknowledge the truth about you, firm up something that feels authentic and put this more honest version of you into the world with assurance.

What this involves for each person varies considerably depending how the last 35 years have gone for you, and yet there are patterns which show through when you know what you're looking for.

If you think of the time from 28 to 35 as the time you built your house the best you could, you may feel it is now time to decorate it, or extend it into something bigger. This would suggest you are fairly happy with what you created. Alternatively you might feel more like turning it upside down, giving it a total revamp. You'd still be pretty happy with the basic structure, just irked by what perhaps feels a bit outmoded, immature or slap-dash about it.

Many however will be thoroughly dissatisfied by their 30's creation. For them only demolition and rebuilding will do. And even the foundations may have to be discarded as a much stronger, surer building is put up. As long as you did not go too far off the rails, it may be enough to underpin those foundations, adding to what you had already laid down.

Whatever you find yourself with at 35, and however radical your building works, the task is one of creating a structure that adds up for you and the wiser priorities you're settling on. Depending how much of this feels shaky, there will be a degree of confusion.

Embracing the Future

Even what you thought you had sorted can turn out to be up for a major revamp. You probably got it right (if you did) based on making something of your history and resources. What went before became the ingredients of your new persona. Now increasingly the future draws you on and life is lived in a space of unknowing.

You can live in fear of this or embrace it as a healthy state, just as you conquered insecurity by embracing that.

Anything in your "shadow" (see Chapter 1) that has not been addressed surfaces now. Work and relationships are the contexts for understanding these deeper, darker aspects of ourselves. We may continue with the role we chose, with more or less dignity, as contexts for this new scrutiny. Or we may feel there has to be a bigger shift and a new context.

Whichever path we choose, major reevaluation is necessary. If we try to fight it, instead of a relatively gentle transition into mature spirithood, we are faced by a mid-life crash rather than just a crisis.

It can be extremely difficult to handle this crisis when all around you are people who are unaware this is natural. You end up fighting it just because they are fighting it. Their fear feeds your fear, and you threaten the safety of the very people whose fears for their safety motivate them to divert you from the sensible course of changing tack.

Somewhere we acquired this wierd notion that we can nail life down like a piece of card, when what life likes to do is flap in the breeze...and even cartwheel off down the road! When your old role no longer does it for you and you start looking out for a change, you're not throwing a wobbly, you're on schedule! When the beliefs and values on which you based your life seem thin and inadequate, you're not losing faith, you're growing up!

The role you found for yourself in your early thirties and felt so certain about is subject to questioning. At one level you may experience just a healthy thoughtful sobering, which barely ruffles the surface. But more commonly this is accompanied by fear and foreboding: is this really it for the next 25 years?! Everything (including sex) can feel routine, and routine is no longer comforting: it feels irksome.

Underneath this lies an even more fundamental questioning of all the beliefs and values that seemed so immovable just a few years earlier.

Sensitive Restructuring
Consider this question. Is there any incongruence between your inner view of yourself and how you operate in the market-place? The conflict between what you have suppressed and what you have become comes to a head now. Few will not find themselves both questioning and trying to complete some sort of structure all at the same time now. What makes it look so different for each person is that some are arriving late after an extended (or delayed) period of experimentation, some fought the demands to 'get a proper job' and never settled to anything, and some have a solid contextual framework (eg a professional career) and are more or less happy with it. All will be drawing on whatever their experience of the first half of life has been to redraw their relationship with reality.

This is a phase when we draw on a combination of two energies - the Blue energy of structuring and organising which was the prime focus for the 28-35 age phase, and Indigo which as we shall see in Chapter 7 is the energy of the intuitive right brain, seeking harmony and searching for the meaning of life. Combined Blue/Indigo seeks a meaningful structure for life.

Most business/work is stuck in Blue/Yellow (and Green if you're lucky), using formalised processes to get results with more or less distorted forms of heart engaged, which is why it is often so frustrating. Indigo helps mollify this and make sense of it.

We are making LifeShifts throughout our lives, but whenever you make your major shifts, it is the energy of this time, the Blue/ Indigo meaningful restructuring, that you use. Now that you have reached this phase (and assuming you have cleared all the earlier territory) it gets easier: at least you have colonised this energy and are less in the dark about what is involved. Remember however that we all have an energy of our own which we tend to exhibit throughout our lives and if for you this is Indigo ideally combined with Blue, you will be someone who is always equipped better to make LifeShifts. You will be someone who always seems to see what adds up. You will always seem to fit your skin.

The Key Time to LifeShift
LifeShift then is the key **lesson** to learn in this phase - 35 to 42. Either you have spent half your life avoiding the real you or making do with second best, or you found something you feel like concretising a little; even so this phase brings a reappraisal which may throw all that earlier certainty into doubt. It's time to weigh up whether the choices you made for yourself at 28-35 are to continue and to come to conclusions about what you will do with the mature 40's. It's a catching up time. Any tasks that were left uncompleted in the previous 5 phases, any attachments that have not been let go, any distractions or pitfalls you fell prey to all need sorting out now. What you have very much on your side is that many of the practicalities and uncertainties of life are better understood and even under control and vision can increasingly take charge.

Just when you were feeling settled and assured, with the consolidation of the last phase comfortably under your belt, life beckons and it's time to move on. Arrival brings with it the inevitability of imminent departure. It's a constant process of evolution towards wholeness.

This pattern of arrival following a period of assurance is well established in human development. Leading up to each new arrival there is a time of awareness that a shift is on its way; and this leads to a period of transition or crisis. What we arrive in at 42-49 as this phase ends is maturity, having experienced an uncomfortable questioning of values which leads to the transitional mid-life crisis.

The shift that precedes this one is puberty, which leads from the assurance of youth via the transition that is adolescence into adulthood. And the first time we went through this pattern was 21 years before that, when we left the safety of the womb, at quickening and hurtled down the birth canal into life!

Life does indeed begin at 40! Because this is the point where the sober questioning of this phase of life comes to a head and decisions are taken about what is to be retained and what replaced. There is more financial or emotional confidence on which to base the decision, and a better capacity for planning and seeing consequences.

This holds the most dread for those whose evolution became stunted somewhere along the way. Peter Pans, academics who never engaged with the big wide world, adventure addicts and establishment figures wary of loss of status and importance...and no doubt many others who rejected LifeShift and decided too soon what they would be for ever.

If the reappraisal can be undertaken vigorously now, the ride through the crisis that marks the start of the 40's can be made less bumpy. Crisis means no more than "time to take a decision" and this is what we need to do around 40. Then the transit into maturity is a positive experience. The sting is taken out of it. For those who struggle with this reappraisal and fight the shift, mid-life crash at 43 is more or less guaranteed. Any later, and it can be a complete wipe-out. Those who think they have cleverly avoided the crisis rites of passage commonly get hit by a massive despondency later on. Any energetic shift we seek to evade gets us in the end! But imagining forward into the next stage of life, building up a portfolio of skills (as recommended in Chapter 4), letting go old outworn personalities and incubating a new way of being prepares the way for a vibrant future.

Rudolf Steiner as interpreted by Bernard Lievegoed saw this phase of life as a major decision point. At the end of it, following a crisis in our values and awareness of our limitations and a sobering or shocking period of transition, we make a choice whether to follow the physical body into decline or soar with the awakening spirit. It is therefore a crucial choice whether life begins for you at 40 or you choose to start dying.

You may feel that you're doing really well; you have a career, reputation, a good salary and many of the symbols of success. You are a very together person who is on top of life and doesn't need help because that's for inadequates with problems. Or you may feel you have enough of it together that it would be a crime to drop it all and risk starting all over again at something new.

Lievegoed says "Career path is like a half-written letter: it doesn't have to be finished." The assurance with which you arrive at this phase can hold you in it, or give you the strength to let go. Growth involves letting go; success in society's terms involves hanging on. It's a tough call, but hanging on only works for 1 or 2% of us. If you don't breathe that rarified air, and even if you do and want the new challenge of evolving beyond Blue structure, LifeShift and a more whole, authentic you beckons.

Make Yourself Redundant

The age at which the system consigns us to the scrap heap comes earlier and earlier. Redundancy is the great fear throughout working life, because it undermines our self-image (0-21), ego (21-28), security (28-35), success pride (42-49) and at 35-42 it's the void we would face without all the stressful preoccupation of career as well as the inability to pay the mortgage and other borrowings that holds us in dread. Redundancy forces us to face our worst fears and attachments. That's why we create it.

Yes, redundancy is always of our own creation. We use it to force ourselves to make changes we haven't been able to convince ourselves to make any other way. As LifeShift is so much about making changes, the topic of redundancy is dealt with here. Why we do it depends on which phases of our previous life have been unsatisfactory and when we hit a phase which is not feeding us. We may act on it straight away or we may make ourselves redundant long after we had good reason.

Even as early as 0-7, a loveless childhood creates grounds for seeking redundancy later. If work is not supplying the love they crave in a way that enables them to reparent and empower themselves, people will absent themselves. An unimaginative education (say 7-14) makes the desire for a more varied, creative experience the spur to leave.

Those whose education has been curtailed before 21, or worse still 18, are deprived of the intellectual personality development which can carry them through the angst of adolescence. The need to be heard as an individual, to answer the fundamental questions of life will precipitate them out of a job if they are not learning about themselves and growing.

Redundancy becomes the rebellion that never happened earlier. We all hanker after whatever we missed out on in our early learning phases, from 0-21. There is this learning gap which we feel impelled to fill, and if the job isn't filling the gap we will dematerialise the job and find another context that does.

For most people in their 20s the work environment is seriously lacking in challenges, responsibilities and opportunities to develop will and a mature relationship with life. Add the disappointment of this to the learning gap tugging at your sleeve and frequent job change up to age 30 should not come as a surprise. And if you don't leave, your wiser inner self will leave for you: redundancy.

The reasons for dissatisfaction with work pile up as time goes by. At 28-35 with the greater assurance and trust in our own judgment, we will leave so we can exercise our talents in a more demanding, exciting environment where they are appreciated.

At the phase we have now reached, 35-42, we are at the peak of our working capacity and the prospect of struggling and striving at the same thing for another 25 years frankly appals. Redundancy now is created so that a new, more social or spiritual life can start. We may fight it and feel very bad about it at an ego personality level but something deeper inside us knows better. We can still miss the opportunity redundancy offers by wallowing in self-pity and recrimination, but we would be just as badly off if we stayed in a job that stunted our growth. At least the self knows it tried. Without a kick up the backside we might go on for ever musing about growing but never take the plunge.

Mid-life crash is of course what happens if we have refused to heed all these calls to fill out the embryonic personality and just have too much catching up to do all in one go. Beyond 43 (and the years this chapter covers) redundancy encourages us to become more of who we could be and more useful to the communities we inhabit. But now, 35-42, is the classic redundancy time because it is the time if ever to make a major LifeShift. Redundancy then is a feature of this phase, to be welcomed as a release from a path that is taking you nowhere.

Redundancy hurts because it seems to represent the loss of everything a job stands for. The job may have provided a sense of purpose and direction, measured and measurable, with its appraisals, career progressions, job descriptions and the assumption that one's role made a useful contribution. Without it you need to find your own sense of direction, take responsibility for it and take stock all the time to mark what progress has been made. Your prize is the exhilaration and spiritual liberation applying your will to your vision offers.

A job also provides regular daily activity and routine, starting and ending at a specified time, with a controlled environment, well documented procedures, pensions, holiday entitlements, tea-breaks and meetings. Lack of routine can be one of the most unsettling aspects of redundancy - all that unstructured time and proximity with family.

Many rely on their job to supply a sense of identity and self-respect and can feel completely worthless without one...which is why it's such a good idea to take charge of your own vision and identity why it's vital you leave and escape this dependency.

A job is also a ready made and elaborately contrived framework for your skills and talents. It is an important apprenticeship period and a common reaction to redundancy is "what on earth can I do now?" The good news is that when you leave you discover you have only been using 1% of your talent so far. The loss of the social context is much more of a blow. Many of your closest friends and acquaintances may have come with the job. This is after all the social group with whom you have spent most of your waking hours. Whatever the situation there has been someone to turn to for advice, confirmation, a chat or to bounce ideas around. If they have been friends who encourage you to keep pushing your personal boundaries stay in touch. Love is not love that changeth when it alteration finds. If they have been a constant drag, restricting your evolution, good riddance.

Probably the major cause for concern, even with a generous golden handshake is the loss of income. There may be huge sacrifices to be made and all sorts of essential life-support mechanisms that have to be jettisoned. This is the end of life as we know it. So you really do have so much to be thankful for. Redundancy is going to reveal to you what life is really about and you are about to be astonished to discover what matters to you and those closest to you.

Redundancy forces into the open all the unrealistic expectations, gripes and resentments that have festered while the excuses a job provides had not been invalidated. You may discover that many of the things you all wanted don't cost, but it will also come clear who is around you for their own purely mercenary reasons and convenience and who is actually rooting for you.

As you become more authentic, you will find you let a lot of your old friends go and acquire a lot of new and frankly much more interesting ones.

Redundancy is merely a reminder to make changes, especially if there has been too little movement thus far. Change, as the saying goes, is the only constant. Working with change instead of running from it all the time is the basis of LifeShift. We need some new strategies therefore to replace all the running away strategies we've had dunned into us. We need a new more positive attitude to change, a better way of looking at it so it's less of an ogre.

Growing through Changes

Change is the only constant, but it can still come as a big surprise! You feel you just have something sussed, and then it wobbles... or a whole new context presents itself...or an old "you" you thought was under control rears its head and suddenly there's something new to work out.

Good news for those seeking a new niche for themselves, because if nothing is changing there are no new needs to meet and no new opportunities to exploit. Good news at a more personal level too, because change means there's something new to learn, and life is learning. Once we've learnt *this*, there's nothing for it but to learn *that!*

Is all change/learning for the best? Probably. Sometimes it's obvious. We've been in a difficult place, and change means we move into a new place. The change is disruptive and unsettling and uncomfortable, but (sometimes!) not as difficult as struggling with that troublesome old place we were in.

Success brings with it as full a gamut of feelings as any failure or tough time could engender. There's learning, pain and things to let go whatever the context. There's no primer that says success is an easier place to be, or a safer place to face the real bogey beliefs! It's just different.

Change is the only constant, but is there anything new? Is there anything for us to experience other than what was already there? It feels like a change to something completely new, because it hasn't risen to the surface before (and because, consciously or not, you made damn sure it didn't!). Memories can take convenient vacations too!

Denial is also change, because something has happened powerfully enough for you to need to deny it. Denial is the harbinger of change. Denial tries to say "That's not me. This isn't happening," but it is you and it always was you and it is happening. You're just not ready.

Has this ever happened to you? Somebody makes a big change in their life or the way they do things and you fight it, resist it, dump on it, complain about it and generally raise all sorts of objections to it. And then you find exactly the same change manifesting in your own life, your own inner reality. You've just been practising denial so you can do a really good job of blocking your own inner change, or handle it more gracefully of course. It doesn't matter which, and you'll learn equally from either response.

The crucial quality is awareness and acknowledgement of what is. You could choose to see your change in a positive light, or you could choose to fight it and make it difficult. Even that's OK as long as you're aware what you're doing and acknowledge it.

Personally my first response to anything I'm presented with has been to handle it in a mental, analytical, conceptual way and get an answer that way. It's important that I (and anyone who wants to help) acknowledge this as OK. That's who I am in that moment. Judging it just damages the judge.

Accepting this opens the door for other responses, which are all possible for me because they are all me and all in me, when I choose to be them. Shutting them out is me too, and that's where I am then, so it's OK to acknowledge that too. I can then gracefully move on.

The pressures of running a business or maintaining a career, even when it's not undergoing a major expansionary shift, can wreak havoc with personal relationships. This combination is a rich and painful learning ground which once you release everything expands your inner consciousness.

The process demands the most rigorous and honest exploration of all areas of your psyche, including several that may not have had a look in before. Acceptance is the key. When we've completed the search in one direction, another direction has room to enter to fill the empty space, always there, even always known and yet unembraceable while the focus was elsewhere.

Others may see it and try to force the pace of change, but this is useless unless they can acknowledge where you are, and unless where you are is where they're looking. Then they can point out what they see and support your shift to another dimension.

Growing through change, and helping others grow through change, starts with acceptance of self and acceptance of other, awareness of change arriving near you as well as in you, then allowing the door to open on a new perspective.

The Importance of Grieving

Redundancy sets off a deeply emotional grieving process, which must be faced if anything more than superficial progress is to be made. This is particularly true for men in our culture who are defined and define themselves too much by what they do whereas for women who we are is what matters. Women seem to find it easier to face the dark, feel what they feel and trust the processes.

Unexpressed feelings and lack of awareness will take the client into a deep depression, all the worse if redundancy was unexpected or unprepared for, or if the job or the separation was unrewarding.

Handling the loss is actually easier if you were happy in your work or parted company on good terms. The better the relationship was, perhaps surprisingly, the easier the grief process seems to be.

There is less hurt and hurt pride to deal with.

But even when you engineer your own redundancy, it can still be a shock to be let go, dumped and rejected. And the pain and hurt of the present traumatic situation triggers earlier griefs that were not dealt with adequately at the time. Sitting on pain and trying to pretend it doesn't exist is a very short term palliative. Sooner or later, depression comes along as a signal that something needs looking at and expressing now.

Comparing redundancy with the work of Elizabeth Kubler Ross on grief, the range of feelings may be summarised thus:

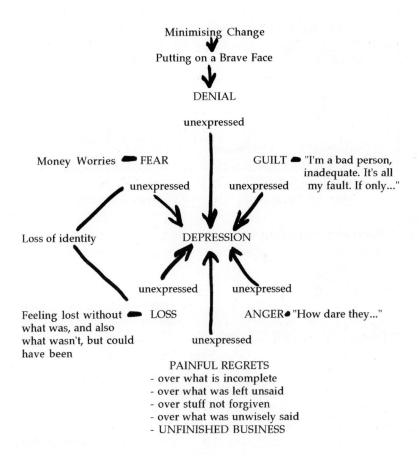

A study of people in transition many years ago by Hayes and Nutman recognised the crucial importance of accepting reality and change, but also valuably mapped out the other stages in the transition process.

Faced with a transition, especially a forced one like unemployment which Hayes and Nutman were studying, the classic initial response is immobilisation. We feel so overwhelmed by the change involved we become unable to reason, plan or understand what is happening. It's shock and we feel numb and detached from reality.

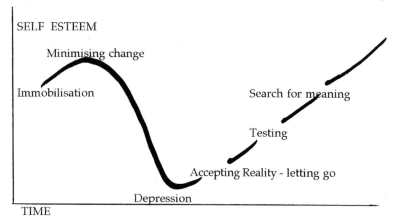

Map of Transition: *Source - Hayes & Nutman*

In an attempt to cope we try to maintain our old reality as if the change or event has not happened. We seek to minimise change.

Putting on a brave face

Self-esteem, which The Map of Transition measures, goes up as we feel better about ourselves blissfully unaware of how we're denying reality. Eventually the effort of fighting the truth overwhelms and we slip into depression. The numbness returns and self-esteem crumbles. Faced with the inevitability of change, but unwilling to face it and lost for answers, the individual feels desolated.

Acceptance, release of obsolete attitudes and experience, is the first step out of depression back into life. We begin to test new possibilities and develop new ways to cope more positively with the present reality. But old narrow stereotypes still carry weight and can get us rejecting new solutions too quickly. Real acceptance of the new requires release of everything from the past which blocks the creation of a new frame of reference. The breakthrough comes when life makes sense again, when new meaning is found. It will have taken the loss of the old and considerable pain to open to this new meaning, but "man can do amazing things if they only make sense to him" (Anouilh). Breakdown is the prelude to breakthrough.

Deserting Familiar Territory

The key then is to accept reality, but this is easier said than done. How do you drop what is familiar and shift to what is unknown and unproven? This whole book is aimed at answering that question, but a key component to consider here is the role of feelings in making the shift.

In the Blue, structuring, organising mode we adopt in the 28-35 phase, feeling can get squeezed out. It seems too floppy and unstructured. Not just lunch but feeling too is for wimps. But now as you refine that structure into something more meaningful and probably deconstruct it in the process, inviting feeling in can be a powerful strategy. It balances all the practical headiness and feeds the search for meaning.

So when faced with one of the disasters that is trying to nudge you forward and relieve you of the pointlessness of getting stuck in the mud, the first instruction, Rule No 1, is "Feel what you feel." You may well not be able to appreciate the good offices of your disaster yet, and you may find the feelings rumbling away inside embarrassing to let out. But that is how you shift out of depressive feelings.

Worry and misery are not going to make you happy. They just aggravate the anger, resentment, fear, rejection, false pride and other nasties that fester and insidiously poison if they're not released. Before you can accept the situation you're in, you have to accept the feelings you're having. Have a good yell. Scream your head off. Cry till you're dry. This is no time for a stiff upper lip. Let the wobbly lower one have a turn. Write letters to everyone you blame for the mess you're in, spelling out all the hurts and misery they've caused - the boss, the bank, ex-customers and the government. Then save yourself the postage!

Because Rule 2 is "Own your feelings and take 100% responsibility for them." Blaming others gets you nowhere (though expressing the feeling is cathartic). No-one is to blame, not even you. But you are responsible. It may well feel like someone else gave you that pain, but where is that going to get you? As long as you feel victimised, living in a world where everyone and everything is out to get you, that will be your reality. You literally won't be able to see anything else. But when you decide how you're going to choose to react to the old slings and arrows, you take charge of your life and hope returns. Out of the old way that doesn't serve you, into a new way which does. Once you own your situation and feelings, you can and must take charge.

Rule 3 is "Count your blessings." Instead of focusing exclusively on the bit of your life that apparently isn't working, recognise how lucky and blessed you are. You had a job to lose! You have a roof over your head. You ate today. You have a body which still works after a fashion. You have friends, family maybe. Somebody smiled in your direction 3 days ago. Think of all the experiences you've had, the places you've been, how much you know about life. List all the skills you have and for this and everything else, give thanks. Don't stop till you've found 100 ways in which you're lucky. This stops you feeling so miserable, because it is very hard to feel grateful and miserable at the same time. It is a gateway because you can step into a more balanced awareness.

Rule 4 follows closely on this. Focusing on the exciting

opportunities of the new rather than mourning the loss of the old or holding on to old regrets is an important step in accepting the situation. Clarify your life vision and get on with it. The only way to do it, and the only way to shift stress and painful feelings too, is to get into action. Then you enter into a relationship with life and it gives you feedback. In how you listen to this and react to it you discover the meaning of it.

Feeling brings humanity to structure. When this is all put together a Cycle of LifeShift emerges. This is highly personal and subjective, so create your own LifeShift Cycle, reflecting your own priorities and drawing on this as much or as little as serves you.

Although this whole process starts with clarity of vision, it is necessary to clear the clag and prepare the ground first. Vision needs a favourable climate in which to grow. There are many ways in which we can block out the possibility of vision, and many more ways in which it can become lost before it is realised. Mostly these blocks to vision are to do with feeling or the lack of it, even where the block seems to be entirely solid and physical.

Whenever progress seems to be blocked, it is vital to get in touch with feeling and work with it compassionately. As long as there is sadness, fear, anxiety or darkness, vision proves elusive. Feelings must be allowed to surface so we can come to terms with them and release the burden of unresolved feelings. If you don't they coalesce into deeper pain and depression, which is OK too because this can be a highly effective trigger to action. Feelings are feedback that something in your belief system isn't working for you. The longer you put off hearing them, the more intense they get, until they resemble a sledgehammer blow between the eyes!

It is commonplace to feel that depression and despair are the end of the road, when in fact they are the beginning. You *have* to do something different. You *have* to change. So celebrate your next low time! It's a gift. And celebrate how the acknowledgement of feelings is the gateway to the flowering of vision, as suggested in The LifeShift Cycle, which is mapped out on the next page.

Notice where you seem to be stuck and look back to the previous activity in the cycle. Check that you have given this previous stage adequate attention before you engage with where you seem to be

THE LIFESHIFT CYCLE

Clarify Vision
- live the vision of a world transformed
- list and act on all your "I'd love to's"

Trust & Let Go
-let go resentments and old scripts,
negatives, victim, fears, anger, need
for approval, anxiety, stress, tiredness,
pressure to deliver, attachments &
addictions, "holding things up"
- trust all is well
- enter every day wholeheartedly

Choose
- choose change
- choose to follow own path
- choose direction you take

Commit Wholeheartedly
- commit to love & service
- open your heart
-focus on the highest manifestation of love each day
- take 100% responsibility
- take risks

Count Your Blessings
- value yourself & your past experience, the
talents and resources you've accumulated
- express gratitude, especially for difficulties
- recognise how even the most unlikely things
serve you

Feel What You Feel
- feel what feelings feel first
- allow shadow & sadness: face the dark
and become a channel for light
- be authentic: speak your truth
- practise loving self-awareness, stay
with heart and let love flow
- express your needs

Connect With Life
- connect in relationship with
self, others, planet & spirit
- open to support
- be with: join in

Do What's Necessary
- ...and only what's necessary
- stop giving yourself
so much to do
- make it clock-work
- do your dream
- secure the future
- realise your potential

Relax And Be
- create a clear, open energy space of still being
- meditate, take time and space to BE: insist on it
- do the inner work
- balance yin and yang

Listen To Feedback
- listen to money & the market
- listen to intuitive insights
- what are you being invited to be?
- if nothing changes on the inner,
nothing changes on the outer

Prioritise Fun & Joy
- look for the good in every situation
- be playful and spontaneous
- more joy and fun gets more done!
- open to sunshine, smiles & success

Open To Abundance
- welcome miracles
- open to the flow & lucky breaks
- allow the vision to manifest & unfold

stuck. And don't try and work on everything all at once. Far better to pick one particular thorn to work with during the day. What tends to happen is that you resolve to "release feelings of resentment" for instance, and by 10 o'clock have had at least 3 things happen that trigger resentment. Gradually you spot what's happening and allow yourself a wry smile.

Notice that before feeling what you feel, relaxing and being is recommended. Meditation, taking yourself for a walk, listening to good music, whatever helps you relax and be still. There is always some state or priority that predicates each step in this process, which is why it's a cycle.

Start wherever you can and work round it, integrating feelings with action and decisiveness.

This work is your Continuous Personal Development, the constant reviewing, regenerating and renewing of your self that needs to run in parallel with Continuous Professional Development. The danger is that without this you have arrived at 35 not with 35 years' experience but with one year you've experienced 35 times. "Experience is as to intensity not duration." (Hardy) A valuable exercise at this point in life, coming up to a watershed, is to write up your CV.

When you review all your achievements and solicit independent verification and testimonials of your talents, you can quite blow yourself away. It's all too easy to deprecate your abilities because you're too close to it and assume that what you've done was easy and obvious. We don't know our own strength!

This then is the task for these years - to review where we've got to, assess ourselves and catch up with anything that's got left behind, particularly feelings. This prepares the ground for LifeShift, if not now then almost certainly by 50. At the same time of course we are consolidating whatever role we chose for ourselves in the last phase. It's a busy and confusing time, trying to be more certain and at the same time questioning everything.

Whatever phase you look at, the energy and inheritance of the previous phase and the pull of the next phase will be at work, to a greater or lesser extent, but nowhere more so than in this phase which is under the aegis of two combined energies. Blue is so strong in our society it tends to drag on beyond its time, while Indigo is knocking at the door. But this happens throughout: Red is still in evidence well into Orange and indeed as long as we have a physical body: Green enthusiasm leaks into structured Blue and so on. The point is that for a certain time (I am suggesting 7 years), the focus is on one energy in particular. The journey of life is to integrate them all into a meaningful composite, on which more follows in later chapters.

It is not just people who are subject to these energetic pulses: whole communities and societies are equally affected. Given how powerful Blue has been for so long, Indigo is the next energy for Western society to embrace. It's what we're growing into. It's the transition from 2000 years of Pisces to The Age of Aquarius.

When we shake the bars of the cage we've created, we're also responding to a long-standing societal shift. This is the context for learning the **LifeShift Lesson** of this phase. We can stay timidly controlled by our fears for the future or we can bravely take a risk and choose to keep learning and growing. We can plead the mortgage as an excuse for not rocking the boat, and continue to carry it as a burden that motivates us to stay put. Or we can think the unthinkable and insist it does not distract us from living.

Count Your Blessings

Killer Mortgages

The **distraction** most likely to be disempowering us at this time is the **mortgage.** 42% of the workforce in a recent survey by Henley Research Centre said they would reduce their hours and accept a lower income if it were not for the mortgage, the debt accumulated trying to beat the system.

Mortgages and debt are how we get to have now and pay later. But they keep the nose to the grindstone now and probably later. And that 42% quoted above + the 12% who are managing to get out of the mortgage trap are a measure of how we pay now by not being now. We defer the happiness of being who we really are and find we have left ourselves so far behind we don't know how to do it when we are released and have the chance. We seem to be faced with an impossible choice - be trapped in poverty and homelessness or be trapped in a mortgage. What is the way out?

Minimise! Refer back to Chapter 2, "Doing the Sums", for the details. The challenges involved in defeating this distraction are germane to the energy of this phase, because you will have to reorganise life so it makes sense. And you have to explain it so it makes sense to the others in your life. You can only do this when you are in touch with feelings, for yourself and for others: attack it harshly and you will stir up resistance: set it out rationally and compassionately and there is a chance of it being accepted and understood.

Indigo adds feeling and fellowship to the restructuring that needs to happen. Face to face conversation, talking to each other personally is key to our evolution. And Blue is called on to help us make those difficult decisions, like standing our ground firmly, stating ultimata clearly and drawing up plans for how our objectives can be achieved over time. It may take time to unpick the ugly tapestry we've woven.

An important component in integrating Blue and Indigo is to communicate with the people around you, in your family, real friends and caring professionals. Involve them. Share your feelings, dreams and fears with them. You will probably be amazed how well they respond. The resistance you feel to doing this is your resistance, your challenge. Withholding how you're feeling does nothing for you or them. If they have a problem with the situation, that is their problem to own, and if you shut down on them, that doesn't help. Once you've shared your feelings, it can open the door for them to share theirs and a new era of communication and mutual support can begin.

The Blue/Indigo energy was excellently demonstrated by a BBC television programme called 42 Up which has been monitoring the evolution of a group of children from very different backgrounds since the age of 7. A farmer's son from the English Dales now teaching science in the States said "It's really important to be constantly thinking what's going on around you and how to react to it." Realism and Review is Blue, Reaction is Indigo. The Blue/Indigo person is constantly on the look-out for new contexts which fit them better, where they can flourish and not just fit in with conventional expectations of them. The Indigo component means that they are noticing what is discordant and what might be a better niche for them. They are busy with the fundamental marketing job of matching their skills and being to a context which fits them like a glove. Indigo also adds back the lost feeling self: it becomes important to integrate what they most enjoy and what they are doing when they feel best about themselves.

42 Up also made clear how environment affected individuals. Those from a more privileged background followed a more predictable path up to 28, and generally ended up where at 7 or 14 they thought they would. They had a set of railway tracks they were pretty well strapped to, which had the downside that taking an independent line off the beaten track came hard. It doesn't tend to occur to them to LifeShift and they find it hard to contemplate anything so disruptive, though they have the resources to make a success of it. Those from less privileged backgrounds had less direction and were less likely to end up in the jobs they hoped for at 7 or 14. But they had less attachment to particular roles, so could adapt more easily, though the lack of resources made the move harder. They also had less confidence but interestingly this became far less of a problem after 35 and all had found their feet and their place by 42, even the drifter though he was least convinced of it! Who has faced their inner material and come to terms with it is going to show up in the next 7 years, as we see who crashes at 43 or later.

The signs of questioning are there and some will have a rough ride.

The support of partners was a make or break factor. Partners who had a clear sense of themselves, whether as homemaker or breadwinner, tended to strengthen the relationship. Partners who were dependent undermined it: they and the relationship tended not to survive, and the break-up tended to put the brakes on the individual's progress too.

By 42 several of the participants in 42 Up had experienced the death of a parent. This concentrates the mind on mortality and reminds us to take stock of our lives, where we will want to have got to before we go and what it all means. All this is pure Blue/Indigo.

Do you have a sense now of this combination of energies? Can you imagine what life would be like without them? It is like being a cork in the sea, with no control over your environment and no awareness of what is going on. Life is a series of unexpected shocks and surprises. And one is constantly mystified by why this is all happening.

Like all the other energies of course this pair can be overdone. The constant search for structure and meaning detaches you from the actual business of living life and generating an income. Intelligent self-awareness degenerates into navel-gazing or frustration at being unable to make perfect sense of life. So nothing makes enough sense to be worth trying. Like any overdone strength it becomes a weakness which blocks progress.

Especially if you're aged 35 to 42, but even if you're not, review where you're at. What works for you and what doesn't? What do you have in place that you are clear about and want to retain? What constructs in your life constrain you and what do you want to do about them? Most things have good and bad in them. Acknowledging this, especially when facing others with what you see needing to happen, helps enormously.

Analyse where the fun, fame, fortune and friendship comes from now and how you want to rearrange it over the next 5 or 10 years. Clarify the implications and cost the alternatives. Let it simmer and then engage others in your LifeShift plans.

Stress Resistance

You have so much that you've worked so hard and suffered so much to get straight. Letting any of this go, disrupting the little peace you've achieved, seems crazy. **Resistance** is rampant and is the great **pitfall** to which you can fall prey especially now. In fact learning to overcome resistance and let go is probably the main ingredient in learning to LifeShift. In The LifeShift Cycle, Trust and Let Go is the step that prepares the way for clarifying vision, which is where LifeShift starts.

To cope with the speed at which things move now, we have to be in the present, unattached and freed up to respond creatively and at breathtaking speed. Society has tried to avoid this uncomfortable conclusion and in distancing itself from individual responsibility has lost touch with the human journey. What we are rediscovering is the wisdom of the ancient philosophers who dedicated their lives to the quest for harmony and meaning.

Throughout all the phases there are attachments to release, but this is the phase of life where the energies you're working with are exactly the energies you need in order to learn how to release. Make the most of it. If it's left undone now it becomes more and more difficult later. Resistance now sets up mid-life crash.

What then is resistance? How do you recognise it? Resistance is what is suffering in you. It lives in old scripts, old self-images, old coping mechanisms.

These were adopted early on in the face of vulnerability, dependency or the need for self-preservation. Sometimes we developed them ourselves to get what we wanted, master our environment or protect ourselves from pain; sometimes outside influences, birth experiences, parental messages and cultural norms (however abnormal) implanted them. They are well-entrenched, so giving them up seems life-threatening, whereas they are what threatens life with extinction and meaninglessness.

These are the subpersonalities running wild in your unconscious, the alien walk-in that has to be dismantled if the authentic you is to emerge. Recognise any of these? Puritan, perfectionist, little princess, Jack The Lad, bossy-boots, people pleaser, rebel, compliant avoider, virgin, vicious killer, heavy father, abuser and the bullying, cynical judge we brought out of the cupboard in Chapter 5. Obsessed with how things look, buttons easily pushed, constantly repeating patterns in relationships? There's a suffering subpersonality about!

If we continue to let these aberrations run our lives, if we deny or dismiss their existence, we become guilty of the worst self-indulgence. We collect others to play out the fantasy with us, we project our own negativity onto others (judging others harshly for instance because we have not resolved our own self-judgement), our poison leaks into the lives of all around us. It is not self-indulgent to become conscious. It is only self-indulgent when we dump our journey into consciousness on others, which may be an early, awkward stage in the process of getting real.

Once we get through this, we can be more compassionate with those who follow us through this embarrassing phase. The embarrassment, and the judgment and sarcasm we attract from others who are still at an early stage of discovering a sense of who they are stripped of the authority their position gives them, these are all things that feed our resistance to engage with this work. Falling apart gracelessly, which is how it looks, takes some swallowing.

The process we need to undergo is well trodden and well-documented. First comes awareness of how we get in our own way, then acknowledgement and acceptance through listening. Once we allow it we can invite a deeper consciousness in and practise this new state until it becomes a habit. Often this amounts to a reassessment, reframing, adaptation, reorganisation and relearning of an old way of being so the good in it is retained and serves us.

As well as releasing all the attachments you have resisted letting go to date, there is one **attachment** which typifies this phase. It happens after you release the soul-destroying elements of your life - the exhausting over-busyness, the intense pressure to get somewhere you don't want to get, the concessions you make to other people's agendas for you.

Stress is now so familiar it's endemic in our systems. We're addicted to it and to all the struggle that goes with it. And there are good reasons why we do it: if our sense of self-esteem is not absolutely solid, we often compensate by working extra hard to try and justify ourselves. So when you reduce the stress-inducing factors in your life, part of you experiences the return of Lack Of Self-Esteem (LOSE) and this brings on withdrawal symptoms. While most of us has decided to slow down and enjoy life, this other part is missing its daily dose. It wants to exchange the gentle, gradual, flowing pace for the old rushing torrent of quick fixes and speeding up to get ahead. Addiction.

Addicted to stress

Stress is what happens when you stretch a rubber band and put it to work. That much stress is good: it turns a floppy piece of resin into something powerful and useful. But stress is insidious. It sneaks up on us and we start overcooking it. We think it's natural, just the way it is, but gradually exhaustion and vulnerability take their toll, stress becomes di-stress, and the rubber band snaps. But by now we're so acclimatised to it, we're completely unaware we're experiencing totally unacceptable levels of stress. And if any awareness remains we may try to do even more in a futile attempt to get ahead of ourselves, out of the vicious circle, but this is counter-productive and saps our strength, so we become even less effective.

Shifting to a less stressful, more personally fulfilling lifestyle, where we can enjoy home, family, coasting or whatever we've chosen can feel like going cold turkey in a rehab unit! Doubts and fears compound to strengthen this backsliding into stress. The loss of structure, literally de-struction, is disorientating and creates hours of time in which little doubts grow into terror, especially if money is misbehaving. We can become paralysed like rabbits in the headlights and can feel we must be doing something terribly wrong.

The shadow side of LifeShifting rears its head and the very reasons why you changed gear present their dark side and frighten you to death. Time for yourself becomes time on your hands that hangs heavy: you get less done in a 16 hour day than you used to in the 3 hours snatched after work! Freedom to control your own life becomes fear of life and you frazzle yourself by recreating your old stressful work patterns. Being your own boss becomes grief there is no-one to direct you or rebel against. Responsibility for your own decisions sets up terror about taking the wrong ones and even resentment against others without responsibilities. Having no-one to judge you leads to harsh self-criticism or pomposity. The dream becomes a nightmare.

Reinventing yourself is clearly not the end of the road. There is always a beyond, and always endless potential for positives to reveal their negative side. This creates a constant succession of challenges to face, even if you manage not to back-slide. The great value of facing these things and positively LifeShifting is that you are better equipped to face the next challenges. It doesn't necessarily remove the pain, but it does equip you better to move through it and out of it. Pruning helps the plant to flower.

Stress is just one of the results of a life out of balance, where key energies are being resisted and the process of integrating life is disregarded. For each energy there is a devastating pain caused by the inability to engage positively with it.

Stress is a distorted form of action (Red energy) which doesn't know when to stop. It is a failure of time management, so referring back to the material on that in Chapter 5 is recommended. Stress is also the symptom of a visionless life out of balance and exposed to an excessive degree of isolation. To get from stress to the clarity of vision which alone can set up a life free of intolerable levels of stress, you have to slow down and relax. And in order to relax you probably have to get physical. You have to introduce a balance of Indigo and Red into your life, and you have to break through from your lofty isolation and allow others in, which is Orange. These are exactly the colour energies which the world of work dismisses, and it leads to all the most negative and debilitating conditions to which we can fall prey.

To get into feeling and express (literally push out) the stress, you probably need to start by shifting the mental picture. Use the language of mind to change the picture in the mind and shift your perspective. Ask yourself whether there is another way to look at what's putting you under stress. This gives your mind something else to do. Gradually the mind can help you take responsibility and own the stress and the sources of stress. You can distinguish between what is yours and what is not yours, and you can own, for instance, that you are angry, rather than that something outside of you is making you angry. You step out of being a victim and into a choice first to acknowledge your own state and then to be and feel the way you want to.

Acknowledging what you feel, eg miserable, opens up the possibility of feeling and expressing. Your mind can see the truth and sense that this is not permanent and will pass. As you connect more closely with the feeling, let it flow through you. Stress is holding on, resisting: let it flow, and let it go. Run it up your spine and out through the top of your head, or down and out through your feet. Allow whatever comes with it, tears, laughter, a smile, wanting to scream. The silent scream is good, preparing everything for the full Tarzan scream - mouth wide open, eyes staring, muscles tense and then screaming without making a sound or into a pillow.

What all these approaches do is to change your physiology. This is what shifts the stress. In the end only doing something physical releases stress. You have to take a break and do something else. If it's not possible to dance or go for a jog, in the middle of a stressful meeting etc, simply leaning back or grasping under the chair you're sitting on and pulling up while you press your body down can do the trick. It gives the adrenaline somewhere to go.

The map below shows what happens otherwise. The inner circle tells you what the symptom is, and shows links between stressed conditions; the outer circle tells you which energy is missing and what is therefore the route to a cure. In stress you keep going round the inner circle until you find a way out into the outer circle. Once you're out, work anticlockwise to gain insight into the situation, or clockwise to express it through action.

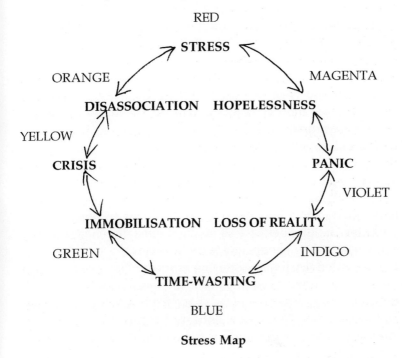

Stress Map

The **pitfall** to avoid now is **resistance** which **stress**, the **attachment** to release now, holds in place. What stops us releasing stress is of course resistance, to slow down, to take an exercise break, to change! And if we needed any excuse for ignoring this cosy dilemma, we need look no further than the **mortgage**, the **distraction** that keeps us stressed and resistant.

LifeShift demands that we solve the mortgage problem and refuse to be deflected by it. It insists that stress is reduced and that we stop resisting. When we have so much invested in the precarious status we may have achieved, this is a tall order. But this has to be faced if we are to keep evolving. What it takes is the courage to commit to the personal strategy that works for us and enables us to let go.

SUMMARY

● The energy of this phase, the energy of meaningful structure, preeminently defines LifeShift.
● LifeShift calls for assurance tempered by an appetite for questioning and unknowing.
● Review and assess your knowledge assets, acknowledge your truth and clear the clag of shadow. This defuses the mid-life crash and prepares the way for transition to mature self-development.
● Transition begins with acceptance.
● LifeShift is a cyclical process through vision, structure, humanity and feeling. Responsibility with feelings is the gateway to the flowering of vision.
● Redundancy is how we release ourselves to face our real priorities. It hurts because so much of our self-image, security and social reality is dependent on our work.
● Acknowledge what is sufferring in you and have the courage to let go resistance and unconscious personality blocks.
● Stress stops you being in a space from which you can act. To release it takes emotional honesty and physical expression. Stress+Resistance+Mortgage is a powerfully destructive trio.

LESSON to LEARN:
What it takes to **LIFESHIFT**

DISTRACTION to TRANSFORM:
The **Mortgage** which usurps the reality it pretends to buy

PITFALL to AVOID:
Resistance, refusing to let go

ATTACHMENT to RELEASE:
Addiction to **Stress**, the depressed relationship with energy

EXERCISE

What works for you and what doesn't?
What stops you letting go of what doesn't work?
What's sufferring in you?
What feels like a meaningful structure?
Read the summary again to find your next step.

Action This Day Space

And what questions and realisations need recording in the Personal Priorities Pages at the back of this book?

CHAPTER 7

The Awareness Years (42-49): The Meaning of Life

The earnest enquiry and questioning of Chapter 6 softened you up for the decision you take as this phase opens. If you took a long, hard look at your life and at least started to put some new criteria in place in the last phase, your 40s are spent consolidating the new you.

There is a tremendous amount to learn but the reward is a more solid understanding of the contribution you might be making. Expanding consciousness can be intensely scary and this can be a time of awful doubts about whether you took the right direction through your late 30s. But you are learning all the time - what works and is you, what doesn't and is not. Making the shift now means you arrive in the next phase with a well-worked version of your transformed, LifeShifted you.

If you have never really had any doubts about your role in life, and have from early on found your work context ideal, with no conflict arising between it and all the other things you want to have in your life, you have probably spent the last 14 to 21 years working your way happily to the top of your profession. People like you are increasingly rare and may be an endangered species given the pace of change and insecurity of the jobs market. Research tells us (cf Chapter 2) many of these "winners" are bored, disillusioned and looking for a LifeShift as much as the rest of us.

If they face this now, the resources and peaceful self-assurance they bring with them are potentially an enormous help. They can afford to take their time delving into the meaning of (their) life, which for all is the energetic focus of this phase. They can even hang on throughout this phase, penetrating that top 2 to 5% of earners and not questioning what they're doing until later. Life is so exciting other things are too low a priority.

As we shall see later on, LifeShift comes to them too and there are still ways in which they can handle the transition: they just have to do it without the benefit of the learning accumulated over these middle phases, and they have other strengths that compensate. If the pressures of the last phase got to you and you decided to defer change in spite of not being on this fast-track to the top, or if you never allowed yourself to slow down and grow wise, disillusionment lies in store.

Up to this point you have created a role for yourself that made use of your talents, but now the question you keep asking is "What does it all mean?" The lack of concern for this question earlier in some ways simplifies things, but lacking the full house of energies to support you is what also makes life difficult to navigate. That however is the journey, and now you have the chance to evolve into a very different realm.

Perhaps if I ignore it, it will go away.

The shift you make at this time is a shift in emphasis away from doing and into being, away from the outer physical world and towards inner concerns. If this shift is not made, preferably now, your choice is to follow the physical body into decline. It is more and more of an effort to keep up physically, and you deny yourself the energy of intuition which could more than compensate.

From 42 on physical performance, eyesight, lungs and muscular capacity may begin to fail, and energy reserves are not so reliable. By 49 you will perhaps be wanting to hand over to others, while you maintain more of a watching brief. If your whole image of yourself is based on your supremacy on the battlefield, inability to raise your broadsword can be a devastating blow. It feels like the ground has been cut from under you and you are stranded. "If only I was 20 again... If I were 10 years younger...", but you're not. Another time has come, another way of being calls.

Fighting it, hanging on desperately to past triumphs, leads you to burn-out, late (and therefore exaggerated) mid-life crash, disillusionment and depression. Women face the added impact of menopause, a further physical reminder that we're not as young as we were. If life has not acquired new meaning, this is hard to handle.

The previous phase was defined by the search for a meaningful structure, something that works at a practical, economic level and fits your vision and value system. This provides a solid base from which one can begin to appreciate and engage with spirit. Without this solidity, spirit is just air.

The Indigo energy which was part of that last phase is central to this one, and the search shifts to a deeper level of enquiry into meaning. There is a growing awareness of what is going on around us and intuition comes into its own, increasingly taking over from too analytic logic.

Without this Indigo energy, the danger is that life becomes a depressing, meaningless experience. No longer able to draw on such a strong connection with physical grounding energy, you can feel strangely disconnected and demoralised. Even those who extend the old structure that defined their lives into this phase may have a disquiet gnawing away at their subconscious: something is not quite right, but perhaps if I ignore it it will go away.

Awareness of how vile, violent and unfair life is grows as both an early stage of tuning in to what is going on around you, and discouragement to look any further in this direction. Life is tough, so I'd better keep my nose to the grindstone and buy protection.

Before you engage with this energy, all you can see are its negative manifestations. When all you see is ugliness, it is easiest to become cynical and sceptical of anything that offers beauty and harmony. It's an excuse for not letting go of familiar, heady strategies, a defence against entering a realm where being and feelings prevail and power politics cut no ice.

The sceptical cynic knows that he dare not look beneath the surface of his own life, and therefore rubbishes anyone who is taking that journey. It is mostly those for whom the system has worked (the top 2%) who resist engaging with Indigo, so the qualities it represents can be seen as strategies of failure. Part of the challenge of growing into this energy is allowing yourself to be less of a frenetic human doing and more a harmonious human being!

As you slow down, you see more of what is going on around you, possibilities and opportunities. Your hunches get better, showing you neater ways to do things, short-cuts that avoid swathes of wasteful busy-ness. As life becomes less of a rat-race, you have less need to be pushy and aggressive, and can be more relaxed around others. All this makes you luckier! We are all lucky, of course: the trick is to see it, which is easier when you're not in such a tearing hurry to get somewhere else.

Indigo is where you connect with peace, harmony and beauty and learn to attune to your whole environment, through the energy of intuition and sensitivity.

As you make friends with this less frantic side of yourself, everything starts to make sense. You exchange external validation for a stronger sense of your own self which comes from inside you.

This is the birth of a new self and often of a new more meaningful vocation. The great asset you acquire at this time is relevance.

Delving Deeper
Previous phases have been about expanding your capacities. Now the emphasis is on deepening your awareness, adding an inner dimension. What you learn now enables you to define the vision you've been working towards more clearly. Because inner work and deep questioning of all the assumptions on which life is based is, as we have seen, the essential force that drives vision. Intuition, inner

listening, shows you not just that change is necessary, it shows you how it can be managed.

Initially you may find yourself wrestling with meaning, aware there is a different perspective, but as yet unable to see. You glimpse first how things don't work, all the negatives. But this is a temporary phase and soon you see the positive connections and possibilities. Give it time and resist the temptation to backslide into the scepticism that cripples all endeavour.

You can no doubt see the problem with making this particular shift. If you have "made it", exchanging doing for being seems to jeopardise all you have worked so hard to accumulate. If you have not, it can look like a counsel of despair, a hole you retreat into to escape the sense of failure.

It's worth remembering that 95% of your work colleagues are having to face this sense of failure with you, because the system can only accommodate 5% of us at 40. No amount of extra doing at this point is going to lift you into the 5% which becomes 2% by the end of this phase. However changing horses and drawing on your inner resources might actually take you there, if that is still important!

Your new vocation emerging now and integrating all the life skills you've acquired earlier could be the vehicle for you to soar to the top. It will certainly make you happier because you'll be being authentic. This, being and doing what you really came here to be is the path to happiness. No amount of money will do this for you. And to be sure the transition is an uncomfortable one, because the sense of self and the happiness are still in the future. Hold onto the idea that if nothing changes on the inner, nothing changes on the outer, that lasting success flows from the inspiration of a sense of personal meaning, that unknowing is the gateway to knowing.

At first you will not know what your life means but still the energy pulsing through you now refuses to let up. It remains mystifyingly important to understand and live a life that makes sense. This becomes the only satisfactory basis for self-esteem. It is only when you have inner confirmation of your sense that you have worth that you can comprehend your connection and interconnectedness with everything else. Gradually from deep within yourself you now find answers to all the questions that confused and perplexed you when you arrived at the watershed of life. It is such a contrast with all the practicalities and negative mind talk that has bogged you down.

There was a time to do, mostly from 21 to 42, and if you tried to avoid this it catches up with you (see below). Now you can allow the initiative and responsibility to pass from you to others, because it is time for you to incorporate your being, and in particular your being *with*. You don't stop doing, especially in these transitional years, but you add more of your being. It's and...and, not either or. Your being with yourself, your being with others, your being with the natural and artistic worlds, your being with your whole environment.

Scepticism cripples all endeavour

Is this intuitive energy available earlier, or does life have to be pointless up to this point? No, you can draw down this energy early and avoid much of the heartache involved in shifting now. In many ways the whole point of reading this book is so that you can make sense of your life, whatever stage you've reached, and you can anticipate what is coming. You still need to live each phase as you come to it, but you can live it with more awareness of what is happening, and of what is to come. And you can find these later energies in your psyche and put them to work earlier.

In addition we all have individual preferences which run throughout our lives, so you may for instance be a natural Indigo and can develop your Indigo powers by reading this chapter. By much the same token you can develop an embryonic sense of Indigo ahead of the phase where it strikes all of us, 42 - 49. Working with a more rounded kitbag of energies and anticipating what is coming is the essence of LifeShift. It is how life is transformed.

So while our principal concern now is with embracing Indigo and the transitional forties, those at other stages of development and with other agendas can adapt this material to their current life contexts, especially having read this book.

Learning to Listen

The **lesson** for this phase of life, 42 - 49, is **listening**. This requires that you meet your inner self, and this in turn requires that you slow down. The wheelspin world of busy doing does not allow in the wisdom of intuition. It is in such a mad rush it can't hear what is being said. When you slow down, you start hearing your inner voice. It warns you of dangers. It suggests other lines of approach and enquiry. It hears what you are about to say and comments on it in advance, so you can decide whether those words are a good idea. It solves problems and answers questions. It tells you what words to type next! It cleared my entire To Do List so that I could be in the right energetic space to write this chapter! It is a phenomenal resource.

To slow down, you will need to continue practising the stress and time management ideas covered in Chapters 5 & 6. Revisit those sections now and identify, if you haven't already, the energy you're most identified with and where you therefore need to go in order to relax. This is stress management tailored to your type.

OK? More relaxed? Or still unable to let go? The first 6 months are the worst. Keep practising and it becomes more and more natural. We'll return to this in a bit, and give you some questions to guide your steps.

This is not necessarily about deserting the real world and retiring to the top of a mountain. We all, well most of us, have to live and engage with income generation. So this is the context in which we have to learn to listen. As with all the previous phases the context in which we're living our lives is also what distracts us from learning the next lesson. And what could be more of a **distraction** than the

noise of everyday life. That is what you have to cope with. And only listening selectively can help you deal with the noise you inhabit. Then you can turn noise into an ally, like grist for your mill.

Noise can help because you have to get away from it! And when you do get away from it, you find the peace where indigo listening can happen. Noise is a constant reminder that you need something else. In the end noise becomes the place where you translate your listening into action. Silence can be too intrusive, which is why those dreadful, sound-proofed, air-conditioned offices have to have "white noise" re-engineered back into them. It's great for deep meditation, but when you want your inner voice to speak or have your mind interact with it, noise can give you some mental grip. So I often seek out a noisy place in order to contact the quiet inside and draw it out. It balances me up in a way that silence cannot. There are limits however: this is being written in a cafe directly under the Heathrow flight path with planes flying about 200 feet above me every minute! Initially you may find it helps to create some peace and quiet, or move between noise and silence.

Connecting with this inner resource changes your relationship with your environment, as you take it out into your daily life. As more and more people tire of the old unbalanced striving against life, a new ethos is emerging. This is variously called intuitive leadership or right livelihood.

Intuitive Life-Planning

Intuitive leadership is inner listening for outer action, a theme covered at a conference at The Findhorn Foundation in 1990. Some of the insights I recorded at the time (I was 43) seem still to sum up the Indigo lifestyle.

Peter Russell described how the human race is facing an evolutionary shift similar to that which took place 60 to 100,000 years ago. Then homo sapiens experienced a shift in consciousness which unleashed his successor 'home sapiens sapiens' on the world. HSS developed two extraordinary new qualities - language and tools. Tools gave more power to the elbow and represent the physical, biological, 'doing' side of our nature, which we tend to attribute to the masculine and to the Red base chakra. Language enhanced our ability to share and communicate, more sensitive qualities that typify the feminine and the Orange chakra.

Riane Eisler's book 'The Chalice and The Blade' makes a similar point. She shows that humanity experienced a remarkably rich, cultured and peaceful society which culminated some 6-12,000 years ago. It was a partnership society where women were honoured rather more highly than men, and where the qualities of both sexes had their place. That is, the Orange, feminine, sharing, community values were served by the Red, masculine, active power and both cooperated. Simplistically man hunted and developed tools to control his environment and make it safe, secure and comfortable: woman upheld justice (or fair shares) and developed a community worth protecting. Riane Eisler called it gylany, because it linked (l) woman (gy) and andros (man).

This harmonious arrangement was crushed by successive waves of invaders, who had developed tools at the expense of the language of sharing. Their code was 'Might is Right' and their creed was greed. Gylany was no more a match for them than were the North American Indians or Aboriginal Australians for the callous invaders from Europe. Yet the dialogue continued and frequently we can see signs of a harking back to that gentler time - Socrates (educated by a woman), Thucydides' Melian Dialogue and Agricola's strictures on the Pax Romana, Jesus too whose value system was eminently gylanic, and our whole artistic and cultural development in uneasy truce with technology and now our own yearning for a better balance between the two sides of our nature.

The rewards of androcracy (where the Red base masculine chakra is supreme) are very seductive - more of everything, growth, expansion, everything one could want for the asking (or failing that for the taking). At last, we have a society where many people are at least within range of having everything they need (rather than just what a tiny privileged minority wanted), and wealth is common enough for us to realise that having everything is a mirage. Those who have everything just seem to want even more, so clearly having everything is a dreadful disappointment. Finally enough of us are learning that gaining the whole world does not profit us if we lose our souls in the process.

We also see that far from gaining the whole world we have very nearly destroyed it. Estimates vary but few give us more than 40 years in our current state of madness, and many believe we have even less before we wipe ourselves out. Nostradamus gave us until 1999, but this may mean that the system he knew cannot last longer than this.

Androcracy has given us powerful leadership in the pursuit of goals and has achieved incredible results. Our discoveries, technology, ingenuity are not to be scorned. They have however been devastatingly out of balance, as we have for centuries - and especially in the last 2 centuries - totally ignored our impact on our environment, the planet, its other inhabitants as well as humanity and people themselves. Without the balance of that Orange level sense of community and justice, androcracy has been a disaster.

The voice of love and care has always been there, but it has taken the threat of annihilation to amplify that voice so it can be heard. Gradually it has grown in strength, as the inevitable conclusions of androcracy out of balance and out of control come home to us, and more and more people are saying "Enough. Our backyard is a mess. It is a disgrace. We have allowed this madness for too long, because we could not fight it - you had to see for yourselves. This is where the skin-encapsulated ego of leadership takes you."

Crisis concentrates the mind wonderfully and as its Chinese symbol indicates there is both danger and opportunity. There are still some saying 'crisis, what crisis?', but they are increasingly marginalised, as the voice of the people and community rises to a crescendo.

The balance is being redressed. The people are taking over the initiative of leadership. We are finally waking up to our ego sh*t, maturing and taking responsibility for it. This is an evolutionary jump quite as great as the shift 60-100,000 years ago.

This is why a new undistorted form of leadership is emerging now, free of ego, in touch with the feminine and community, more sharing or following than leading. 6,000 years of increasingly brutal androcracy have finally convinced us - all it leads to is more war, more devastation, less fulfilment and less humanity. It increases the separation between us and everything else. And it hurts more than we can bear any more. The bribes of the old way have lost their seductive power: and as always when an old civilisation dies we see its worst excesses in its final reactionary death throes.

In the old civilisation, inner well-being is determined by outer well-being, doing more is supposed to enhance being; changing the world is the only way to change the bad feelings inside. So there is an obsession with money and other addictions: all designed to achieve peace out there but all it does is shift the focus a bit. This has had to become so out of control that it is obvious even to the most addicted that it doesn't work. The 'spiritual aridity' of it is finally clear.

The shift to redress the balance is long overdue. Urgency is further increased by the speed at which things are happening now. Changes that used to take 50 years now take five. Those that in the 90s take five years will only take one in the next decade. There is no longer a tide in the affairs of men: there is a flood. This is why it is time now to find a new way.

The new way is intuitive leadership, which means allowing the inner voice to lead. It therefore has more to do with following the inner voice of intuition than with leading and the outer fix of logical, rational mind.

"You can't work these things out" said one conference speaker. "Mind will always come up with reasons for not doing what the intuition urges". Peter Caddy reiterated his well-worn theme that we must act immediately on intuition, not allowing mind to interfere. This brings us closer to our higher, divine self, "seeking first the kingdom of heaven" with which intuition connects us: only then "shall all else be added unto us."

This entails doing the inner work and working out our inner response to what is happening on the outer levels before taking on the world. We can only contribute to resolving crisis if the personal inner preparation has been done. In fact the inner work is our contribution, because when we are all at peace within, there will be peace on the outer.

As intuitive leadership means doing the inner work, it includes all the work we do on letting go of past memories and of projecting the future out of the past, releasing pain and doubt, opening our hearts, seeing and learning the lessons in everything.

As long as the inner work is not being done, intuition cannot be heard and all we are left with is struggle and pain. The only way to cope then is to close down emotionally and focus on achieving change in the outer world in the forlorn hope it will make things better on the inner. This is not just forlorn, it is suicidal. If for instance we just focus on mending our environment without mending ourselves, Gaia will quite simply take us out. We're the problem and all our specious talk about saving the planet is bunk. It's us we're trying to save. "If you want to save the planet, it's very easy," says Peter Russell, "just organise the mass suicide of the human race tonight." Our only other hope is to allow the spiritual, the inner voice of our intuition, to come through.

Intuitive Leadership allows the initiative to pass from one to another and just holds the energy and the vision. It creates a space in which people can empower themselves, allowing all to lead and take decisions about their work, which generally increases income, as each person steps into their power and the group grows, co-creating the company, as creatures not pawns.

It allows pain, fear, conflict and anger to be expressed, getting things clear on the personality level. It does not allow fear of mistakes to hold you back, nor technique or bureaucracy to take over; they block the spirit and energy of people. Consensus, attunement, appreciating people take the place of rigid authority. Faith and goodwill, the courage to be uncomfortable, the freedom to be authentic and the responsibility that goes with it all are encouraged under the rule of Intuitive Leadership.

Intuitive leadership is about really giving people their heads. What makes this possible is spiritual purpose, bringing spirit into matter (the Kingdom of Heaven down on Earth). All purposing and planning is an intuitive process, since the numbers are just calculated guesses and certainly beyond one year a totally intuitive activity. Centred purpose orders the energy of one's experience, providing a stability which is stronger in its very vulnerability and dissolves conflicts as one might vaporise a cloud.

Many aspects of contemporary business need to be dropped or rebalanced.

In the list that follows, items on the left obviously represent aspects of intuitive leadership, items on the right represent the traditional approach whose stranglehold can with benefit be released a little now.

Meditating on a pile of invoices	Worrying yourself sick
Focus is What to Be / Create	Focus is What to Do
Holding Goddess Energy	Applying God Energy
Co-Creation	Hierarchies
Inner Silence	Outer Noise
Starting with the Inner	Skidding along on the outer
Going Deeper	Broader (or Shallower)
Letting go, letting God(dess)	Holding on tightly
Harmony	Discord
Being natural, authentic	Being false
Intuitive philosophy	Analytical technique
Feminine in balance with masculine	Masculine distortion
Orchestrators	Leaders
Plan as start point	Plan as rigid container
Company as merely context	Company as prime Content
Keeping the space open and empty to be filled each moment anew	Stuck in the past, projecting more of the same into the future.
Holding the energy so people can empower themselves,	"Empowering people" which actually disempowers
Trusting your needs will be met	Distrust: salaries and profits being a focus for anxiety
Being a custodian (for assets, debts etc)	Possessive, acquisitive, accumulating
Money as a workshop in self-esteem	Money as an end in itself
Values, above all else	Values mostly monetary
Welcoming crisis as much as success	Being overselective in favour of success

Mistakes are OK	Mistakes are NOT OK
Process is important	Goals are all that matters
Commitment without attachment	Attachment without love
Detachment and Release	Obsession with continuance
Natural succession	Succession battle
Ecstatic reasoning with grace	Analysing it all to death
Metaphor & Metaphysics	Brass tacks and tight logic
Following hunches	Practical, progressive, physical action
Listening	Focusing opinions
Consensus	Control
People before Organisations	Organisations before People
Seeing the light in all of us	Looking to Gods, Gurus and Leaders
Allowing the pain	Suffering pain by resisting
Going with the flow	Allowing the mind to dam the river
Acting instantly	Framing excuses for inaction
Here and Now	Past and Future

The world of work, organisation, money and concept is the place to do this inner work of discovering intuitive leadership because these are the things that block our progress. These are the excuses people put up as reasons for resisting and rejecting the intuitive leadership approach.

Everyone can lead. You just have to get out of your own way and do what matters to you, so you set an example for others and enable them to empower themselves... like the kid who gave up his most treasured possession, his baseball glove, as a protest against nuclear power - and started a national campaign in the U.S. Real leadership now is each of us taking a stand, being our own guru, without any ego shit, growing up and maturing.

When we each do our own work, we achieve transformation in our outer environment. We can't convince those who don't see this.

As Eileen Caddy put it, "Don't try and take the dirty worn out old toy away from the child: it loves that old rag and will resist tenaciously. Just put the new toy in alongside it. If it's rejected or thrown out, just offer it again...and again. When they tire of the old toy, the new one is there, already familiar and safe to turn to. You can't force people to change, but they are hungry for love and intuition and will respond to a good example."

The Swedish word for business is NARINGSLIV, which translates 'nurturing life'; now there's a concept if you like, and it's where intuitive leadership takes you. "When you work for profit, there's a smile at the end. When you work with intuition there's a smile at the beginning".

If not us, who
If not here, where
If not now, when
If not through truth and love, how

When you adopt the balanced, sensitive Indigo approach to life, you live in commitment to right livelihood. These are the values and the lodestar of that lifestyle.

This is the new world that is now emerging, as indigo energy is more widely embraced. How do you respond to it? How far have you gone with it? Take some time after reading this for some further reflection on your personal situation and state of play.

The Right Livelihood Commitment

● We respect, support and value all the people with whom we have dealings, both inside and outside our business.

● We practise the highest standards of integrity, emotional honesty and loving care in meeting the needs of our customers, ourselves and everyone involved in our business. We seek mutually rewarding relationships with them all and communicate the same message fairly and honestly to everyone.

● We are creating our workplace to be loving, joyful, friendly, open-hearted and free from fear and negativity. Our aim in this is to help all to learn, grow, win and fulfil their potential. We are committed to enhancing quality of life.

● We welcome advice, criticism and suggestions from all quarters and will do our best to respond positively. We proudly walk the extra mile in our search for excellence in everything we do.

● We strive for authenticity, integrating our spiritual values in our work, and taking responsibility for learning our lessons from life.

● We are committed to service, and trust that through service all our needs are met.

● We accept our responsibility to preserve, protect and enhance the environment, its resources and our community.

● In everything we do, we will remember that we are all members of one world-wide family and act accordingly.

The questions you could usefully ask yourself at this stage are:

● what are you doing when you feel best about you?

● what would give your life greater meaning?

● what does your inner self tell you about the direction you might take?

● what do your toughest problems tell you about your life purpose?

● what inner work are you doing? what have you ever done, and

● again what does your inner voice recommend?!

● what's going on inside...right now?

● how would you describe your inner self?

● what is your connection with this inner self and with the natural world around you?

● how do you relax?

Invite your inner voice to tell you how to connect with it. It is the only place you will get an answer. Let it tell you what your next step is...now and whenever you need some help.

Stay in Balance

The **pitfall** you must avoid at this time is landing so heavily in this glorious new tableau that you lose touch with any semblance of physical reality. The pitfall is **polarisation**. This in a way is one of the pitfalls associated with every phase and every energy you colonise, but it's raised here because the shift from Blue structure to Indigo sensitivity is such a dramatic one with so much investment to release that it is the right moment to invite awareness of the dangers of polarising.

There is such a thing as over-being! It is the classic weakness of all the flaky New Age stuff which puts most of us off Indigo for lifetimes. It has no balancing groundedness and is in constant danger of floating away into the blue yonder. With all the religious fervour of the new convert, the overdone indigo lives in a cloud cuckoo land, populated by metaphysical entities and fantastical ideas. Nothing has any substance, and in fact nothing has any meaning either as there has to be some connectedness for there to be meaning. This is one of the opposite poles to which you can disappear.

The other is over-doing, fighting the shift, resisting the arrival of wisdom, workaholics heaven. You can't hear anything from this space, let alone your inner voice! Which is why it's such a popular avoidance mechanism, and why it's so fiercely defended by winners however disenchanted they may be.

Staying polarised, refusing to come into balance, is the obstacle to overcome for those in their 40s. It's the principal cause of a disastrous mid-life crisis, whether you succumb to it now or make it even worse by delaying it. Over-doing and over-being are both ways of trying to shut out reality. Over-doing avoids hearing inner wisdom; over-being avoids acting on it; without this vital reality check the inner message becomes more and more of an aberration, detached from the wisdom it claims and prey to ego masquerading as sage.

Polarisation is the problem now in the 40s because we tend to have become too strongly attached to our own way of doing things. We know what works and are not about to risk everything by throwing that overboard and starting all over again with something untried, untested and unfamiliar. So whether I've learnt to get by by being a hopelessly addicted workaholic or an equally hopeless space cadet, I'm going to resist like crazy dropping my guard.

At every moment from 40 on, there is a choice whether to turn towards spirit or turn towards matter. I can always choose the route which makes most money, or I can opt for what enhances the spiritual welfare of mankind. These are the two poles of existence, and it is the tension between them that creates the variety that is the spice of life. Always turning one way, only ever choosing the materialistic or only following the path of spirit, makes you one dimensional and stunts your evolution. Put simply you will be a raging bore!

The Tragedy of Success

Spiritual being needs tempering on the hard edge of human existence; human doing needs leavening with the yeast of inner meaning. Attachment to either stops us growing into mature adults. It's a poor sort of success, but that's the choice we make when we remain attached. We deny ourselves the sort of success that will see us out, that is sustainable beyond the confines of a career. Unhealthy pride, pomposity, holds us in there. But if we can let go of the limitations of worldly, or esoteric, success and all its trappings, we can open up to the real success of wholeness.

Success blocks us in another way too. Anything new we do allow ourselves to try has to be done on a grand scale that reeks of success. It has to be big and impressive. When what you're shifting to is an unfamiliar acquaintance with being, the last thing you want is a big show and trumpets blaring. The difference between loud doing and soft being can be yet another factor which makes the transition an abyss to draw back from. **Success**, everything you have built up to this point, is the **attachment** you have to let go. The chances are it is what you are most reluctant to let go, and that makes it top of the list.

Just as you find yourself experiencing some success, life has moved on again, and it is time to tune in to a deeper level. The internal conflict is intense. But maintaining that success probably means staying in over-doing. And you cannot get to being from there. The 40s is the time to complete your career and connect with the meaning of life and your reasons for being here.

It is a time for new interests, especially artistic or environmental ones, a time for new values as what seemed important becomes jaded. It is a time for seeking a moral philosophy, a wise mentor, a new perspective on life. It is a time to expand your sphere of influence and maximise your impact on your selected community.

When this strikes earlier in life, it is crucial to remember that there is also an energy relevant to that phase of life which must also be honoured. And it helps to be aware that there will be a time later when this engagement with inner reality will be the prime focus.

Chapter 6 covered the transitional years into the 40s, when the task is to integrate more being with the doing which is still the context in which life and learning is happening.

This chapter covers the 40s which is when being takes over from doing. These are the transitional years out of doing, whereas the late 30s are the transition into being.

Even the most active person around 40 can be open to being, without much outward sign that a change is taking place. Even the most inactive person can resist the challenge of being, at the same age, and end up at 43 in mid-life crash. Being is not just not doing. There is an intensity of being that is centred and healthy just as there is a healthy form of doing that is intense but not excessive.

Life does begin at 40

The 40s is the time to complete the four phases of life dedicated to doing, while learning how to be more in touch with the being side of your nature.

The mid-life crash previewed in Chapter 6 happens now if the preparation for this phase has not been done by the age of 42, if being has not yet been allowed in. Doing only does it for you if being is getting a look in. If you still hang doggedly on to the fight and inner life continues to be ignored, even what appears on the outside to be a worthwhile existence grows irksome and unrewarding to the soul. You have a choice, whether you slip gracefully into the super-efficient flow of being or have to be dragged reluctantly into it. Mid-life crash is kicking and screaming against the natural transition into mature wisdom.

Life begins at 40, because the apprenticeship with life is completed then and the rest of life is about making sense of it. "The first 40 years furnish the text. The next 40 are the commentary." But 50 is an even more significant milestone. The fight is over and it is time to start reflecting and giving back from the insight accumulated. Each phase is both an experience in itself and a preparatory learning for the next phase.

Inner work is the basis of being, just as much as outer work, engaging with the material, physical world is the basis of doing. They are not in conflict, nor is one better than the other, but there is a time for one to be the priority and then for the other. The thumb and forefinger are in conflict, going different ways, with for all we know different belief systems: but in the context of a hand, does it matter? After all, the contradiction is what enables us to grasp things.

Doing is the essential grounding for the inner work which develops your being. Problems arise when we get polarised in either being or doing, and it arises now because around 42 is the watershed. Doing is gradually less important from this point on, and being is more important. Inner work takes over from outer work.

Inner work means taking time to be with you. Some of the ways this manifests have been touched on above. Slow down, relax and reflect; listen to the inner voice of intuition; deepen; question; engage with your artistic side and the natural world. Whatever else you include in your personal programme of being, time sitting quietly with yourself is more or less obligatory. The technical term for this is meditation, which is not unlike sitting in front of the television, with the set turned off.

A Brief Guide to Meditation

● Set aside an area or corner for quiet reflection.

● Go there daily for at least 1 minute. If you want to stay longer that's fine. But think of it as 1 minute; then there's no excuse for not doing it every day.

● Sit with your back straight and self-supporting.

● Take 3 deep breathes, filling and softening your belly and allowing your chest to expand. Breathe out through your mouth.

● Close your eyes if this helps and notice what is going on with your body. Move and stretch as you wish. Consciously relax each part of your body in turn, especially the brow, jaw, neck and shoulders.

● When you find an ache or some physical discomfort, stay with it. Let it be; don't try to stop it; let it grow, shift or reduce as it wants and be aware of what's happening.

● Imagine a taproot or cord connecting from the base of your spine into the ground.

● Move your attention into your belly, imagine an inner door opening to your feeling self and allow any feelings that are there to be present. As with the physical sensations, let them be, grow, shift and diminish as they wish.

● Move your attention to your solar plexus and be aware of all the nervous and mental activity going on in you. Allow and listen to it. There is no need to reply or fight it; just hear it out. If you get no further than this for the first 3 months, that's still a considerable achievement.

● Open your heart to yourself, and allow your chest to breathe.

● Open your throat, all the time assessing what is going on with you - physically, emotionally and mentally.

● Move your attention into your forehead and invite your intuition to make contact. This is where you connect with the energy to which this chapter is dedicated. Let your inner voice communicate in any way it wants - words, pictures, colours, sensations, insights.

● Raise any questions you have for your inner self and be open to answers. What do I need to look at differently about this vision? Is this for me? Why? What is a significant step I can take to be more with this vision? What's blocking the way here? And always finish by asking "Is there any other information for me just now?"

● Practise checking your intuition. Try posing yes-no questions, and imagine that you have some internal traffic lights. Take the question straight to the traffic lights and see the colour. This can cut through the mental analytic process and allow intuition through. You could use scales instead, or spin a coin in your head.

● Say thank you and bring yourself back, aware of the ground under you, the tips of your fingers and toes, the hair on your head.

Once this much is in place you can if you wish go deeper, into a state of deep peace, silence and totally relaxed consciousness. For further guidance still, William Bloom's book Meditation in a Changing World is recommended.

This practice sets up a connection you can then draw on throughout the day. It builds trust which supports letting go, as The LifeShift Cycle suggests (Chapter 6). Whenever you want an intuitive insight, pause, breathe and invite it in. Notice where it seems to come into you. I feel it enters me through my right temple; others are aware of a committee above and to one side of them; all that is valid is your experience; there are no rights or wrongs. You can also pose two options and imagine one to your right and one to your left. Then step into each in turn and notice which feels right, with which you most identify.

You cannot force intuition. If nothing comes, nothing comes. Turn your attention elsewhere. Intuition often arrives when you're not expecting it and haven't even asked for it. Its main problem is getting through all the noise of analytical process and hyperactivity. The more you practise taking a break from left braininess, pausing, breathing and meditating, the better the connection with your intuitive inner voice becomes.

How do you know when it's intuition and not just ego talking? Intuition whispers, ego shouts. And if there's any doubt, it's ego! But you'll never know till you stop doubting and try it. If in doubt, ask to be shown, not asking what to do, but how to see it differently.

The seven years from 42 to 49 are the classroom for this vital ingredient in learning to LifeShift. This is the domain of poets and poetry, expressing the inexpressible, bridging the abyss between the worlds of spirit and matter.

SUMMARY

● The 40s is the time to complete your career and make the shift from doing to being. It is time to connect with meaning and sensitivity to your surroundings.

● Now you consolidate the new you and discover your reasons for being here.

● The 2% of winners resist this Indigo energy because it seems to jeopardise their accumulated pile. Instead of moving on and growing they hope to get better and better at doing the same old thing. Success blocks growth.

● A new way of being calls - intuitive leadership and right livelihood. The arts and community become more important. Mentors are advisable.

● You can draw down any or all of the energies early to anticipate life and mould vision sooner.

● As you slow down and listen, your inner voice becomes available. Ask it what your life means.

● Over-doing stops you hearing; over-being stops you acting on what you hear. Out of balance either way you're a raging bore.

● Meditation is where you learn to work with your intuition.

LESSON to LEARN:
Listening inside and out

DISTRACTION:
Noise, until you turn it into an ally

PITFALL to AVOID:
Polarisation, the imbalance which causes mid-life crash

ATTACHMENT to RELEASE:
Success, when it stops you taking risks

EXERCISE

Refer back a few pages to the questions following The Right Livelihood Commitment and take them into a 5 minute meditation.

Here as usual is the Action Box, this time to record any insights from your meditation and reading.

Transfer key ideas and action points to your Personal Priority Pages.

CHAPTER 8

The Visionary Years (49-56): Growing Wise

The main problem we have with directing our lives is that we don't have any clear idea in what direction we want to take them. This phase, from 49 to 56, is when we discover that direction. We now have the experience and maturity to understand why we have done what we have done and what we might usefully now do with that. The great paradox of life is that it is only at the end of a career that we see the point of that career, or, if we have missed out any crucial phase along the way, the pointlessness or incompleteness of it.

A key purpose of this book is to explain the energies we only otherwise discover at the end of our journey, so you can at least be aware of them at the start of your journey, and take that journey in a more fulfilling direction.

By being open to learning throughout the years of engagement you have the opportunity to see the whole picture now. In particular you can now see the why that has been at work all these years. And you can also see what you have scrupulously avoided!

As we grow up we tend to get stuck. At some point we decide that we have found our niche, the energy with which we feel comfortable and have resisted moving on to new and often uncomfortable experience. If this is the case, the 50s can be an awkward time. We lack the rounded access to all the six energies covered in the previous chapters, and find it all a bit mystifying.

There is certainly no point carrying on in this unenlightened state. If all else fails (and if you have refused to learn your lessons it will have done) try being you. The fight is over, the battle out there won or lost; it matters not a jot which.

Even those who have kept up with the changing phases and their tasks and lessons have a sizeable job to do in the 50s, consolidating it all. Not every phase will have been equally well integrated, so the task now is to fill any gaps and catch up.

Completely empty phases have to be absorbed in double quick time, though the flavour or colouring of this phase with its helpful insights into why things were and are as they are is an ally.

As you integrate whatever you skimped earlier you have the energy of this phase to help you. The better connection you've made with your self and your environment helps you make contact with your vision, the why behind your life, your purpose for being here. The meaning you searched for in the last phase comes clearer and it becomes easier to let go of any doubts. Where doubts do still linger it will be because some earlier energy has not been properly colonised, but your clearer vision will help see you through the process of integrating these other energies.

This is what really matters in this phase, being clear what does matter and what is important. It is no longer sufficient to do something without knowing its meaning. It is no longer sufficient to be asking what it means. Only what has meaning and clearly enables you to put your vision to work is worth doing now. It will not be a knowing, but an intuitively harvested insight.

It is time to stop compromising your own needs to fit around others who lack the vision to make anything of their lives without getting you to do most of the work. It is time to be less conscientious, drop unproductive commitments and responsibilities, realise what a mug you've been and resolve to do only what furthers your vision.

It is now entirely natural that you insist on working your creativity. Only when you are transforming something that you care about in a way that inspires you and inspires others is there any sense of fulfilment, and if there's no fulfilment you're just not going to do it any more. Activity that once held you enthralled palls now if it has no meaning, and is not 'working your why'.

50 and a New Life
Now in your 50s you become a visionary, the dreamer who does, the spiritual entrepreneur, creative, transformative and inspiring.

The context in which you live your life, evolved over the previous 30 years is where you apply this transformative energy. You transform your surroundings, whatever they are - boardroom, dole queue, village or inner city slum. This is your arena. And the energy you bring to it is uncompromising. You have earned the right, if you have done the work, to be cantankerous and bloody-minded! This all gives you the unfair advantage of resilience; they just can't keep you down any more! You have taken everything that life has thrown at you, paid your dues and reached the point in your journey where you discover your spiritual dimension.

Spirit is what feeds your soul and soul is your self only more so. Spirit is like an ocean, of which your inner wisdom is the cupful you bring with you, constantly replenishable whenever you wish. Soul is the website, spirit is the Internet extrapolated forward to infinity. If all you've ever known is that one website, that one first cupful, you will be unaware of the vast reservoir beyond. Your inner self can open this up for you, consciously inviting the bigger picture to present itself. There's always a beyond. So spirit and soul wisdom are closely connected.

Soul is known by many names - inner self, inner voice, inner wisdom, centre, and when it draws on spirit higher self or wise being. It is a place deep inside you, to which you gain access when you complete the outer work. You started to connect with it when you started listening to your inner voice. Now instead of making the odd telephone call you're wired in. The cupful of inner wisdom is expanded by its alignment to the reservoir of spirit. If you're still trying to play the old materialistic game your soul and your spirit sink. Once again you have to move on from familiar, successful territory to unfamiliar land where there is no guarantee of success.

From this spiritually deepened inner core you can reach out to consult your intuitive inner voice, your own authority, your heart, mind and feelings, your vitality and your physicality. Now when you act you act from a space of deep inner alignment. You do from a space of be. You build what you do on who you are. Growing into this energy gives you personal charisma. It is time for a burst of creativity, a new vocation, a new rounded self to emerge.

Social responsibility, artistic and literary qualities, respect for the natural world and compassion the absence of which is such a feature of the workplace attract you now and it is likely you will turn your attention in those directions. You have taken so much, in so many ways. Now the imperative is to give back whatever you can.

Build what you do on who you are

Paradoxically opting out of other people's agenda for you and insisting on working your own why makes you infinitely more valuable to your community. Having put god in charge, you become more available to your self as well as to others, more congruent, a better listener in better relationship to the all (god again).

When you're taking this energy into your life earlier than age 49, bear in mind that the energy of the phase you're in chronologically will also be acting on it. This energy that you inherit at 49 (once you have done the previous work) is the Violet energy of visionary creativity and transformation. It draws on all the previous energies and integrates them into a quality that at its highest level of manifestation enables you to achieve results simply by envisioning them. Potentially you have access to a whole new relationship with life. By being wholly present you can stop having to flog yourself to death.

Clear vision is the beginning of any new venture. Once you have clarified your purpose, in general and for the specific venture you now have in mind, you can and must make your way back down the sequence of energies you have just been climbing up. Clear purpose (Violet) makes it easier to tune into your niche, the place where your vision can land and be successfully applied (Indigo). And the close match you create between vision and niche, between what you have to offer and who wants it, enables you to plan the form and structure that will work best (Blue).

It is much easier to make the commitment when you have a clear plan for how something that you really care about can happen. Whole-hearted commitment is the next step (Green). Once you're really committed you can sail through the details (Yellow) and engage with others enthusiastically (Orange). With so much going for you, it is much easier to keep going and turn vision into action (Red).

As you work back through these energetic steps you will spot where you are unenthusiastic and need to do some more work. Doing it is in the end the only way to do it, to identify where you are vulnerable and need to give some attention. Doing it is also the only way to see what's next.

Learning to See

The task for this phase then, the **lesson** to learn is **insight.** How can you see all the things you have missed so far? How can you tap the alignment you now have with spirit to show you what you need and what you can become?

By listening.

You should have spent the last 7 years learning to listen. This practice gives you insight now. And still you are learning to listen. The context in which the learning happens is still the workplace. We never stop learning and growing, but now your insight evolves to help you. As you learn your insight grows. As your insight grows it helps you learn. You become more aware of the reverberations and repercussions set up by your actions. You come into better relationship with disappointment and frustration. They spur you on to new directions and new heights. Your progress accelerates, and you emerge with a road-tested model for a wholesome life, greater self-awareness and strategies for transforming the arena you have chosen.

Initially as you start to work with this energy, you can feel intense frustration at your lack of imagination and discouragement in the face of others who seem to be more evolved than you.

Failure in colonising all the previous energies will aggravate this. If you give up on it now though, you are left with resentment and self-recrimination. That's what's left when you lack this Violet energy. If you opted out of growth at 40, you are now in a far worse state, grimly struggling against a world that feels very threatening (men especially) or obsessively engaged in furious, ill-conceived activity (women).

But the sense of urgency to be stimulated creatively will overcome these early stage distress symptoms. And the growing sense of your own capacity for transformative vision will spur you on to asserting yourself in the world, even if you haven't before. Your experience of developing the previous energies will help too. You will recognise and remember the difficulties in the early stages of working with each of those other energies and know that you emerged from that and will emerge again. You may even remember that each energy can be overdone and catch yourself slipping into fanaticism. Just ease up and bring yourself back into balance and back into reality.

This transformation takes place inside just as anxieties may be building on the outside regarding what you are going to live on in "retirement". The **distraction** from engaging with your trans-formation to a spirited being is the **pension,** or lack of it. If you have found an activity that feeds your vision, this will be less of a worry. You will be happy to see your work continuing for many years yet. People only retire from jobs they never wanted to be doing in the first place. But even so you might like to feel that you work for the fun of it rather than to meet some financial imperative.

By now too, money may not be such an issue. There are less costs to cover, and there is less time to go, so less to worry about. You can be less frazzled, less preoccupied, less desirous of the trinkets of fame and influence because you know your own worth. If others don't recognise it, it really doesn't matter that much.

If you won the last game, you may have more money to make this phase comfortable. The trouble is, if you're comfortable you probably won't want to jeopardise that by moving on to the scary but exciting and uniquely rewarding work in this phase. And even the rich worry where their income will come from for the next 30 or 40 years. Money blinkers us to the real rewards and tasks.

All you can do is use the quality of insight this phase gives you to create a stream of income for the future. No amount of doing will create it now. You need to be smarter. Review your position. Pull in your horns. Reorganise your assets and finances, for instance selling off what you no longer need and facing the unacceptable. As ever the challenges of the outer experience are your growing edge. This is where you learn to be insightful. Seek insight from your inner self and its spiritual connection. When outer resources fail you, look within. There is so much wealth inside, if you will work courageously with it.

The question raised at the beginning of this book, 'What is it you most want to have happen in your work and in your life?' is germane now. But you're returning to it with greater awareness of the energies required and the strengths and quality you bring to it. Keep asking yourself this question, and also why? Why do you want this? If you had it, would you want it, and everything that comes with it? Be sure the answer is what most inspires you, what you most care about, what you most keenly intend. Nothing less will do. What you are really asking now is, 'Am I willing to be who I really am? Is this more important than all the old attachments? Am I willing to be stripped of all that?' Most people still back off from this, and then complain that life has gone sour and they can't make ends meet. You can't have it both ways.

Once you are clear what the one thing is that is in front of you, it is worth asking what stands in your way. This obstacle is worth removing. Why waste time removing obstacles to getting places you don't want to get to?! And yet much of life is like that.

Take these questions into your spiritual practice. This is where you work on your violet connection with your deeper purpose. It might be meditation or taking yourself into nature and being aware of your place in the overall scheme of things. Anything can be a meditation. It's wherever you connect with a heightened sense of self and discover your inner journey. What is it for you? Gardening, chopping wood, doing a cashflow, creative pursuits such as singing, painting, music, reading or studying?

You are working your violet energy when your priority is to free up space to do your inner work, and connect with heart and your soul purpose. This is how you come home to your connection with spirit.

You need to find silence, no matter how much noise there is around you (see Chapter 7). Violet energy gives you inner silence. Make time to be silent, so you can hear what your higher self has to say about your intentions and how to break through the obstacles.

You came here with a contract. The Violet in you knows what it is and how the connection with spirit it represents translates into your soul purpose. (If this is too much for you to take on board just now, don't worry. Violet energy can still be accessed even if you don't buy it altogether. The why may be a bit more mystifying without the explanation soul contracts provide, but you can still benefit.)

The time you spend in meditation tells you what the contract is, and though you might have liked to know this earlier, part of the contract is that you will do your best without full (or even partial) knowledge of what it is. What happens next is none of your business! The journey is more about how you respond to what happens and what you learn. Even now in your 50s.

The context for this learning is more and deeper, inner and meditative. You might like to refer back to the brief guide to meditation (in Chapter 7), as preparation for this next section on creative visualisation, which is the next level of meditation and is core to the colonisation of Violet energy.

Creative Visualisation

Creative visualisation is a technique for sharpening your focus on desired results, so that your entire being is so directed and open to the realisation of those results that the probability of achieving them is enhanced. It puts to work your powers of imagination. This is powerful stuff indeed! Imagination includes in its etymology the Magi, the wise men of the East, magic, "the art and science of achieving change through an act of will", imago and image. It is the force that produces transformation.

To tap this force you must be aligned with spirit and attuned with your inner wisdom. You need both to get imagination working. And you need the stillness and relaxed concentration of meditation to create the space in which you can listen to this vast wisdom.

Having stilled yourself as briefed, instead of posing questions for your inner self to answer, or after using questions to gain clarity about your vision, invite yourself to see a picture of your ideal desired situation. See yourself in this situation, as you want it to be and as if it already is. "I am now...", not "this person who is not really me will, if all goes well and we don't screw up again!"

"My bank manager/boss/wife understands me perfectly and we have a mutually rewarding relationship." begins to make that a reality, whereas "S/he thinks I'm an idiot" supports a frame of mind that constantly confirms that you are indeed an idiot. What you see is what you get. If you're looking for negatives, you'll see the one bad report you get and brood over it for weeks. If you have a positive picture in front of you, you notice the 99 good reports and glow all over. It even works when the numbers are reversed! Focus takes out random results, so what you focus on expands. It's quite simple and scientific...and the trick is all in the imagination.

Allow this picture to develop. Colour it in and notice all the details. Notice who is there, what you are all doing, the atmosphere. And notice what is not as you want it. Ask the problem what it wants, what it is trying to tell you, how it serves you and how it can become an ally. Invite it to change. As you do this, resistance may show up in various forms. Listen to what interferes with your imaged vision, because this needs acting on in order for you to arrive where you want. Notice also what comes as a surprise. There will be all sorts of brilliant ideas to incorporate in your planning.

It is important that your visualisation is broad. It should include giving as well as receiving, serving and sharing as well as achieving, being open to let go as well as arrive.

Creative visualisation has had a bad press and quite rightly. Early versions of it wrapped it up in a lot of muck and mystery; disciples were encouraged to create treasure maps of status symbols and material goodies, which they would get if they were advanced enough. Little or nothing was said about the work you might have to do. And the focus on society's trinkets gave away how immature this approach was.

What is proposed here is quite different. First it is stressed that life purpose is understood as something more sophisticated than a pile of tokens. Second imaging is used both to clarify and focus on desired results, and to identify obstacles. This reveals the personal growth work, the clearing of old trauma which needs facing, not suppressing like an embarrassing boil.

Creative visualisation helps set a new agenda for you. Its value lies first in ensuring that you have got still and centred enough to be there for it. More important still it gets you back in the present. When misused it leads into fantasies about the future, but done properly it identifies what needs to be given your attention now in order to create the situation you want. It raises questions about whether what you visualise is appropriate or even that desirable. It does this by enabling you to see the implications of what you are taking on. It shows up where you are allowing ego to take hold instead of putting inner wisdom in charge.

Creative visualisation works best when the desired result is not happening. Then you seek guidance on what you need to do, what you need to look at differently in order to move ahead. The result itself is relatively unimportant! What matters is the way the process holds you in the present, working on what is the priority now. Vision is now, not some distant dream. It's all in being here now, working on what's right in front of you.

With the clarity you keep getting as you return to it, you have tasks, issues and visions of course to express and share with others. Only share with people who have done considerable work on themselves, can listen and match your honesty and integrity. For the others the way you are will communicate your vision and energy.

A word of warning. Once you move into listening to your initial tranche of inner wisdom and dip your cup into the vast reservoir of spirit, you invite spirit to engage with you. Those who feel drawn to deepen their experience of themselves, to engage with a deeper, inner dimension, to gain insight into higher worlds and the realm of spirit are the lucky ones who have seen there *is* more.

When the desire to redress the balance and rediscover who you really are takes precedence over comfortable retirement, there are rich rewards, and as always when you make a choice, there is a price.

What happens when you engage with inner work?

When we enter inner work, the first effect seems often to be a collapse in our outer life, and not just a temporary blip. When we choose change on both fronts at the same time, inner *and* outer, as is common, we really are asking for trouble! And there is really no option, because to break through to a whole new life, the only life that is actually worth living, we *have to* reduce our pre-occupation with the outer and increase our availability for inner work.

The very first step inside commonly involves facing the fear the mortgage keeps alive. Which is why many never take it, and judge it as weak and vulnerable so they will have an excuse for not looking at the emptiness of their own inner lives. We judge what we fear or fail to understand. Those who take the step inside have realised that however fearful they may be of it, there is no life without understanding of self. The engagement with inner work is no soft option, and it is a path without end that raises increasingly tough challenges. Though it can take many forms, it is the only path that leads to life.

"Vulnerability is perfect protection" (Transformation Game)

So what does happen when you engage with inner work? Carolyn Myss gave a wonderful insight into this at another Findhorn Foundation conference in 1987. "When" she said, "you ask yourself 'What is my life purpose?' (a fairly typical step when entering inner work) this is not as you might have thought a question. 'What's for dinner?' is a question, but when you ask 'What is my life purpose?' that is an invocation, and your Guardian Angels show up! And what they do first is take you and your cleverly skin-encapsulated ego apart! *They start with the chakras (energy centres) where you are weakest and most vulnerable, where you leak.*"

But it has to be done. You have to take your power back chakra by chakra in every aspect of your life. You get to look at your unmet emotional needs, your addictions, your private ego agendas, your sense of self, your attempts to have intuition conditionally with strings attached, every part of yourself that may interfere with your spiritual self - your mind for instance. "Mind, "says Caroline Myss, "can never get you out of trouble. It only ever gets you in!"

There can be a lot of blood and gore, energy bleeding all over the place, and there are no half measures, no ways of protecting yourself from mistakes, failure, injury etc. If your intuition needs you to foul up so it can break through your material world barbed wire, get ready to foul up spectacularly.

If the traffic (money for instance) of your outer life is still years later not running freely, it is because your Guardian Angels still have the road up, so to speak. You are weakest both where you have done *least* work and where you have *most* work to do, which may or may not be the same thing. So what you experience when these chakras come under the loving attention of your Guardian Angel is both the pain of losing what you are most attached to *and* the early stage distress involved in developing an unfamiliar chakra. This is what it looks like.

CHAKRA	ATTACHMENT ATTACKED/LOST	EARLY STAGE DISTRESS EXPERIENCED, WORKING WITH A NEW LEVEL OF ENERGY
CROWN	HOBBY-HORSE	FRUSTRATION AT OWN LACK OF IMAGINATION
BROW	UTOPIANISM	DISCONNECTED FEELING: EVERYTHING IS UGLY
THROAT	STATUS	OBSESSION WITH RULES/TIDINESS. SARCASM
HEART	MONEY	VICTIM COMPLEX. OVERSENSITIVITY. BLACK HOLE
MIND	ANALYSIS	BUTTERFLY DISTRACTEDNESS
FEELINGS	RELATIONSHIPS	ISOLATION; TAKING NO PRIDE IN SELF
BODY	PHYSIQUE	OVER-STRESS; ABUSING BODY

To take some examples, suppose you have a heavy investment in the status your job gives you, the angels will go for the throat and strip away that job. You will have to find a more real you, while you handle the humiliation of losing the respect your status gave you. At the same time, you will be invited (press-ganged is more how it will feel!) to work with an energy that is less familiar, because you have never given it enough attention. Let's say this is relationships (because that's the most likely). You will be acutely aware how lonely and isolated you have become and think pretty poorly of yourself.

Take another example. You are attached to money. Having it is good and makes life OK: not having it is disaster. Most people in a society built on ambition, greed and acquisitiveness are attached to money and find that when inner work calls, this is what goes first. And perhaps you get to start working with the brow energy, and as you look around you see nothing but ugliness and injustice. It all looks meaningless and you don't feel part of anything.

If you fight this (and you probably will!), life gets tough. But it's a great life if you weaken! As you accept the lesson and let go the old attachment, you find a new, more real, not externally validated relationship with yourself to replace the old distortion. And as you develop your energy at the weakest chakra, you get in touch with it and handle it more naturally.

Then a second tier of attachments and weak areas will come on the agenda, and give you your next lessons. So while you're improving in some ways, you can feel got at in others, and may wonder if the problem you're having with say relationships is caused by your slow progress with say money. Oddly, it's probably because you've made better progress than you give yourself credit for with money, that your next lesson, relationships, has arrived! At the time it's very confusing and you are *very* likely, no you're *certain*, to end up at some point saying 'Well what the hell *am* I meant to be working on?'

If your angels think you're ready, you may be really lucky and experience The Dark Night of the Soul. This is a wonderfully awful time, wonderful because only by going right through your darkest, murkiest, most revolting shadow can you emerge into the light, awful because you wouldn't wish it on your worst enemy. All your worst fears are realised all in one go.

Giving too much attention to your inner development will result in Inner Burn-Out, a complete depletion of all your inner energy, so it is important to balance the intense inner work with playbreaks, creative pursuits, good old-fashioned work and R & R. To repeat, this is not a soft option. You're being tested to the limit on the inner and in completely unfamiliar, uncharted territory. And your outer life is in collapse. The more you hold on and try to put it back together again, the worse it will get.

Your only hope is to let go what you're most attached to and what you're most reluctant to let go. This attachment is a distorted form of a potential pure energy, which can also manifest positively, once you have gone back to basics with it and started again. You will probably find that you have to re-enter this energy field and experience the early stage distress of working with this energy too.

Together your least developed chakra and the one to which in a distorted form you're too attached create your personal curriculum. They create the context where your lessons lie. You are being invited to respond constructively and authentically. Splurging, tantrums, despondency and deserting the battle will only make it worse, though you may well have to find this out for yourself. Nothing beats personal experience , but do try and remember you have a map of the territory, and that your experience is not unique or delinquent.

What are you most reluctant to let go? Is it your hard-won claims to fame, your power-base? Or is it all the belief systems that underpin life as you know it? Is it money and the financial structure of your life that interferes with your ability to be human, in communion with yourself and other? Or is it your guru? People and relationships, whether of dependency or constraint, physical obsessions, hyperactivity and everything that gives structure, meaning and purpose to life can all be distractions from you discovering and being you. Let 'em go.

The more 'doing' has taken over your life and squeezed out 'being', the harder it will be to engage with the change. But continuing the imbalance of being and doing (let alone doing even more) will only aggravate things.

It's a great life if you weaken

The first challenge is likely to be fighting the feeling that being is a waste of precious doing time. But as you learn that twiddling your thumbs is probably the most constructive use of your time (as long as you don't get out of balance the other way and do *nothing* but twiddle your thumbs), sanity slowly returns. You will need to combine this with a complete reorganisation and downshifting of your life. This reduces the overpreoccupation with the outer, without completely destroying it and retains just enough viability for your physical existence while you engage with the inner work.

Outer work is not in conflict with inner work. It's the only place you can do it, unless you opt for the space cadet route, which is a distorted attachment at the other end of the spectrum, and therefore a dead-end too. What conflicts with inner work is attachment to something external. The outer with all its adversity, perversity and misfortune is exactly the place to do inner work. And it can often be very unclear how to proceed when the perversity of the outer world gets the better of us.

How can we draw on deeper levels of our being in the face of adversity and outer distractions?

● Be still and listen. No transformation is possible without this. Use meditation, gardening, walking in nature as times to ask for insight. Then listen and act immediately.

● Childlike wonderment is good when asking for this inner help: what do I need to know now? how could I look at this differently? how would my inner businessman (etc) behave here?

● Make friends with your intuition too, and listen to its promptings. Intuition is what happens when mind and feelings coalesce, so the more you learn to feel what you feel and express it, the better your intuition will come through.

● Put out clear intention, but be careful not to be attached to it or to any particular result, and affirm your connection with the all first. Otherwise it's just another ego-contaminated mission statement. Rudolf Steiner, of whom more later, says "Work undertaken for the sake of results is the least likely to produce them" (because there is attachment and no reverence for the work itself).

● Create a positive environment, not swayed by others' projections and interferences, not phased by the appalling chaos that probably surrounds you. And allow a new support system to enfold you.

● Every night, review progress and resolve on what you intend next. Then check in the morning how this needs to be modified.

● Keep practising! Forgive yourself frequently as you shift from being bogged down in doing to being in touch with your higher creative self.

● Remember when you give up, it's not failure, it's complete. Your personal development is drawing you on elsewhere. It's OK to make mistakes, because that's how we learn. "I am good" is a given. If there is "success", this is confirmed, but your being is not validated by any of the outer show or success. If there is "failure", there is just another challenge and maybe a need to change direction. There need be no loss of faith or face, just forgiveness.

● Also finally remember we're made of much tougher stuff than we know. You can survive this.

How to know higher worlds
Rudolf Steiner had some fascinating, and for his day unusually lucid and accessible perspectives on this subject, particularly in the most

readable of his many books "How to Know Higher Worlds" (Germany 1912, England 1923, reprinted by Anthroposophic Press 1994).

I first read this at a time when my attempts to bring spirit into matter, develop a rich inner life and take a higher awareness into business were being so confounded by the demands and frustrations of said business that I had ground to a halt. Dark Night of the Soul beckoned once more, and my knowledge that this was an essential step on the way to emerging into the light was *not* helping. Knowing what's going on does not necessarily make you either immune or comfortable.

Steiner seemed to be confirming that there was no incongruence between the spiritual life and engagement with the material. Indeed he is clear that the material, workaday world is the *only* place to begin and continue the journey. Spirituality starts (and maybe ends) with the attainment of a balanced relationship with the material, natural, human world. Balance is the beacon. Cultishness, New Age flakery, guru worship, copping out of life à la new age traveller, spiritual fascism and all the other distortions of spirituality have no place. Whenever we enter *any* new realm of energy, we tend to land heavily and overdo it, rejecting all other ways of being, especially anything to do with the establishment.

What follows is very largely based on Steiner's writing, with my own comments/additions shown in brackets.

Reverence is the key in esoteric training. The capacity to gain insight into higher worlds lies dormant within each of us. Enrolling in the esoteric mystery school is to be approached with reverence, discernment and sincere will. As you develop a richer, inner life and find your ideals and values, this must feed into the outer world of duty, sharing and ennobling humanity.

Preparation for esoteric training requires this balance and inter-action between inner and outer life, and a calm, measured, reverent approach to their integration. So you need to balance activity by creating moments of peace, solitude and meditation, drawing on spiritual texts for strength. Take time to be in communion with natural objects - stones, plants, animals, seeds. Practise listening selflessly, without the judgments and analysis of the self.

(Krishnamurti is also *very* hot on this. '*See* the tree without awareness of eyes.') Learn to distinguish between the essential and the inessential. As you find a new, undistorted foundation for who you are, your self-confidence, courage and single-mindedness can grow, (what I call responsible self-fulness).

Relationship with others is another crucial arena for esoteric training. Listen with tact, says Steiner. Practise communing with others' feelings as you did with the natural objects. Do not restrict others' autonomy. (Interfering in other people's lives is just a displacement activity for avoiding getting on with your own; and you don't want others interfering with you, so mind your own business, in every sense.) Steiner commends feeling responsible for the all, but not political activism.

Be patient. "One day when I'm ready for it, I shall receive what I am to receive" is a good attitude. Fast-track approaches (the quick-fix sheep-dip style of the '80s and '90s) are to be abjured; they open up unhealthy side-effects and dark powers which they are not equipped to handle. Coming over time to understand why life is at times hard, connecting with life as it flourishes and with the fading into death is what leads to illumination and paves the way for initiation.

This well-balanced enhancement of your physical, mental and spiritual health is the groundwork for esoteric training in the higher mysteries of life, but obsessional asceticism is not in the programme. It is off-balance.

Preparation, for Steiner, is completed where love meets work. Love what you do however menial and stick at it. Love is the only motivation for action. But take satisfaction in the act, not just the outcome. Work undertaken for the sake of results is the least likely to produce them, just as learning unaccompanied by reverence is unlikely to advance us far.

Love for the work, for what is in front of us now, not the antici-pated result moves us forward. And the path to love is gratitude, which leads to calm, inner peace - the basis for further action. Keeping thoughts and feelings pure develops a helpful heart and inner firmness. And all this sets the scene for initiation to begin. One needs to be in balance, organised harmoniously, performing one's duties perfectly up to the limits of one's abilities. One needs to be mindful, discriminating and thoughtfully active, in touch with life and inner truth. Then one begins to see.

There are strong resonances here with other messengers of the perennial philosophy:

'To love life through labour is to be intimate with life's inmost secret ...Work is love made visible.'

Kahlil Gibran: The Prophet

'Only the intelligence of love and compassion can solve all problems of life...In order to act rightly, there must be right thinking. And right thinking can come only in understanding ourselves'

Krishnamurti

'Work is love in action. Love where you are. Love what you're doing. Love who you're with.' *Peter Caddy, Findhorn Foundation*

' Perfection is anything done whole-heartedly and with love.'
Eileen Caddy, Findhorn Foundation

'Love is all there is.' *John Lennon*

The desire to engage with inner work *as well as* to make a success of the outer world is both the means whereby we 'keep body and soul together' and our main context for growth.

Inner work is a lifelong commitment with endless lessons to learn in both inner and outer dimensions, though there may be some respite between challenges.

Reading this you could be forgiven for feeling there is just too much to do. Don't get overwhelmed. Recognise the parts you have engaged with and give yourself some acknowledgement. After all most people maintain a brave face and a stiff upper lip rather than face the truth about life. Rather than hanging on grimly to denial, you have dared to step into the challenge of change. That calls for some recognition. So celebrate and then simply pick out the next challenge for you. It will probably be the bit you least like the look of!

Facing The Truth

Around 50 it is transparently clear whether you have made it into the magic top 2% the system honours, or are trailing along with the other 98%. We are now all faced with what we've achieved or not. Either you face this and keep growing, or you feel overcome by regret. The 50s is the time to brood over all the mistakes you've made, to relive them over and over blow by devastating blow. All those goals you set and never achieved come back to haunt you now and undermine your already fragile sense of self-esteem.

By now you have probably got as far as you're going to by the route you've taken so far. It is quite possible that if you let go and fly off in a new direction, you may yet scale the heights, but for your career to date accept that's it, and move on gracefully. It is not uncommon to find your talents being appreciated in some quite unexpected places, and a whole new career evolving.

There is no point staying attached to regrets about this, or squirming with shame about this and all the other missed opportunities. Your road took many turnings and you made your choices on the best evidence available at the time. If not the turning you took it would have been another, and you have no proof this would have worked any better. Forget it! Lives you never lived are lives you never lived.

Regret, brooding, shame cannot change that, though sadness and tears may have a beneficially cathartic effect. Even so there definitely comes a time to bring the sadness and grieving to an end. Then releasing your **attachment** to **regret** can free you to take advantage of the next round of opportunities and the surprising invitations you may find you now receive.

To release this attachment, recognise that regret is a reminder that there was a lesson crucial to your whole life which you could have got years ago. Forgive yourself and acknowledge the good there was and what you *have* done and learnt, even without that insight. Recognise also that there is a crucial lesson NOW that you are in danger of missing. Don't put off facing this new lesson, as you did the one you now so bitterly regret.

The same applies to regrets over all those foot-in-mouth remarks you made, the awful hurts you inflicted whether unconscious or not, the stupid mistakes and near misses you die over daily. For all their ability to curl you up with cringe-making horror, all you can usefully do now is let them go, and resolve to be more aware. The same goes for guilt. It has its place; it tells us what we need to look at and change about ourselves. But if it takes over (perhaps not being heard and acted on in time) it can be crippling.

Now if not before is the time to let all this go. How? Acknowledge and accept it, listen to the lesson and forgive yourself. Find in yourself a sense of gratitude and invite it to leave you in peace. Talking it through with a trained counsellor will help you get complete with the past and re-engage with the present.

Releasing this **attachment** to **regret** is not an admission of defeat. You're not giving up, packing up your marbles and going home. Or at least you don't need to see it that way. The great **pitfall** in this phase is **separation.** If you hold on to your sense of failure and regret, or if you give up with bad grace, the danger is that you disengage from the world. Separation. Don't write yourself off just because you got a B and not an A+++. Your value lies elsewhere. The contribution you make is of a different order, and it may be yet to come. There's a million better ways to "make it" than join the generally miserable top 2%. Meanwhile your job is to be you to the best of our ability. And this involves staying in the world, not separating from it.

An important variant on this external disengagement is separation from your inner self. When the lesson is to develop insight, it would be a tragedy to shut out the sources of this insight, out of fear or unfamiliarity. All through our lives we have to keep learning to become our opposite. Headcases need to find their hearts. Physical perfection needs to find other forms of inner beauty or skill. Managers must discover the warmth of human companionship. And vice versa. We must all link up the dots, and keep making connections.

LifeShift NOW!

Let the impetus of this time separate you from past glories or regrets, not isolate you from your fellow man or from the inner man or woman. The same sort of break with the past you made around 28 comes around again as this phase ends, 56/57. You can use it to connect with people and yourself more, or you can isolate yourself feeling there are so few others like you or all too many. Men hit their version of the menopause around now just to aggravate things.

The polarisation which you have to avoid in your 40s rears its head again in the 50s as a dysfunctional exclusion or separation from either the world or your inner self or in extreme cases both. 56 is a new start, and like every phase that has preceded it this time from about 49 to 56 is preparation for what follows.

By honouring your past and connecting intimately with your present life, by wisely reviewing what's missing and becoming more of a fully rounded person, in particular adding inner insight to what you have made of your external world, you now arrive at a vision worth living. Awareness of this compounding of qualities earlier in life is what enables you to discover vision and incorporate it in your personal growth and LifeShifting at 20 or 30 rather than waiting for the end of your career to get the message. Even so the actuaries say you have another 30 years left to enjoy the vision you take into your second childhood, after 56.

SUMMARY

● With the violet, visionary 50s, the meaning of life is the priority, and all becomes clear...for now, though not if you got stuck and stopped growing earlier.
● It is time now to catch up with any unworked energies, integrate them all and stop flogging yourself to death.
● There are Seven Steps, each governed by one of the colour energies, which create a framework for turning vision into action.
● The heightened sense of self that silence, meditation and creative visualisation give you now reveals to you your soul contract, your next challenge and the way forward. Inner wisdom expands when you tap into spirit.
● By imaging the positive, the negative block is clear. The desired future result is relatively unimportant; transformation of the present is what matters.
● Giving back, socially and creatively, which began to be more important in the last phase, becomes critical now. Initial frustration with lack of imagination soon passes.
● Drop what (and who) drains you. Work your why, and be careful whom you involve.
● Be careful also before you invite spirit in.
● When you engage with inner work, you get to take back your power chakra by chakra, starting where you're weakest.
● There is a perennial wisdom which marks the way through these mysteries.
● By 50, unless you're in the top 2%, that's it for career, but 56 is a new start with a new rounded you, and you can still do something worthwhile if you LifeShift now.

LESSON to LEARN:
Insight to develop your growth

DISTRACTION TO TRANSFORM:
Pension: No, find a job you'll never want to retire from

PITFALL to AVOID:
Separation, disengagement from inner or outer worlds

ATTACHMENT to RELEASE:
Regret for all that might have been

EXERCISE

Creative Visualisation

See your self totally positive about every aspect of your life.

Notice where you don't convince yourself.

Pick the main resistance and ask it what you can do to allay its fears.

Write any actions in the usual box, and transfer whatever you need to your Personal Priority Pages.

CHAPTER 9

The Wholeness Years (56-63) Finding Balance and Fulfilment in relationship to life

When you integrate all the seven levels of energy there is a wholeness which yields a powerful fulfilment.

The concept presented here is that over the years we learn all that we need to learn, but that rather than wait to the end to find out what will fulfil us, we can anticipate and draw down what we need, to create a fulfilling career much earlier. This brings us into an infinitely deeper relationship with life.

In a very real sense we get to have two lives for the price of one! By knowing the outline of the seven energies at 25 or 35 instead of 65, we can apply all these energies to each of the phases of life as we grow up through them. Our understanding will not be complete. Perhaps it never is. But we will have that sense of "working our why" all through life.

We can also have a more mature understanding of the strengths and weaknesses that come with our own personal "colouring", the energy/ies we tend to exhibit whatever phase we're in. We can avoid getting stuck in one energy because it's comfortable, and can consciously balance it with complementary energies.

The ability to anticipate which this gives us is one of the principal ways in which change is managed without stress.

There are many routes to this point in your career, the years leading up to conventional retirement.

You may have arrived here financially successful, but unevolved lacking one or more of the seven energies you need in order to feel fulfilled. You could just carry on until they give you a huge golden handshake and you retire to the tedium of world cruises. You perhaps have a hobby or pastime that can keep you amused, and there is such a thing as blissful ignorance. The trouble with a life dedicated to making money however is that you never seem to be able to stop. There is never quite enough and the only satisfaction comes from making more. It is hard to step off the treadmill, and when eventually you have to, it's a dreadful wrench.

You don't get to the top without a strong sense of responsibility. This is a large part of what drives you, and as you head into your '60s there can be real pain that you don't seem to be able to have an effect any more. This powerful energy seems to have nowhere to go.

The recommended strategy is, even now, to set about filling out your personality. Spot what you have left undone so far and resolve to catch up on it now. Since success is so much about Blue and Green, you probably need to brush up on Indigo. The most difficult thing for a captain of industry is to relax, commune with nature, indulge in artistic pursuits. These are the people who cannot go for a walk in the woods without calculating the value of the lumber!

The money makes life comfortable, but there is likely to be an empty hole where fulfilment ought to be. By working Indigo (Chapter 7), you get to work with Violet (Chapter 8) and get a handle on the Why of it all.

Much the same applies to the person who got stuck somewhere and spent their life getting better and better at doing something they (and probably everyone around them) grew out of years ago.

Some never get beyond Red, physical manual labour. They will need to engage with Orange, making more of an effort to communicate and join in. Others stick at Orange, and would do well to bring some intellectual rigour to the Ab Fab gossip culture which has possibly degenerated into bitchiness by now.

The stuck Yellow, the academic who never ventured out could try it now. There's a brilliant fundraiser just waiting to get out, a dynamic social entrepreneur. And so on. Whatever level you stuck at, the job is to move on through the levels or decline into a miserable trudge to the grave.

You might on the other hand have worked all the energies and have an integrated, balanced capacity in all of them. Included here are those who grasp the nettle and catch up in their 50s / 60s.

You may even have your whole self present *and* have the success that society honours, money. As noted above (Chapter 7), success is what often gets in the way of the personal growth process, but it is possible you spotted this and managed to keep growing while you worked the system to your benefit. It can happen, and what a wonderful result, to have realised your potential as a whole human and met the criteria for social success.

There are two most likely routes to such success. You could have focused single-mindedly on getting to the top, taken responsibility and had the courage to let it all go and LifeShift into a whole new you sometime between 35 and 63; or you could have acquired this knowledge at the start of your career and made such a good job of activating your vision that you rose effortlessly to the top!

Vision is the Task for Life

Vision is something that evolves with us as we grow up. We only finally discover it at death, and are right up to that point constantly unwrapping more and more layers of it. Engaging with this awareness from the start turns any life into a wondrous adventure. Constantly you are asking "What is this meaning? How is this serving me? What am I to learn from this?"

Whether you get to the top or not, the crucial point is that you arrive at 56 with all the seven energies under your belt, or catch up with any that are missing no later than 63.

By whatever route you get there, we now arrive in the phase of life when the whole is understood, 56-63. All seven energies have been lived through, and now we integrate them into a holistic process. That is the **lesson** of this seven year period up to the end of the third grand 21 year cycle - **integration** of a life's learning.

When Violet, the colour of vision and spirit is mixed with Red, the colour of action and grounding in reality, you get Magenta. This is the colour of this integration phase. What matters is deepening all life's experience, growing wiser still, and reviewing what remains to be done. It is a time of reckoning. What are all the things you always meant to do, and which are left undone and absolutely must not be left undone any longer? Where will you apply that sense of responsibility your career used to give you?

The tragedy of the conventional route is that even if we do discover vision at this point, we have less of that doing energy from the years of engagement to create and prepare the ground in which this late-found vision can flower. We have to adapt whatever we have done before to make the most of the realisation that comes with this phase. The greater tragedy is that as indicated above, many never colonise all the seven energies and are left at this time only partially evolved and mystified by their lack of fulfilment. They may need a quantum leap to catch up.

Your body may not appear to be helping you very much just now, and this can further undermine your physical energy reserves just when you really need them. If your health is suffering, you will need to pace yourself...which is exactly the message your body is giving you. Illness is a wake-up call: you cannot go on like this. "Death," says Woody Allen, "is nature's way of telling you to slow down." So listen to this early warning, but don't focus all your attention on the illness: that just makes it worse. Focus on well-ness and on all the things you *can* do even while you're being ill. Nurses report that patients are commonly so busy being ill, they forget everything else including their spirituality: this is not a good way to get better.

There is an extra resource you acquire now however, to counter any lack of energy. A renewed burst of creativity is common. A full quiver of all seven energies helps, but creativity can supplement what you've lost or missed earlier. Experience of life, however unbalanced, helps you get stuck into the new visionary insights you get now. As you act on vision you learn what you ignored earlier. It can seem overwhelming but starting is the key.

Integrating all the energies means turning vision into *action*. Now is the time, if never before! And you have a lot of new resources to help you if you're prepared to engage with life's progress. Concentrating all your energy on one thing helps too.

Creativity adds a dramatic new dimension to the tapestry of life you're colouring in. In the creative tension between the inner spiritual dimension of heart and will, and the outer structures of money and resources, we learn and grow and find our power. Work is the place we create as a context for this, so there is no question of it ending now. It may just be engaged in with less frenetic urgency.

Having things more in balance removes the principle stressor; it is imbalance which separates us from others and sets up the isolation and lack of support which makes for stress. The answer to stress is not just to be more subdued; there must be intense inner work if we are to find balance.

Odd then that this phase of life is equated with retirement. There may well be a different, less driven relationship with work, but retirement is something people only contemplate when there is a gulf between what inspires them and their work. The sort of work you're going to organise for yourself as a result of reading this is not the sort of work you'll lightly give up. Feeling resigned to resignation is not on our agenda.

Retirement, especially the assumptions colleagues dump on us, is both the **distraction** and the context in which this creative reawakening happens. Far from resigning we are consolidating, continuing and deepening our understanding of the journey of life. The potential exists for more pleasure than you have ever experienced before, for growth, learning and inexpressible joy.

Retirement can give you more time and space. If others assume you are relinquishing control, they may be happy for you to be less in evidence. So you can make your contribution selectively, and work smarter. This gives you time to allocate to your new ventures. One way and another you feel more free.

Further Fine-Tuning

Now we can see more clearly how all the parts contribute to a vibrant whole. What a time to give up! No, this is the time to weigh yourself in the balance and correct the polarisation that threatened your growth in the 40s.

If inner life is ignored and "heavy" emphasis placed on outer life, you have workaholism, obsessive, driven, pressured and unable to see the inner destitution; "If I can't count it, it's not real." The Myers-Briggs Personality Type Indicator calls this the "Extrovert, Sensing, Thinking, Judging - ESTJ" type. Nothing that cannot be rationalised and acted upon decisively has value. It's the aberration of life that prevailed during the Industrial Age.

This ESTJ is the stereotypical Managing Director of the past, thrusting, controlling and completely immune to intuitive feelings, alternative possibilities and half-glimpsed perceptions. Women almost more than men may still tend to see it as the way to win. But the new leaders are more rounded: they value intuition and have a deep sense of social responsibility.

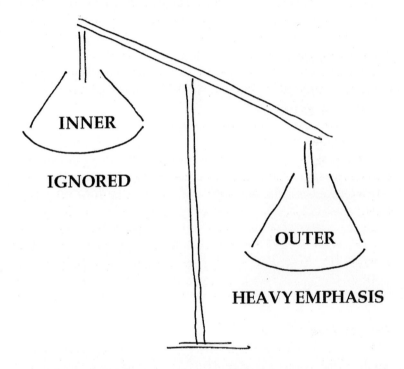

Equally unbalanced and aberrant is the heavy emphasis on the inner and dismissal of outer reality, shown immediately above. These are the cloying, claustrophobic, unworldly people, lost in deep inner process, ungrounded, out of relationship with reality, the Myers-Briggs extreme INFP (Introverted, iNtuitive, Feeling, Perceiving) types, who are so in touch with deeper realities they are unable to cope except in a sort of dreamland.

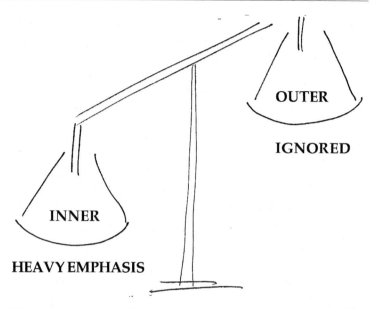

OUTER

IGNORED

INNER

HEAVY EMPHASIS

Most of us need to "lighten the outer load" and "gain weight" inside. This is classically the job at this time. But it can be that your journey takes you the opposite way, discovering how the world works.

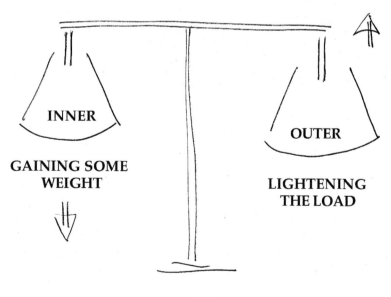

INNER

OUTER

**GAINING SOME
WEIGHT**

**LIGHTENING
THE LOAD**

The task is to balance not just inner and outer, but all three strands of human experience - Think, Feel and Do. When we act with conscious feeling we weave these strands together and are present in spirited mind, the fourth strand which connects us through soul to the ocean of spirit. This idea of balance has parallels in other philosophies, for instance the Chinese concept of Yin and Yang. Yin is like the softer inner side, and Yang the harder focused outer, but each contains the other. Combining all of this can be represented like this.

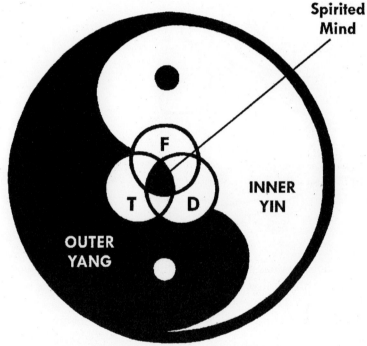

It's like being on autopilot, always correcting a deviation from the central path, constantly assessing how you stand in relation to Think, Feel, Do and Spirited Mind. This describes the Magenta person. Like an expert martial artist standing on a train, apparently motionless, but actually reacting with thousands of imperceptible movements to changes in their relationship with the world. Restlessness of Being. Spirit in Action.

The Magenta person is the calm, contemplative sage, wisely surveying the scene, taking in everything even when they seem to be asleep. Their aim in life is simple...and deep. They seek wholeness and the fulfilment this gives them. The fascination of intellectual discussion, the excitement of enterprise, the joy of enthusiastic company are all part of it, and none of it. The Magenta *is*. Without this quality of wholeness, we may attain the heights but without much satisfaction. There's nothing for it but just to come back down again.

Calm, contemplative sage

It is hard to imagine overdoing this, but if one could it would look like a stillness that is closer to death than life. And we are meant to live until we die. From the space of intense being this phase invites, there is much that might be done to arouse sleepy energy centres.

RED: It is important to balance the intense Magenta being with doing. Keep yourself in good physical shape. Even the most evolved spirit needs effective arms and legs. Plan in an hour a day of exercise - walking, Tai Chi, swimming. Break up the day. Even wisdom needs to be done.

ORANGE: Especially if your life has been one of decisive action or thinking, reach out to others. It is natural to want to be active in the community at this age, and you have extra reserves of creativity and time to apply now. Use this natural tendency to arouse your feeling self. Watch what you're feeling from moment to moment and allow new feeling experiences to move you. (See also below the material on relationships)

YELLOW: Give your mind exercise too, especially if your life has revolved around other people's agendas. It can get out of practice, and when you come to read all those books you always meant to read, you can find that you just cannot maintain concentration. You have another 30 years to go, so you can't afford your mind to wander. Develop contentment of mind.

GREEN: Open your heart. Heart energy tends to be directed towards the fray, battling for love and money, and taking on a very distorted form. Now let it open to you and from you expand out into the world with compassion. Meditation is a good place to practise this. Visualise the lower three chakras opening and feel the sense of relief. Then see your heart opening, first inwards to you, then outwards to the world. Notice what interferes and engage with it. The journey into heart is largely a journey through the attachments and obstacles we hold on to. Let go.

BLUE: The strangest thing about this phase is having so much time. Most of the things we busy ourselves with are behind you now, and you can be tremendously focused, but also disoriented by the lack of distractions! It's that restlessness of being again. Just another of those early stage distress reactions as you enter a new phase of life. It passes and sitting quietly becomes a joy in the end. Organise your day into chunks that are not yawning great chasms of time. Build in plenty of possibilities for connecting with others and sharing your wisdom with those who are ready. You can make good use of an hour, but fritter away a whole day!

INDIGO: This quiet, reflective non-judgmental way of being is still a priority. Any symptoms of stress remind you to slow down, relax and be. Keep on keeping on with calm consistency and commitment.

VIOLET: Keep on also reviewing what has reverberated through your life, what you seem to keep coming back to. The places, activities, ideas and types of people you have always been drawn to and also the dreams you maybe never quite engaged with are top of the list now. It is never too late to do your dream. The stillness of meditation should by now be a daily practice. It is where you can best become aware of your direction and how to be in this particular moment of it.

Keep working through the seven levels, as above, but in both directions, ie up and then down the sequence. Working up from Red to Violet is how we learn and grow "up". Working down, from Violet to Red, is how we integrate and take our vision out into the world.

We can now set out the whole of what has been covered in the previous chapters, with reference to three components:

ENERGETIC FIELD, the quality to work with
and the *primary task* to engage with at each step.

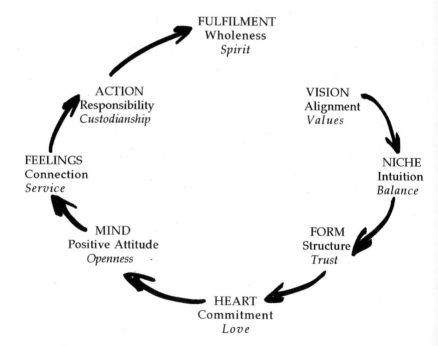

FULFILMENT
Wholeness
Spirit

ACTION
Responsibility
Custodianship

VISION
Alignment
Values

FEELINGS
Connection
Service

NICHE
Intuition
Balance

MIND
Positive Attitude
Openness

FORM
Structure
Trust

HEART
Commitment
Love

BECOMING WHOLE

A further expansion to this seven or eight step process is to recognise that each step or level has a masculine and a feminine dimension to it. You may see masculine as rather more Yang, and feminine as more Yin, but masculine and feminine do not equate to male and female, men and women. See how the table below chimes with you, and how each level comes to life for you.

Level	Masculine	Feminine
RED	Physical strength	Sensuality, stamina
ORANGE	"The Lads", noisy, ebullient	"The Girls", warm, consensus
YELLOW	Logical, systematic	Flexible, fascinated
GREEN	Assertiveness, power over	Conviction, inner power
BLUE	Structure, leader	Concept, vocation
INDIGO	Fit, justice	Psyche, mercy
VIOLET	Visionary, magus	Envisioning

Successful implementation of any idea therefore requires the integration of energies in both their masculine and feminine forms, as shown in the following diagram (where the *feminine* is shown in *italics*). This sequence of steps shows the way to fulfilment.

The classic hard focus masculine style on its own consistently misses the point. It shuts out opportunity, new possibility and easier options. It takes the balance of masculine and feminine to change, create or re-create anything, and in all human undertakings it is wise to start with the feminine and press home with the masculine. When you combine both approaches you set up the real possibility of macro-transformation.

Over-emphasis on the more masculine energies has reeked havoc, but exclusively feminine energy is equally flawed. What this looks like is set out in the table on the next page - "Further Manifestations of the Seven Levels". What we need is "gylany" (Page 150). We can all find both masculine and feminine within us, just as we can all find each of the seven levels. We just have to dig deeper for some.

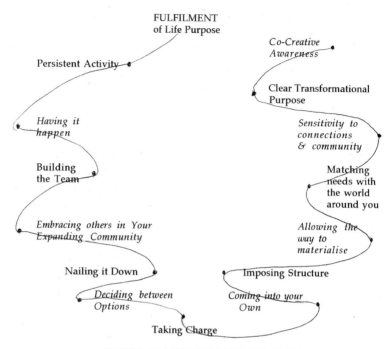

FULFILMENT
of Life Purpose

Co-Creative
Awareness

Persistent Activity

Clear Transformational
Purpose

Having it
happen

Sensitivity to
connections
& community

Building
the Team

Matching
needs with
the world
around you

Embracing others in Your
Expanding Community

Allowing the
way to
materialise

Nailing it Down

Imposing Structure

Deciding between
Options

Coming into your
Own

Taking Charge

TABLE: MACRO-TRANSFORMATION

Does this ring any bells for you? Does it suggest where you need to fine-tune or bring certain elements of your make-up into balance? Record any thoughts in the Action Plan box at the end of the chapter.

Let us return now to one of the major themes of this book, how Vision is discovered and realised. The energy of vision and defining a clear, powerful, transformational purpose is held in the crown chakra on top of the head. Chakra is a Sanskrit word meaning "spinning wheel", since our energy centres are like coned vortices which spin energy in and out. We need to get each energy centre "spinning", operational, in turn. For this one the question to ask is "What inspires me?" We visited this briefly in Chapter 8, and can now reveal more of how deeply this model resonates with our inner spirituality.

Once your **vision (Violet)** is clear, not necessarily final or perfect but clear enough to work with, you can and must begin grounding the vision in reality, by finding a place on the planet where it can land.

It needs a context in which to operate, a harmonious **niche (Indigo)** to grow in, like a seedling needs a growing medium. In terms of career or enterprise, this means a market or job opportunity for the skills, talents and energies you bring to it. Not everybody will be ready or open to what you have to offer: not everyone will have your offer at the top of their list of priorities. You need to allow your intuition to find your place, where for some you are the tops, where some people are if anything even more enthusiastic (a greek word meaning 'filled with god') than you are, and will insist you share your inspiration with them. They help you define your vision even more clearly. This chakra, in the brow, is about aesthetic sensitivity to connections.

From this, organically, the **form (Blue)** your contribution needs to take becomes clear. The marriage of your potential with their need for it clarifies broadly how your work can best be organised, and how your life can work around it. This prospect should empower you to voice your plans and decisions. Blue is throat energy, where we speak our authority.

The excitement you feel at having a plan for realising your vision makes your heart sing and activates the heart centred chakra, from where you can and must make solid **commitments (Green)**. It requires you to assert your true self in the world, which can be scary as well as exciting. It involves taking risks, though these are well calculated, because of what they are based on. Joy and fear live in the same place, so feeling fear means joy is not far away. Fear is frozen excitement: melt a little! Because this joy is what creates abundance in your life, like a sunny day gets people smiling. As you face the challenge to be real, personal growth and self-empowerment occurs.

Once one is committed, it is safe to let the **mind (Yellow)** loose on your vision, sorting out all the details, thinking systematically about precisely what is involved and nailing down the realities. Without commitment you will sink or succumb to doubts. But

Overleaf: Further Manifestations

1. COLOUR	2. REALM	3. MASCULINE APPROACH	4. OVERDONE MASCULINE	5. FEMININE APPROACH	6. OVERDONE FEMININE	7. UNDERDONE STATE
VIOLET	VISION	Clear purpose	Megalomania	Co-Creative awareness	Fantastical	Aimless
INDIGO	INTUITION	Matching (Market) needs	Lacking commercial reality: science fiction	Sensing connection, valuing hunches	Flightiness	Irrelevant
BLUE	FORM	Imposing structure	Planning strait-jacket, committee management	Allowing the way to materialise	Becoming a victim to circumstance	Chaotic
GREEN	WILL	Taking charge	Autocracy	Coming into your own	Smothering others	Feeble
YELLOW	MIND	Nailing it down	Getting bogged down, analysis paralysis	Deciding between options	Indecision	Ill-conceived
ORANGE	FEELINGS	Building the team	Communication blitzkrieg	Embracing others	Great party, no progress	Heartless
RED	ACTION	Persistent activity	Working oneself into the ground	Having it happen obsessional tidier	Fidget,	Dead

Three further overall comparisons may also be useful...

-	-	Making it happen	Pushing the river	Letting it happen	Being swept out to sea	-
-	-	Sharp sun light	Destructive	Diffused moon light	Fading away	-
-	-	Individuality and separation	Isolation	Interconnected-ness of all things	Loss of self	-

commitment on its own is not enough to carry you through. You must also be mindful, mentally sensitive and crystal clear about precisely how it all hangs together, otherwise you will not be able to communicate the vision effectively to others, which is the sixth step. This analytical chakra is centred in the solar plexus, the body's nerve centre.

You now need to exude the warmth and vitality that is the stuff of magnificent interpersonal **relationships (Orange)** and networking. Your full feeling self needs to be present, generously connecting and engaging with others as the final link between your inner vision and its outer realisation in the physical material world. This connection comes from the adrenal centre.

At this point, the seventh grounding step into the base chakra which represents **action (Red)** happens, and the realisation of a life founded on vision, instead of mindless, heartless, visionless busyness, creates a deep sense of fulfilment. The vision can then be seen more clearly still, and having come full circle, you set off once more on the Seven Steps, experiencing each part of yourself, the worlds of Being and Doing, living your personal vision.

The task throughout is to build an expanded team, interconnecting with others in the transformation of life. Crucial to the integration which is the learning priority for this phase is the sharing of talents between you and the rest of your expanding community.

Vision also develops in close collaboration with values and beliefs. Here as an example and to give you a start point for framing your own vision and values statement is The Breakthrough Vision and Core Beliefs as formulated in June 1996.

THE BREAKTHROUGH VISION

To facilitate the transformation of the world of work into a place that is joyful, open-hearted, free from fear and negativity, empowering, emotionally honest and dedicated to service, where we can learn and grow, as we earn our livings, without compromising our spiritual values and inner truth.

The world of work and money can be a tough task-master, constantly challenging us to face new lessons. With each challenge comes a fork in the way - towards spirit or away from spirit. Yet success is not succumbing to either route, but constantly balancing spirit with matter - inner life with outer task. From time to time we lurch one way or the other.

The demands and exigencies of the material world distract us from the true path. There is always a way back, but the more forks in the road we have taken away from spirit, the more challenging will be the journey back. Materialism has a seductive hold, and we fear all is lost if we loosen our hold. We may know intuitively that the opposite is true. It still takes courage to let go and trust. One can feel anything but joyful, fearless and empowered.

Those who have opted for a more spiritual route can have similar misgivings about engaging with the material. Yet it must be faced, as the material world is where the inner steel is tempered ... and where we earn our livings.

Five core intentions flow from this Vision Statement. We intend:
-to live our vision and support/recharge others in finding and activating their vision/soul purpose.
-to offer a safe space of love, service and learning where all can face, express and release the difficult feelings, fears, patterns and belief systems that sabotage.
-to provide simple, effective, practical strategies condensed from our learning and experience.
-to be a Centre of Inspiration and Demonstration that a rigorous path of personal spiritual growth creates fulfilment through inner peace and outer success.
-to create an extended community of holistic enterprises.

In actualising our vision and intentions, we draw on a set of core beliefs which may be summarised as follows:
- All we need lies dormant within us and can be accessed.
- In the practice of silence, both individually and collectively, we can access ageless wisdom.
- We have an outer duty or task which is enhanced by inner work.
- "If nothing changes on the inner, nothing changes on the outer."
- Entering the dark shadow is as necessary as living in the light.
- Work is a place we each create in order to learn and grow.
- Work is love made visible.

- There is only love.
- Our prime responsibility is to serve with love and open-heartedness.
- To love is to will the good of oneself and of all others unconditionally.
- In learning to love where we are, what we are doing and whom we are with we find peace.
- It may take time. We need abundant supplies of patience, persistence and perseverance.
- We are part of a co-creative purpose, moving from fear, conflict and separation to peace, trust, respect and inter-connectedness.
- Humanity is undergoing a major evolutionary step to a transformation of consciousness.
- The business world is the primary arena for the new paradigm.

You will see from this what underpins the writing of this book, since the statement of vision and core beliefs is a summary of much of the book's content. So much of our society polarises between those who represent material and financial success and the virtues of ambition and ruthlessness on the one hand, and those who in one way or another put people before profit. The task for the 21st century is to build bridges between these two extremes. We are pioneering a person-centred philosophy of business, work and life.

Relationship is all there is
Inform anyone they have 6 months to live and the chances are their priorities will revolve around people and relationships. This is partly why various relationships become much more important in this phase. And this is partly why the theme is covered here, but only partly. The main reason is that we have now reached the point where all the ingredients of your individual vision have been aired and you can have some clarity about who you are and why. Without the close relationship this gives you with yourself, relationship with other is impaired or impossible. As well as gaining the understanding of personal vision which makes so much more sense of life, you also gain the basis for healthy relationship.

We are in relationship from the start and learn the fundamentals in our first 14 years. Yet the understanding of self which provides a firm base for relationship comes later. We are learning about, while inevitably being involved in, how to be with others. So the subject is covered here even though it has to be lived very much earlier. Just as does our vision. Relationship is the other great arena in which you do your work, learn and grow. To be in relationship is to be a context for our own and each other's growth. It starts with self.

All that has gone before has been a blueprint for resisting the distractions and coming into right relationship with your self. Letting go of others' agendas for you, questioning assumptions and obsolete cultural value systems, facing personal challenges, releasing the blocks and learning your lessons. The end is to come to centre, which is where you come to love.

When we don't love ourselves, we cannot love or come into relationship with others. Communication is distorted, the negative feelings we have about ourselves are dumped on others, negative core beliefs interlock and interactions become inappropriate. The dictatorial boss, the recluse, the group dependent, the addictive helper whining their catch phrase "I was only trying to help", all are symptoms of unrequited self-love.

All relationships and experiences reflect and mirror this Lack Of Self-Esteem, until you get the message and learn to love yourself better. Letting go, which has been such a strong theme throughout this whole book, is the key to this learning and moving on to unconditional love. Meanwhile you cannot give others what you're not giving yourself. And you cannot receive from others what you refuse to receive from yourself. A good test of how you're doing with this is to check whether you're loving where you are, what you're doing and who you're with, but without dependency. Needing someone and needing to be needed is not love, but more a form of selfishness. It blocks intimacy.

Some of the ways you can improve your relationships with yourself and others are completing relationships before you move on, to avoid just repeating the same old mistakes; recognising responsibility rather than looking for who to blame; expressing hurt without judgment; forgiving yourself and others; loving the unloveable, but avoiding those who don't love themselves.

You cannot give others what you refuse to receive from yourself

And funnily enough conflict is when you can learn most about relationship, because what stops you being intimate is then painfully self-evident. The worst thing you believe about yourself rises to the surface and there's nothing for it but to face it and release it. Celebrate conflict; it's an opportunity to grow. Centre and breathe. Connect with your heart and be open to an answer.

The demands of working life are a principal cause of conflict in primary relationships, so it's worth looking at a different way of coming to terms with partners - more honest, realistic and true to both of you, a better holistic balance of work and life.

Whatever work you and your partner (and other close associates) are doing, there must be mutual understanding. Either you must both have the same perspectives and goals, or you must both enthusiastically support each others' perspectives, goals and evolution. Then there can be a healthy interdependency. Conflict arises when only one partner wants to make a change and the other feels betrayed or left behind.

Conflict may have arisen because the attempt to fund the relationship takes too much time away from the very relationship it's supposed to be helping. But conflict can also arise when one party decides enough is enough and LifeShifts. Even if both agree initially, the shift is stressful. It involves letting go of an extravagant lifestyle, taking responsibility, making a powerful inner shift. If the other half is reluctant (or backslides into the apparent security of the dependency culture) resentment can blow the relationship apart.

At least "bringing home the bacon" is deemed a reasonable excuse for being an absent partner. But when you LifeShift and perhaps opt for more free time and less obsessive chasing of the uncompromising dollar, partners who have not bought the same trip can be very disruptive. Their self-image may be very tied up with high income and they can feel threatened in other ways too; people taking charge of their lives are charismatic and suddenly attractive. Especially in "Worker / Shirker (Winner / Sinner)" dependency relationships, the modern hang-over from the clearly defined Breadwinner / Homemaker contract of the 50s, anxiety is inevitable. To make it work you have to be totally clear yourself and communicate with clarity, compassion and sensitivity. And you have to listen and respond. All pretty important lessons and skills to learn!

Here is the plan for LifeShift in relationships:

A Define success and vision for yourself.

B Invite your partner to do the same.

C Compare visions and implications: no unilateral declarations!

D Recognise it can take time and involve sacrifices.

E Allow difficulties to stay on the table: no rushed solutions. When an impossibility arises, ask "How can we overcome the problem that....?"

F Plan what you can, over time. Keep insuperable problems tabled as such, with clear intention to find a resolution that works for both of you.

G Get support - an objective place to go for wise counsel.

H Keep talking.

A family council, meeting at least weekly is unreservedly recommended. An excellent formula for these meetings is to start with a "Daily Temperature Reading", as invented by Virginia Satir. Each person gets to speak on each topic, and is heard out with respect and without any response.

Start with Appreciations and trust that everybody will get

appreciated, or that it will be OK for someone not to get appreciated.

Then invite New Information, things that need to be made public because they may affect others. Puzzles are next, anything you don't understand. This is the only category to which there may be a response, if it's short and simply explanatory. In a way, Puzzles is a way of inviting New Information.

This clears the way for Complaints with Recommendations, heard out in silence with no response, excuses, hectoring or bullying allowed! Finally each family member expresses Wishes, Hopes and Dreams, again heard in silence.

Especially early on this might take up all the time available. But if time allows each member shares what's up for them, what's good, what's bad and what's so awful they can't even talk about it.

Families, partnerships and close friendships are places where we feel safest about showing our true selves. This is where you practise being you, so you can take more of you into other contexts, where it may not be so safe to expose the bits of you you're not very proud of or feel embarrassed about. This then is good preparation for entering into real working relationships.

Relationship is where you do your work

Work is the essential grounding relationship, where we learn to value ourselves, develop all our energies, make a contribution and activate our divine co-creativity. The great pain at the moment is that the real purpose of work has been lost in all the madness of materialism, and other relationships are diminished as a result.

If we cannot come into a healthier relationship with work, we can forget all the rest. The misery more than half the population suffer when they go to work is destroying community and relationship, for all of us. Why? Because we are failing to see work for what it is - a challenge to respond to, the key place to learn about relationships.

The problem with the old world of work was that there was too little love there, not tacky office affairs, but real love - willing the good of all including oneself, responding to what happens with emotional authenticity.

Business/work is defined by its relationships. Marketing is

principally about fostering relationships in which our visions merge and are given form. The organisation is an abundantly rich bundle of relationships with whom I have to accommodate myself. Generating money, publicity and sales starts and ends with relationship. Every task I want performed, every meeting, every project stands or falls with the quality of the relationships involved. Everything else is arithmetic.

Yet the most important relationship lessons work presents lie in how I respond to its challenges. Will I depend on it for external validation? Will I stay even when it abuses me beyond anything I would accept in a personal relationship? Will fear or lack of trust take me over? Or will I get complete with it and leave it with love and gratitude for what it has given and taught me?

Work then is a primary arena for learning about relationships, letting go and being authentic. It is a fertile and comprehensive field, all too often ignored. As with all relationships, success at work and how we even define success demands that we come into a healthier relationship with our selves.

We have to start somewhere, and that somewhere is the relationship with self, constantly reviewing how whole we are, which energies need to be aroused or released, what is out of balance. Work and vision are like two poles that need to collide. As they do other polarities come up for consideration - head and heart, masculine and feminine, linear and organic, commitment and non-attachment, responsibility and release.

All this needs to be integrated, and consciously or unconsciously we each create our work specifically for this purpose. The fact that work is so closely bound up with our economic viability adds to the piquancy of the whole thing. We really are on the line in every sense - spiritual, practical, self-evaluatory and economic. This is why work is such an important learning ground and probably why we get so hot and bothered about it! All my stuff is coming up, all my buttons are being pressed, all my worst nightmares are coming true and there is no getting away from it! I either face this or I stop eating!

How then can we come into a healthier relationship with our selves in this crucial context of work? Here is your starter for 10.

1 Review your key results over any time period you care to.

2 What has "worked" and what apparently hasn't?
What have you learnt ?

3 State your "core values" - what really matters to you?

4 Compare 1 and 3. To what extent does each key result reflect your values? Score each result/value match out of 10.

5 What emerges as your vision/soul purpose? What is truly in front of you? How might this be harmonised with your environment: planet, community, market, family and other relationships?

6 Having flexed your feminine intuition, balance it with your masculine structuring logic.

7 Now open your heart to yourself ... and to what you might be.

What distracts you from being who you might be? That is your next task. Get your head in gear, connect, connect, and be in action.

Relationship is all. Every context with which we interrelate is a space of learning and growing. In fact to be in relationship is to be a context for our own and each others' growth. Being in work is the same. LifeShift is a holistic undertaking.

The Green Challenge of Responsibility

As we press on from our '50s to our '60s, none of us can shirk our responsibilities. Whether we are losing the responsibilities and authority of a traditional job, or only now take on the mantle, our job is to be a model from which others can learn. In the new emerging world of holistic enterprise, responsibility is absolutely key to our relationship with others and with nature. The ethics of this mean that you will never take advantage of anyone or treat them with anything less than respect. Your word is your bond. Your obsessions are reliability and sticking to your commitments.

The major failing of otherwise holistic enterprises is loss of commitment and the acceptance of mediocrity as a standard. The challenge for many is to be as good as their word, and on the rare occasions where a commitment cannot be kept, to make it the highest priority to put things right. Keeping appointments, doing what you have said you will do when you say you will do it, walking the extra mile, paying bills to order and behaving with integrity is not negotiable. It is the basis of the new holistic enterprise and the priority it places on connecting in real relationship with others.

Funnily enough this is why holistic enterprise has no argument with the concept of profit: because profit is the result of good relationships - treating customers and suppliers well and not making enemies. Profit secured any other way these days tends to be short-lived and brings you little joy.

In the past, profit was the top priority. Caring for customers, staff and other stakeholders was seen as a cost to be met out of profit. If profits were under threat, the costs of relationship were the first to be cut - staff were laid off and the survivors worked harder, advertising and after-sales service suffered and community / charity contributions ceased. Suppliers were squeezed and waited longer for payment. Even shareholders could find their dividends reduced.

This was not totally stupid because if there is no profit, that's the end of the story for any business. The holistic enterprise recognises that service and listening to people come before profit, because they create it. If any costs are to be cut, it is unproductive, non-servicing admin and ego-boosting extravagance that goes. And people are kept firmly in the picture.

We work *with* people, not against them, and behave as if people rather than the preservation of the organisation at all costs matter most. Businesses like everything else have a life-cycle, and if in spite of prioritising service and people the business is failing, it is time to change it to meet people's needs rather than fight for the survival of something that has had its day. Organisations too often stagnate into bureaucracy, out of touch with their past supporters and reality. The holistic approach involves facing unpalatable truths sooner rather than later, and finding new needs and new services. The same applies to jobs and skills: when an industry is in decline, people have to adapt their talents to develop new skills. Holistic enterprise is hot on continuous personal and professional development. It rarely stands still for long.

When new customers, opportunities, skills or suppliers are needed, the first recourse is to networking, since networking is relationship in action. Networking typifies the new ways people are coming into relationship with each other. Valuing each other, sharing and honouring each others' value systems, giving rather than simply taking, interdependency are the stuff of networking. The information and connections obtained are based on personal experience. We discover the truth from an insider and learn fast.

Whatever work or enterprise you're involved in, holistic means being whole, wholly present, your full feeling creative self as well as the practical, mental human that is traditionally all we're allowed to present at work. The holistic approach draws on the whole person, all their energies and talents, changing, learning, growing and adapting as the individual evolves and faces the challenges of their environment. Fighting change is atrophy. And the greatest challenge is commonly to let go. Change requires us to know ourselves, be in close, clear relationship with ourselves and brutally honest.

Most jobs only call for a very limited range of our full potential, probably less than 1%. This limited scope for personal expression and growth is at the root of the widespread frustration with work. We have grown and work has not. To be fully functioning, we need outlets for our creativity and imagination, our intuitive, analytical, managerial and design abilities. We need to be able to assert who we are, to feel good about the work, follow our hearts and dream a little. This builds a whole relationship with ourselves which equips us to give of our best.

The attraction of portfolio careers is that we may exercise more of our skills. I might be an accountant with half a dozen regular clients receiving 40% of my time. I might also play in a band twice a week, write a column on poetry for a literary journal and run a network of artists. And to keep fit and use my physical intelligence, I might pass on my passion for windsurfing or tennis to others at the weekend. When I have a moment I can give talks on all these things, and of course I can organise my time so that I can spend a proportion of my time in the country or even in *another* country!

Some of these activities are paid, some are not, but all overlap and set up opportunities for each other: a windsurfer needs an accountant, an artist belongs to a society that needs a speaker, a client turns out to be the stand-in bass player we need next Tuesday. Life is full, rewarding and more secure, because I am no longer restricted to one stream of income. As one strand goes quiet, another wakes up. Vision has many strands.

We need to find a healthy balance between the individual and the collective, where we connect with our individual selves at the deepest level and discover there our inter-connectedness with all that is. A healthy inner reality then creates a healthy outer context for life which supports and is supported by inner truth. "External difficulties, obstacles and problems correspond with inner blocks on self-awareness." (I Ching, Hexagram 39. It goes on to say "Get help.") One of the most important early lessons to learn is that our inner and outer worlds mirror each other.

The healthy, holistic outer environment this creates is of a human scale. It neither suppresses the dreams of individuals and their attempts to live them, nor does it reduce people to the deadness of the 'dependency culture', where personal responsibility is denied, someone else is always to blame and solutions to all problems are handed over to the collective leadership. When will we learn that nobody else has the answers?! We own our lives and take responsibility not just for their evolution, but for everything that happens - to us, to humanity, to the planet. Because we *are* humanity, and we *are* the planet.

This is where holism meets the green philosophy. The core common ground of all green thinking is concern for the natural environment. "Dark Green" sees this concern as spiritual, an attack on nature being an attack on god or however you care to define the infinite, holy, sacred: since we ourselves are inseparable from this sacredness, an attack on nature is an attack on us. If the planet hurts, I too experience that hurt, and am brought face to face with my responsibility, just as if my friend or lover hurts, I hurt and learn compassion and grow through the experience. Not to be green is to act against yourself too.

The integration of human-scale, green thinking and enlightenment leads to the sustainability which is fundamental to the holistic approach. To seek anything more than what is sustainable and 'sufficient unto the day' is to fall prey to fear of the future and distrust of the goodness of life. Sufficiency need not be life-threatening. In fact anything *more* than sufficiency is what threatens life.

*If the planet
hurts, I hurt*

Elegance is not inconsistent with sufficiency. Aesthetics, beauty do not undermine sustainability: the ugliness of thoughtless development and built-in obsolescence do that. Living with awareness, sensitivity and mindfulness of the impact of our actions sustains us and our environment.

Green is about the way we relate to each other and to ourselves.

Our primary relationships interconnect something like this.

Seven Levels of Relationship

As we grow through the seven levels we change, and so does everyone round us. This has strong implications for all our relationships. Our way of relating reflects the stage of evolution we're working on and also the energy colouring that pervades our lives. A Red in relationship is physical, sexual and down to earth, or exploring that aspect of themselves through relationship.

An Orange is sensual, flirting, reluctant to be too restricted to just one person, though the friendship with others is unlikely to threaten the primary relationship.

A Yellow relationship is a meeting of true minds, often based on a common interest. Greens expect a lot, are passionate and excitable, but also exploring, so their commitment may be no more reliable than any other colour. Blues are concerned with things looking right and not rocking the boat; their solidity is very attractive to their opposites, Oranges, who will however get fed up with the coolness they experience from the Blue.

Indigos are deep; their relationships go with the flow and they are hard to pin down, while Violets are only happy if their powerful presence is matched by an equally powerful partner.

We are growing through this and so at least every 7 years a crisis is likely as both parties to the relationship shift to a new life focus. Success requires an understanding of how each is changing and what this new dynamic demands.

The main challenge to learning in relationships, and at the phase of life we're reviewing here (56 to 63) is Habit. You will often hear older people say "You can't teach an old dog new tricks." This might be true if we were dogs, but we are humans so it's just laziness. We just get stuck in our old ways, almost determined to get left behind instead of continuing the learning and growth adventure. **Habit** is another **attachment** to what is familiar, what we've got used to, a restrictive comfort zone that excludes us from new exciting vistas. Habit is a way of dying early. Creativity does require some of the structure that habit and routine supply, but it also calls for the spontaneity, newness and serendipity addiction to habit kills.

Habits can be changed. Apparently anything you do every day for 28 days becomes a habit, so it's even quite quick to release the habits that keep you a prisoner in the past.

The Pain of Perfection

One of the reasons why we might be reluctant to drop old habits is that we have got rather good at them. We can do them without even thinking. Change means risking a long learning curve and still getting it wrong. Better to do the obsolete well than the new and relevant badly. This leads us straight to the **pitfall** to be avoided. **Perfection.** We have to learn that if a thing is worth doing it's worth doing badly! (Abraham Maslow)

Be Perfect Syndrome is a killer too. Like habit, perfection grinds you to a halt. It is like living in a museum, but failing to realise that perfection is always on the move. You have to keep learning and risking getting it wrong in order to keep up with the ever expanding potential of perfect possibility. Holding on to perfection is holding onto the past, whereas anything you do wholeheartedly is closer to perfection than this. Recognise that perfection is never achieved and any perfection you think you've reached is illusory. It kills new ideas, creativity, any prospect of continuing to evolve in life.

The perceived pains of kicking the habit and battling our way to a perfect new high conspire to block consideration of any initiative. We know how long it took to acquire our currently treasured perfection, and how much effort it takes to maintain it. Wild horses will not persuade us to embark on another epic voyage. So don't! Make habit and perfection work for you. Set out each day to make a perfect mess of something new. Make a habit of it. Success is to have done it as badly as you possibly can. What will happen is that having lowered your defences you surprise yourself. You will find new activities that quite entertain you. And in spite of all your worst intentions, you may not make such a dreadful mess after all. Worse still you may actually enjoy everything more once you're released from the necessity to get it all perfect. Honour imperfection.

Age is on your side now. You have earned the right to get things wrong, need some help and make a total pig's ear of whatever you attempt. Many people love to help, especially when they see someone making an effort. So if instead of sitting hopelessly in your frayed, worn out old habits, you reach out for some gay new gladrags, all manner of wonderful meetings and new vistas can present themselves.

The run up to 63 is not necessarily a headlong descent into oblivion and "unregarded age in corners thrown". It should be an intense learning time in preparation for the next Grand Cycle, from 63 on to 84. Develop some new routines that will serve you in the next phase. Drop the harsh self-judgment that restricts you to enjoying only what you can do perfectly.

What you bring to the party now is a rich smorgasbord of experience; this is vastly superior to a small plate with one indigestible monoculture lump on it.

There's a whole world out there to taste, and this time you have fewer financial worries and far more time at your disposal, so have a feast!

It is time to embrace the wisdom that reveals what we may be when we exercise our excellence and collaborate in interdependency. We may also become more open to what nature can teach us.

The Goose Story

Next autumn, when you see geese heading south for the winter, you might consider why they fly along in a V formation. As each bird flaps its wings, it creates an uplift for the bird immediately following. By flying in a V formation, the whole flock adds at least 71% more flying range than would be possible if each bird flew on its own.

People who share a common direction and sense of community can get where they are going more quickly and easily because they are travelling on the thrust of one another.

When a goose falls out of formation, it suddenly feels the drag and resistance of trying to go it alone . . . and quickly gets back into formation to take advantage of the lifting power of the bird in front. If we have as much sense as a goose, we will stay in formation with those who are headed the same way.

When the head goose gets tired, it rotates back in the wing and another goose flies point. It is sensible to take turns doing demanding jobs, whether with people or with geese flying south.

Geese honk from behind to encourage those up front to keep up their speed. What do we say when we honk from behind?

Finally, when a goose gets sick or is wounded by gunshot and falls out of formation, two other geese fall out with that goose and follow it down to lend help and protection. They stay with the fallen goose until it is able to fly or until it dies. Only then do they launch out on their own or with another formation to catch up with their group.

If we have the sense of a goose, we will stand by each other too.

SUMMARY

- Understanding the seven energies gives you two lives for the price of one.
- There are always new facets of ourselves to be explored, old qualities to be rebalanced and enhanced by new ones. It's never too late to do your dream. 50-somethings rediscover creativity and round out their experience to find fulfilment.
- It takes masculine and feminine, yin and yang, vision and values to find fulfilment.
- Relationship is all there is, and all relationship starts with your self. You can only love or relate to others, when you love yourself and have clear vision. Green is about the way we relate to each other and ourselves.
- Business is relationship. The future is integrity, sustainability, networking.
- People only retire from doing things they never wanted to be doing in the first place. At 63 your career has barely started!
- Don't be a goose!

LESSON to LEARN:
Integration of a life's learning

DISTRACTION TO TRANSFORM:
Retirement

PITFALL to AVOID:
Perfection, Be Perfect Syndrome

ATTACHMENT to RELEASE:
Habit

EXERCISE

Consider these three questions:
What is the major issue to work on in *your* spiritual development?
What is the most difficult situation you face in your working life?
Is there a connection?!
Your work and your relationships are the two main contexts to work on both these sets of issues.
As usual, write any action points that arise from this in the box, and transfer whatever you need to your Personal Priority Pages.

Chapter 10

The Self-ful Years 63+:
Human Being

LifeShift requires the wisdom that a whole life gives you. Even if you have not acquired this wisdom earlier, your experience of life now provides you with the tools to discover new depths and direction to your life, piece by piece. 63 marks the biggest LifeShift of all. This is where we have been heading throughout this book, because the phase you reach post-career is the time when you consolidate all the learning of life and integrate it into something new and deeper. To make an end is to make a beginning; the end is where we start from.

If you're not yet 63, the contents of this chapter are "not needed on journey"! If what follows makes sense, that's fine. But there is no need to be concerned if it seems strange. Think of this as an exciting prospect for later in your life; as long as you have engaged with all the earlier phases, you will be well prepared to enjoy this phase.

Those earlier phases sharpen you up. They contain the grit that is essential to the production of the pearl you come to realise now. The task of life is to work with that grit, not pretending you can get to a deep spiritual level of understanding without ever engaging with the material world of work. Work up to 63 is the training ground for the final enlightenment.

It is all grist to the mill. Life exposes you to all the energies that constitute humanity and gives you a feel for them all, even if you rejected some of them at the time for fear of rocking the boat. You therefore have the necessary resources at 63 to see yourself out. You may just have to dig deeper for some elements.

Infallibility is rare

The quality of your relationship to the knowledge you have collected decides how serious are the dangers that go with this final phase. Being too knowing closes you down to new information, new insight and the wisdom and support others would love to share with you.

It may be true that you have a superior working knowledge of the world or at least your bit of it. Even so nothing stands still and others have knowledge which can complement yours and keep you up to date. Networking with others is the fastest way to learn and you have good stuff to trade. It is as dangerous for you to assume that everything new is worthless as for the rest of us to assume that a lifetime's learning is obsolete. 95% of the time we may both be right! But the 5% lurking in there is pure gold, and we will be wise not to reject it.

Even so your knowledge is probably less solid than you pretend. More bluster than blunt fact. More bravado than brain. The more you protest your superiority the more questionable it probably is. The truly wise being seeks insight from all sources however unlikely.

Whether you really do know a lot or not, pretensions of infallibility are a great temptation and a great danger. If you don't want to look ridiculous, drop the saintly self-image. Trying to hold on to an outmoded self-image is always fatal. But it can be desperately hard to let go this pretension of wise and wonderful senior citizenship, because of the fear of appearing senile, and because others insist you keep up the act.

This blocks new learning and is a very poor exchange for real wisdom. It's also dishonest and lacks the integrity you should by now know better than deny. The **attachment** at this age (or whenever you feel you have colonised all the Seven Energies) is **infallibility**.

Infallibility is like habit and perfection taken to excess. It's all the most destructive patterns of the final career years rolled into one great blunder. Admitting you may not be perfect and may have just one more piece of information to acquire makes you human. Admitting there is something you don't know makes everything you do claim to know infinitely more credible. Infallibility just makes you a joke.

Ignorance is bliss

Ignorance is the beginning of wisdom, according to Socrates. With the well-rounded experience of life you have behind you, you are well-placed now to understand why you have done what you have done and how that 'why' has informed your whole life. But you also have the wisdom to recognise that this knowledge has no depth to it. It's a superficially meaningful explanation of your life's purpose, adequate indeed essential to that level of evolution, but it says little about the deeper meaning of life.

If you are at all honest with yourself, you will know that you don't really know anything, or not anything of any value. Unknowing is far more realistic a conclusion to have come to now. The task is more now to be with that sense of not knowing, and be comfortable with it. The more we learn about life, the less we seem to know. Every new fact raises whole universes of new unanswered questions. By all means share your understanding, and at the same time be open to correction and improvement.

Ignorance is bliss

This introduces what we need to be focused on for our last 20 or 30 years. We need to be constantly unfolding more layers of the tapestry of life, wrestling with what our contribution to that is and has been, furthering our understanding and vision of ourselves in relation to 'the all that there is,' (pan in Greek). There is so much uncharted territory to explore. Our job is to attempt to understand and share our understanding of the meaning of existence.

Divinity is common

This is no time for faint hearts! The **lesson** we have to learn now is our own **divinity**. It is why we went through all that preparation in the tough mill of career. It is why we took so many hard knocks and suffered so many humiliations. It is why we struggled, so we might appreciate the relative freedom of our final years.

Throughout especially the last 3 chapters a constantly repeated encouragement has been that you be yourself. As you gain a deeper relationship with that self, you may realise a closer connection with something inside that feels different to the outer reality you present. And the closer this connection becomes the more you may realise it is what is variously called your inner self, soul, divine spark. We touched on this briefly in the last chapter. Now as the pressures of the daily round recede it is time to make the development of this relationship with the divine your priority.

Your relationship with the divine creates a context in which you learn about your life purpose, the meaninglessness of much of our existence and ways in which you might respond even to this meaninglessness...and grow. At the same time you are a context yourself for a piece of the divine to manifest, for a spiritual being to engage in a human journey, for a 'droplet of divinity' to find its ocean.

It is our divinity and our readiness to own it that overcomes everything outer forces throw at us. David Spangler quoted in The Kingdom Within says uncompromisingly, "If you think something in your environment is keeping you from being, then you are operating under illusion - the illusion of your own powerlessness and lack of divinity." Outer forces are no match for your inner power once you tap it. And once you're working on your inner material you can make a valid contribution to any outer context you choose.

Owning your divinity is heresy in some quarters. And heresy is not a bad word for the rejection of convention. You are grasping a freedom which allows you to think the unthinkable. As long as you combine this with a complete absence of infallibility, you will not go far wrong, though nobody says heretics against society have it easy. Heretics just insist on selectively being themselves. Many would rather you didn't.

You know what's best and can decide what you will keep, what the priorities are now and where you will apply your energies. You will reinvent yourself in the way that works for you and enables you to make the most powerful contribution in your community. Many fear the rise of individualism as a diminishing of the collective community. Nothing but nothing could be further from the truth. Only by being you can you be of any use to you or anybody else. Individualism just means you are no longer run by the collective, that tiny minority of people who are not reknowned for being in touch with their divine inner selves!

As you investigate your own divinity you quickly discover that your divinity connects you to the divinity in everything and everyone else. "I am god and so are you," as Professor Charles Handy put it in his Radio 4 series in 1998. "Heaven," he went on to say, "is a gift, a place to recreate my life here on earth. <The task is> being god in our own time." This is not vainglorious or pretentious. Nor is it any sort of soft option or opt-out. The burden of selfhood, the weight of responsibility you undertake when you own the depths of human experience as a multiplex spirited mind can be heavy. Its weight can only be sustained by connecting with the whole of which we are a part.

Those who make this final stage of the journey of life exhibit a stillness, certainly compared to the wheelspin world of career. Career after all means an out of control gallop! But the stillness of this age is a vibrant stillness. The whole human bristles with energy even in their stillness. They may appear White to the eye, but that whiteness contains all the colours of the rainbow perfectly melded into the pure unity of White, the "colour" of this phase.

Rudolf Steiner's "How to know higher worlds", already reviewed in Chapter 8, is an excellent guide to the inner learning which is central to this phase (especially from Page 151 in the Anthroposophic Press edition, 1994). It sets out a series of meditative foci in harness with rigorous external action. There is throughout an injunction to replace illusion with full consciousness, impatience and irritation with compassion, balance and forbearance; to exchange discipline and self-mastery for cravings, harmony for discord.

Through Steiner's process, the student gradually sees a separate level of reality beyond normal vision including metaphysical qualities of shape, heat, light and colour and distinct images of the physical, etheric and soul bodies. This however feels like a concomitant of the deepening awareness of self rather than an end in itself.

Unappealing alternatives
Now if never before your spirit guides are most ready to respond to your invitation to join you and support you in your discovery of the deeper meaning of existence. The more inner work you have already done, as outlined in earlier chapters, the more this spiritual energy will seem to be working with you rather than unkindly challenging. Whereas earlier spirit maintains its activity however slovenly your own response, it now accepts defeat if you're not prepared to cooperate. When this happens the stillness becomes stagnation and the vibration either disintegrates or reverts to the nervous anxiety of human life deprived of meaning.

Without the meaningfulness spirit gives the over 60s many stay here absent-mindedly while spirit waits to see if they will get the message and while the human refuses to let go and move on.

If you sit in this particular waiting room, comfortable in your infallibility and steadfastly resisting the invitation to explore your divinity, an intense boredom sets in. It is that state of numbing desperation where all you are aware of is the loss of faculties, "mere oblivion, sans teeth, sans eyes, sans taste, sans everything."

Boredom is restlessness *without* being, without the connectedness that is at the root of the work to be done at this time. This restlessness is the precise opposite of the vibrant stillness that can permeate this phase of life. Boredom is another danger that comes with the assumption that it's all over and there is nothing more to learn or experience. Just because career is maybe less active, just because physically you may not be as vigorous as you were, just because remembering things may not be such a high priority, there is absolutely no reason or excuse for closing down. The decline of certain aspects of life clears the space for other priorities and foci. To give up now would be like doing the training and not applying for the job.

The **pitfall** at this time then is **boredom**. It's another way of trying to slide out of taking responsibility for your life. What you need is a new project, something to get engaged in, something to do and be. As noted in Chapter 9, few will completely retire from work at 63 or 73 or ever if it was work that fulfilled them, but in addition there is the work that is especially germane to this time. Check that you are not outstaying your welcome in the old work for fear of engaging with the new, deeper work. Avoiding boredom does not necessarily mean you are doing the right thing.

There are four qualities that might counter the risk of boredom and the stresses it sets up. These are the four qualities Roger Cooper said enabled him to survive 5 years of imprisonment and beatings in an Iranian gaol. (Interview on Radio 4, London: 1998) First was Optimism, the ability to see the most positive possible outcome. Humour was essential to counter the grimness of his circumstances. And he kept his Mind active by playing memory games: this will also have assisted him to stay optimistic as the mind decides whether the glass is half full or half empty. Cooper's fourth essential quality was Self-Esteem. It was vital for him not to allow the process to dehumanise him or make him feel anything less than good about himself. To feel and express love for oneself is the beginning of all relationship. Optimism, Humour, Memory/Mind and Self-Esteem spelt OHMS, a mnemonic that reminded him he was performing a significant service.

This cycle can just seem boring compared with earlier excitements. Outer concerns are likely to be less in evidence now, but the inner world expands. The meaning of life and existence may seem a bit tame after the heart-stopping glamour of high finance. Or so I'm told! But this is the recommended way of giving up everything so you can have it all! Now if never before you do your life's work.

At the end we will finally know ourselves

Starting afresh

A good place to start with this is to review where you have got to and what now are your priorities. This is relevant whatever age you are, having completed the earlier learning. First review the achievements of your life. What do you feel you did brilliantly? Of what are you most proud? What have you learnt and what have you contributed? What have others learnt from you and what do they see as your great strengths and qualities?

Take the time to acknowledge how far you have come, and appreciate yourself. From this you may begin to see what your growing edge is now, and where your priorities lie.

This exercise is called "Missing Persons". Which bits of you have got left behind? What are the gaps to be filled now? It makes most sense now, but can be used at any time.

VISION: Are work and the skills you apply a primary life builder or has it become a distraction from living your true vision of a whole, wholesome life? Where is the godhead in it? How can you re-integrate your essential self?

Your answers might indicate retraining or a more meditative approach.

LIFE CONTEXT: When you look inside yourself, is there perfect congruence with what others see when they look at you? And does this congruence extend to what you see when you look outside, into your market or workplace? Does your work bring you more or less in touch with your true inner self, creativity, your artistic side and feeling for nature?

Any uneasy feelings need taking into counselling.

LIFE PATTERNS: Review all the Seven Level phases and identify the age/stage you've reached. Where are you heading next? And what is the structure of your day/week/month? Is it balanced? Does it jar when you look out into where you work and then back into the inner you?

This sets you to drawing up new plans for every slot of time from hour to decade.

HEART ENERGY: Does your heart feel open? Do you love yourself, your fellow man, the planet? Is your labour where your love is? Have you released attachment? And where do you still sabotage yourself?

Your answers tell you the shadow work you need to do.

MIND: Is your mind at peace, serving your heart? Or is it panicking, stifling and controlling? Does it positively support or negatively undermine you?

Witness your mind at work and "accentuate the positive."

EMOTIONAL LIFE: How are your relationships? Squeezed out or prioritised? Have you learnt from them and separated the sheep from the smelly goats?! Who is served by your relationships? You at all? Is your timing right? Where do you hurt?

The job is Feel, Feel, Feel!

HEALTH: Are you well? Taking care of yourself? What is your body trying to tell you?

The answers are obvious as are the actions you need to take.

FULFILMENT: So what is most fulfilling and what are your next challenges? Is your being in balance with your doing?

Of course not! But what is most out of balance? That's the next priority. At the very least, this analysis may spare you from another danger at this time, which is being so out of touch with your own inadequacies, challenges and uncompleted tasks that you insist on interfering in everybody else's life. Motes and beams remember!

Foot-loose and befuddled

At every other phase of life, there is a context in which we both learn our lessons and are distracted from that learning. Now the **distraction** is that there is **no context**. There is no job or row of little pigs at the trough waiting to be fed. There are few expectations of us, and no routine to keep us on the straight and narrow, though we can create one of course. The lack of context conspires with the limitations we may see in ill health to set up worries about welfare.

Freedom is also the absence of constraints. It can be a wonderful release or it can worry you sick. It's the upset that portends the crisis of retirement in which we are reborn into wisdom. So while initially there is a loss of competence, assurance beckons once again. Death which follows this is one more transition. With death we complete what Ian Gordon-Brown used to call "the individuation away from the collective, owning more and more of ourselves and our personality."

Ian depicted the life process as analogous to the rising and setting sun. The unconscious sits before birth below the horizon in darkness. Life is about becoming conscious and then returning to embrace the unconscious again. As the sun rises the conscious self "annexes" the physical, emotional, mental and at high noon the intuitive dimensions of itself. Each Saturn return (every 28 years) the self is initiated into a new level of consciousness. 63 is the beginning of wisdom and 70 marks the point where the sun sets and the journey from there on is deeper and deeper into the unconscious.

Ian and The Centre for Transpersonal Psychology he founded with his partner Barbara Somers have been crucial influences in explaining the centuries old tradition of life cycles and the journey of the soul through consciousness.

Change, said Ian, is primarily an inner shift that manifests in the outer. A key idea is that there may be interludes while the self prepares for change. It may appear that nothing is happening at certain times. This is like a pause between in and out breath, a solstice (which literally means that the sun stands still). At these times forcing the pace is counter-productive. This agrees with Steiner who warned against delving too deep too soon, because forces would be released that would run riot with the inadequately prepared self. Change also can be frustrated, by apparent lack of control over our lives, endogenous childhood traumas and griefs, aberrant control patterns, depressions and the impact of the collective; and some people are collective lightning conductors.

Our later years are a new beginning, the time when we resolve the material we carried through our earlier lives. Inner life is more and more annexed and understood. Those still in the grip of outer concerns will find this preoccupation strange and even unhealthy. It is a whole new world. Our job in the early years is to engage with consciousness and personality in the outer material world. As we do, essential inner lessons are presented which we can choose to learn or reject. Accepting them will make more sense of the journey. But if we keep rejecting what life tries to teach us, we run the risk of missing the point of the later years.

There is therefore a time to be outwardly active and then a time to give priority to inner life. That creates balance, and that in turn makes for fulfilment. Each step along the way calls for a challenging, often painful and confusing LifeShift. The greatest shift of all is the one into the unconscious which presages death.

"At the end we will finally know ourselves." (Aristotle)

SUMMARY

● Life begins at 60! Now you have the freedom and the resources to make a new start.
● Ignorance is the beginning of wisdom.
● Inner spark or outer dark.
● The self-ful individual is not run by the collective, but contributes powerfully to it.
● Connecting with the divine relieves the burden of selfhood.

- The quality of the '60s is vibrant stillness.
- There is now an invitation to go deeper into the unconscious and allow your spirit guides to join you. The alternative is numbness.
- Especially now, it is time to review all seven dimensions of your life, acknowledge and appreciate your achievements and map out the future.
- Don't be a missing person.
- "At the end we will finally know ourselves."

LESSON to LEARN:
Divinity, connecting with the inner spark that in turn connects us to everything else

DISTRACTION TO TRANSFORM:
That there is **No Context**

PITFALL to AVOID:
Boredom

ATTACHMENT to RELEASE:
Infallibility, fighting learning and forward movement

EXERCISE

This is a lengthy exercise to round off the book.

The quality of your connection and presence with your inner self defines your relationship with the outer world and how you are perceived and recognised by it.

The solution to all the problems you face in life starts when you reconnect with your core being. From there, you open your heart to yourself and others. When you feel OK with being with yourself, warts and all, others feel OK with you. So the first part of this exercise is to identify what is in front of you now, what challenge you need to face next, whatever your age. Connect with your inner being and take this problem

there. Open your heart and be with it and with you in it.
Breathe.

Chances are some obstruction has presented itself. Some
aberrant behaviour, denial, negative mindset, myth or drama.
All the way through life, moving forward requires us to gently
release layers of obstruction. And this requires us to let go of
something the absence of which we cannot imagine, and to
enter a new state which is equally unimaginable.

It is hard to let go. It is hard to admit life is not working for
us, to admit we're stuck. It is hard to realise there is help at
hand if we only ask for it, and it is hard to actually ask for that
help, without 'poor-me' self-pity, other control dramas or acute
embarrassment. Then it is hard to understand that the only
way others can help is not by rescuing or gratuitously advising,
but by insisting you help yourself, with their help. It is also
hard to allow something into your life that looks even worse
than the pain you were already sufferring.

It gets worse! We have to give thanks for the darkness
because it's the only place to learn. We have to overcome
pride, shame, feeling stupid, shattered self-image; and find
the courage to face them. Finally it is hard to persevere when
there appears to be no early result at first, and in the end
there erupts the strangeness of a new you free of the pain you
were addicted to. It is hard.

Identify where you seem to be with this now and work
with that. This is the first step, to recognise where life is not
working for you, what is missing. **Accept** this is the case and
name it, eg "I can't face making all those new calls," or "I lack
joy." **Acknowledge** the predicament you face. **Listen** to it,
open to understand what it could be saying to you. And **Invite**
the quality you need to come through.

Vicious circles are the principal block to LifeShift.

There is for instance a vicious circle of financial pressure,
reinforcing sadness, undermining joy and closing the heart;
the coldness and anxiety this sets up drives money away and
aggravates the financial pressure, and off you go again! There
is also a virtuous circle which starts with inviting joy in to

counter the negatives and stop driving people away. Gradually the negative gives way to the positive.

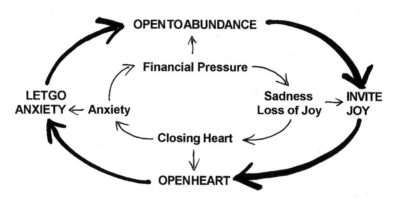

Try this with your current obstruction. And remember to be compassionate with yourself and to celebrate.

Now record here how you might bring more being into your life, whatever age you are, and review your Personal Priority Pages.

Keep taking whatever has spoken to you from this book into your daily life. Take it a step at a time and enjoy each step on this 'journey of a thousand miles.'

May your life continue to shift!

The journey of a thousand miles

FOLLOW THROUGH SUPPORT SERVICES

A unique feature of this book is that communication with the author is actually encouraged! There is a range of affordable services that support you as you create and implement your LifeShift Action Plan.

LifeShift with Andrew Ferguson

Thoroughly practical ways to create the life and work you want

● LifeShift miniWORKSHOPS
 - clarify your vision   - remove blocks to fulfilment
 - connect with others   - define your next steps

● 121 LifeShift Counselling
 -rebalancing work and life   -clear the decks for action!
 -explore possibilities and new more fulfilling directions

● LifeShift Counselling by Telephone
 -all the benefits of 121 Counselling
                          plus ad hoc access over the phone internationally

● Breakthrough, The LifeShift Network
 -pioneers of holistic enterprise in the UK
 -team up for mutual support and connections
 -stay in touch with Andrew Ferguson's ideas
 -relieve the isolation of ploughing your own furrow

Andrew Ferguson has been counselling and supporting people with their personal and career development since 1983. 8000 people have experienced his "life-changing, creative, practical, sensitive" skills. He is among the country's leading advisers on the new flexible ways of working, a Chartered Marketer and qualified Business and Therapeutic Counsellor, with first hand experience of how life and work interface.

For affordable on-going access to ideas and inspirations
Call 020 8347 7484   (GB+20 8347 7484)

Andrew Ferguson MA(Oxon), MCIM, MIBA, Dip C
Breakthrough Tele-Admin Centre
Wester Marchhead, Elgin, Moray, Scotland IV30 8XE
email: breakthr@dircon.co.uk
www.lifeshift.co.uk

LIFESHIFT

Chapter	Lesson to Learn
1. Living the rhythm of life	Vision
2. Change is the only constant	Re-evaluation
3. The Grounding Years (0-21) Catching up with yourself	Re-invention
4. The Breakout Years (21-28) Stepping into your vision	Passion
5. The Song-Bird Years (28-35) Creating a life that works	Determination
6. The Crucial Years (35-42) Positive mid-life	LifeShift
7. The Awareness Years (42-49) The meaning of life	Listening
8. The Visionary Years (49-56) Growing wise	Insight
9. The Wholeness Years (56-63) Finding balance and fulfilment	Integration
10. The Self-ful Years (63+) Human being	Divinity

SUMMARY

Distraction	Pitfall to Avoid	Attachment to Let Go
Busy-ness	Negativity	Shadow
Smokescreen	Procrastination	Aberration
		RED/ORANGE/YELLOW
Exams	Disappearing	Self-Image
		GREEN
Money	Disempowerment	Ego
		BLUE
Convention	Judgment	Security
		BLUE/INDIGO
Mortgage	Resistance	Stress
		INDIGO
Noise	Polarisation	Success
		VIOLET
Pension	Separation	Regret
		MAGENTA
Retirement	Perfection	Habit
		WHITE
No Context	Boredom	Infallibility

Resource Index: People & Places
Organisations and Contact Names

2000 X 2000 Initiative, London UK; **Kate Holloway**
Social Transformation; 020 8983 3816
a sense of place, Liverpool UK; **Ronnie Hughes**
Leading a more creative working life; 015 1734 3796
Academy of Natural Health, London UK; **Anja Dashwood**
Healthy Living, Holistic Massage Courses; 020 7720 9506
Acorn to Oak Foundation, London UK; **Pennie Quaile**
Self-Healing; 020 7794 6652
Action Life, London UK; **Kleo Green**
Person centred business counselling; 020 7790 7647
Alternative Voice, London UK; **Editor**
Promoting yourself to the media; 020 7222 1561
Alternatives, London UK; **Jane Turney**
Monday Talks by New Age leaders
www.alternatives.org.uk; 020 7287 6711
AMED (Assoc Management Education Devel), London UK
1600 Counsellors & management developers; 020 7235 3505
Angel Learning Experiences, London UK
Presenting leaders such as Shakti Gawain; 0800 973203
Archway Bookstore/Holistic Centre, East Sussex UK;
Rachel Lewis; Booksellers
Association Humanistic Psychology, London UK
Accrediting body & Educational Charity; 034 5078 506
Atlow Mill Centre, Derbyshire UK
Residential Conference/Course Centre; 013 3537 0494
Barchester, Wilts UK; **Geoff Griffiths**
Ethical Financial Advisers; info@)barchestergreen.co.uk
017 2233 1241
Bells Associates, Devon UK; **Peter Campbell**
Holistic Publishing; 101752.2142@compuserve.com
017 6958 0899
Blind Business Association, Middx UK
Blind business organisation
rhoda.carratt@btinternet.com; 020 8427 3052
Body & Soul, Edinburgh Scotland
Booksellers; 013 1226 3066
Books for a Change, London UK
Booksellers; 020 7836 2315
Bowden House, Middx UK; **Dr Brenda Davies**
Healing your relationship with the world; 020 8966 7000

Brainpool, Edinburgh Scotland; **Isabel Willshaw**
Lively gatherings; 013 1229 1576
Brainwave; London UK; **Mike Considine**
Festivals of Holistic Living; 020 8677 8000
Breakthrough LifeShift Network, London UK; **Andrew Ferguson**
On-going support for LifeShifters
www.lifeshift.co.uk; 020 8347 7484
Briarpatch, California USA; **Roger Pritchard**
The original holistic enterprise network; 001 510 527 5604
Brightlife Institute, Isle of Man UK
Personal Development Centre
brightlife@enterprise.net; 016 2488 0318
British Association for Counselling, Warks UK
Directory of counsellors, some holistic; 017 8855 0899
Business by Design; Middx UK; **Cathy Lasher**
Co-Active Coaching; cathy@925.com; 020 8952 7522
Business Connexions, France; **Brigitte Cassigneul**
Teleworking group; 0033 (1) 46 96 09 95
Business for Social Responsibility, California USA
Green business association; 001 415 865 2500
Business in the Community, London UK
Umbrella Org. socially responsible companies; 020 7224 1600
Business Innovations Research, Cornwall UK; **John Wilson;**
The Escape Kit; 017 3679 7061
Business Inspirations, Worcs UK; **Andy Denne**
Holistic Corporate Training & Development; 016 8454 1542
Business Link, UK
Business Advice; 034 5567 765
Cahoots, Manchester UK
Holistic connections; 0161225 2410
CCAM (Council Complementary/Alternative Medicine), London UK
Access to holistic practitioners
Centre for Alternative Technology, Powys Wales; **Rachel Banks**
Inspiration for sustainable lifestylers
cat@catinfo.demon.co.uk; 016 5470 2400
Centre for Human Ecology, Edinburgh Scotland
Community Empowerment Think-Tank; 013 1650 3470
Centre for Mens Development, London UK; **Mike Fisher**
Holistic Mens Development; 020 7686 1293
Centre for Social Development, West Sussex UK; **Anita Charton**
Steiner based courses; 013 4281 0221
Centre for Tomorrows Company, London UK; **Mark Goyder**
Shaping big business; ctomco@ctomco.demon.co.uk;
020 7930 5150

Changes Bookshop, London UK
Booksellers; 020 7328 5161
Coach U, UK; **Elizabeth Rowlands**
Coaching list (£125-300/month); 012 7381 8632
College of Holistic Medicine, Glasgow Scotland; **Ron Rieck**
Holistic Therapeutic Training; 014 1554 5808
College of Psychic Studies, London UK; **Administrator**
Personal Growth; www.psychic-studies.org.uk; 020 7589 3292
Compendium, London UK
Booksellers; 020 7485 8944
Complementary Business Association, Hants UK; **Paul Baker**
Holistic Enterprise Association; 012 0229 7301
Conference Cassettes, Glos UK; **Philip Royall**
Mail order & conference tapes
confcass@licone.net; 014 5376 6411
Cooperative Bank, Manchester UK
Career Development Loans & Banking services; 034 5212 212
Cortijo Romero, Spain
Holistic Holiday Centre: Spain; GB 014 9478 2720
Cranfield Network European HR Mgmt, Beds UK; **Jos van Ommeren**
Progressive business group; m.mills@cranfield; 012 3475 1122
Creating Your Life Centre, Herts UK; **Bryan Andrews**
Personal development/Creative Visualisation
BryanCYL@aol.com; 014 3871 8602
Creative Alternatives to Violence, UK; **Trish Dickinson**
Peace-making; 012 1454 6231
Creative Dream Company, London UK; **Brian Davis**
Creative Development; credo@dial.pipex.com; 020 7288 6141
Creative Leadership Ltd, Wilts UK; **Chuck Spezzano**
Psychology of Vision
106417.3713@compuserve.com; 013 8082 8394
Croydon Business School, Surrey UK; **Lynne Sedgmore**
Holistic business thinking; 020 8686 5700
Dean Clough, West Yorks UK; **Sir Ernest Hall**
Centre for Arts, Education, Enterprise
Sir Ernest Hall@Dean.Clough.com; 014 2225 0250
Debtors Anonymous, UK
Introductory events for debtors only; 020 8960 9606
Dillons UK; Booksellers: National Network
Earth Stewards, Washington USA
Community in action; 001 206 842 7986
Emerson College, Sussex UK; **Belinda Hammond**
Steiner/Waldorf Training; www.emerson.org.uk; 013 4282 2238
Essentials for Health, London UK; **Gill Tree**

School of Massage & Aromatherapy
essentials.forhealth@virgin.net 020 8556 8155
Farnham Holistic Centre, Surrey UK; **Arvid Willen**
Healthy living; 012 5273 4445
Federation of Small Businesses, Lancs UK
Businesses Services; 012 5372 0911
Findhorn Foundation, Moray Scotland
Personal and spiritual development
spd@findhorn.org; 013 0969 0311
First Impressions, Cambs UK; **Patrick Halpin**
Self-employed network; 012 2381 3121
Flint House, East Sussex, UK; **Caroline Dorling**
Course Centre; 012 7347 3388
Foundation, Hereford UK; **Francis Macleod**
Personal Leadership & Team Development; 014 3226 4777
Four Winds Centre, Surrey UK
Personal development; 012 5125 3990
Freelance Centre, London UK; **Roy Sheppard**
Support for creative enterprises
100044.1602@compuserve.com; 020 7820 8511
Freenet, London UK; **Arieh Kronenberg**
Artists Support Group; 020 8374 8353
Friends of the Earth, London UK
Environmental pressure group; 020 7490 1555
Gaunts House, Dorset UK
Personal development; 012 0284 1522
Gekko Design Studio, London UK; **Graham Whatley**
Product Graphic Environmental Design; 020 7701 5159
Golden Bough, Surrey UK
Book and other sales; 020 8667 1944
Grimstone Manor, Devon UK
Personal development; 018 2285 4358
H & L Balen & Co., Worcs UK; **David Balen**
Insurance Brokerage & Drumming; 016 8489 3006
Hampshire TEC, HantsUK; **Venika Kingsland**
Enterprise support; 013 2922 6155
Hatchards, UK; Booksellers
Healing House, Dublin Ireland; **John Kenny**
Healthy Living
Heart at Work, London UK; **Nick Williams**
Courses on work, money, abundance
hello@heartatwork.net; 020 7287 6711
Henley Centre, London UK; Research into holistic lifestyles
future@hencenf.co.uk; 020 7955 1800

Home Business Alliance, Cambs UK; **Len Tondel**
Micro-business club with holistic leanings; 019 4546 3303
Human Potential Research Group, Surrey UK, **Dr Josie Gregory**
Personal & professional development
J.Gregory@surrey.ac.uk; 014 8325 9760
Humana International plc, London UK; **Caroline Steele**
020 7872 9044
ImagiNation, Scotland; **Ian Kellas**
Self-Employed network; 013 1661 7886
Independent on Sunday, London UK; **Kate Hilpern**
Full of interesting case histories; 020 7293 2370
Industrial Society, London UK
Early promoters of people centred business; 020 7479 1000
Inner Bookshop, Oxon UK; Booksellers; 018 6524 5301
Insight Seminars, London UK; **Stacey Medalyer**
Personal Development
london@insight-seminars.org; 020 7706 2021
Institute of Business Advisers, Yorks UK; **Brian Dunsby**
Assoc. professional SME advisers/counsellors
www.iba.org.uk; 014 2387 9208
Institute of Creativity (ex Actors Institute), London UK
Ann Woodhead; Successor to the famous Mastery
fractals@netmatters.co.uk; 011 8977 6130
Institute of Noetic Sciences, California USA
Changing paradigms; 001 415 331 5650
Institute of Personnel/Development, London UK
Professional association for human resource; 020 8971 9000
Iomlanu Centre, Ireland; **Dolores Whelan**
Restaurant, bookshop, courses; 00353 (0)42 32804
Kinharvie House, Scotland; **Rachel Reekie**
Personal & Professional Development
KinharvieH@aol.com; 013 8785 0433
Lantern Consulting Group UK, London UK; **Roy Maunder**
Intuitive awareness; Lantern@compuserve.com; 020 7385 4401
Leadership 21, Oxon UK; **Francis Standish**
Enterprise Development; 012 3553 5326
Lifeforce, Iceland; **Geir Vilhjalmsson**
Spiritual development
Lifeworks, London UK; **Darren Linton**
Holistic LifeTransformation; 012 4546 0057
Lios Dana, Co Kerry Ireland; **Michael Travers**
Retreat & Development Facility; GB 020 8340 4321
Little Grove, Bucks UK; **Alan Dale**
Personal Development Centre; 014 9478 2720

LiveWIRE, UK; Advice for young business people;019 1261 5584
Living Magically, Cumbria UK; **Gill Edwards**
  Personal-spiritual development
  www.livingmagically.co.uk; 015 3943 1943
Local Enterprise Agencies, UK
  Contact for business help, sometimes holistic; 012 3435 4055
Local Enterprise Agencies, Scotland
  Contact for business help, sometimes holistic, 012 3645 2777
Local Enterprise Companies, Scotland
  Contact for business help, sometimes holistic; 014 1248 2700
London Business Centres, London UK
  Easy access business premises (14 sq m +); 020 8377 1154
London Business School, London UK
  Executive Programmes; 020 7262 5050
Lower Shaw Farm, Wilts UK
  Courses & workshops (wide range); 017 9377 1080
Man Woman Centre, Oxon UK; **Jane Duncan**
  Personal Development Trainings; 018 6989 603
martinleith.com, London UK; **Martin Leith**
  Innovation; www.martinleith.com; 078 0877 3713
Maynard Leigh Associates, London UK; **Michael Maynard**
  The actor at work; 020 7385 2588
McKenna Breen Ltd, London UK; **Paul McKenna**
  NLP, personal development, hypnosis
  happening@mckenna-breen.com; 020 7704 6604
Message Company, New Mexico USA
  International conferences on spirit in business
  message@nets.com; 001 505 474 0998
Millenium Exchange, London UK; **Dave Sharman**
  Alternative Strategies where time begins; 020 8305 2196
Monkton Wyid Court, Dorset UK; **Michael Jeffries**
  Personal development; 012 9756 0342
Motley Fool, UK; **David Berger**
  Investment Guide; motleyfool.investment
Muswell Hill Bookshop, London UK; Booksellers; 020 8444 7588
National Association of Volunteer Bureaux Birmingham UK
  Matching volunteers to charitable organisations; 012 1633 4555
Neals Yard Agency, London UK; **Ulrike Speyer**
  Key Personal Development Publication; 07000 783703
Network for Social Change, London UK; **Vanessa Adams**
  Putting money to good use
Network Ireland, Co Clare Ireland; **Ruth Marshall**
  Access to holistic enterprises in Ireland; 00353 61 921642

New Academy of Business, Bristol UK; **Gill Coleman**
Business transformation
www.new-academy.ac.uk; 011 7925 2006
New Approaches to Cancer, Surrey UK; **Colin Ryder Richardson**
Ideas on working with awareness; 019 3287 9882
New Economic Social Network, London UK; **Martin Summers**
Business in the community
New Economics Foundation, London UK; **Ed Mayo**
Focal point for sustainable thinking
info@neweconomics.org; 020 7407 7447
New Learning Centre, London UK; **Noel Janis Norton**
Courses for families, parents and children; 020 7794 0321
New Life Promotions Ltd., London UK; **Graham Wilson**
Mind Body Spirit Exhibitions: UK & Australia; 020 7938 3788
New Ways to Work, London UK
Advice on flexible working; 020 7226 4026
Office Promotion pour Travail à Domicile, France, **A Benoit**
Teleworking advice; 0033 30 91 49 12
Open Centre, London UK; **Mike Wibberley**
Body-centred psychotherapy; 020 7251 1504
Open Centres, Wilts UK; **Cara Voelcker**
Lists 153 spiritual centres + 61 other contacts; 012 4972 0202
Open University, Beds UK
LifeShift requires retraining; 019 0885 8585
Openings, UK; **Administrator**
Cooperative of counsellors & psychotherapists; 012 2544 5013
Ownbase, Cheshire UK; **John Coleman-Smith**
Homeworkers Club; www.ownbase.org.uk
Oxford Centre Environment Ethics Society, Oxon UK
Conferences: sustainable economics
ocees@mansfield.oxford.ac.uk 018 6527 0886
Oxford Psychologists Press Ltd., Oxon UK
Myers-Briggs Type Indicator®
orders@opp.co.uk; 018 6551 0203
Passport, London UK; **Janie Wilson**
Creating a personal life and career passport
janie@passport.co.uk; 020 7228 1982
Pellin Institute, Italy; Holidays: Italy; GB 020 7720 4499
Pen Rhiw, Pembroke Wales; **Lis & Steve**
RetreatCentre; penrhiw@stdavids.co.uk; 014 3772 1821
Personal Development Show, Surrey UK; **David Jones**
Career Development Exhibition
www.personalshow.co.uk; 020 8332 0044

Personal Finance Educational Services, Oxon UK; **Jean Hicks**
Solution Focused Financial Coaching
jeanhicks.pfes@virgin.net; 018 6524 4156

Personal Strengths Publishing (UK) Ltd., Lincs UK; **Simon Gallon**
Relationship training
PSP4SDl@compuserve.com; 017 8076 4762

Phoenix Community Stores Ltd., Moray Scotland; **David Hoyle**
Best selection of holistic books anywhere
dhoyle@findhorn.org; 013 0969 0933

Positive Living Groups, London UK; **Colin Underwood**
National programme of meetings; 020 8575 6480

Praxis, Beds UK; **Jacquie Drake**
Responsible self-management
m.mills@cranfield; 012 3475 1122

Princes Scottish Youth Business Trust, Glasgow Scotland
Courses and grants for young entrepreneurs; 014 1248 4999

Princes Youth Business Trust, London UK
Courses and grants for young entrepreneurs; 080 0842 842

Prosperity Club, London UK; **Shaun De Warren**; Wealth creation

Prosperity Press, Queensland Australia
Enterprise Development Texts; 0061 (0)7 266 7570

Rainbow Centre, Co. Down N Ireland; **Helen Grant Johnson**
Personal Development Centre

Re-Vision, London UK; **Chris Robertson**
Counselling courses - short & long
revision@dial.pipex.com; 020 8357 8881

Redfield Community, Bucks UK; **Simon Pratt**
Courses, straw bales building
Redfield_Community@compuserve; 012 9671 4983

Relaxation Centre of Queensland, Queensland Australia
Lionel Fifield
Living lightly and self-responsibly; 0061 (0)7 3854 1986

Renaissance Business Associate, Idaho USA
Soul in business; staff@rbai.com; 001 208 345 4234

Richard Barrett & Associates LLC, NC USA; **Richard Barrett**
Transforming the Business Soul
richard@corptools.com; 001 828 452 5050

Rivendell Centre Healing/Creativity, Essex UK; **Stephanie & Nick**
Workshops, courses & classes; 012 7737 5797

Runnings Park, Worcs UK; **Tony Neate**
Centre for Health, Healing & Self-Development; 016 8457 3868

Sailing with Spirit, Northampton UK; **Keith Beasley**
Local connections; tigger@gn.apc.org; 013 2734 2566

School for Social Entrepreneurs, London UK; **David Stockley**
Business with a purpose
School of Business & Economic Studies, Leeds UK
Prof. Peter Nolan; Future of Work ESRC Project; 011 3233 2614
Schumacher Society, Devon UK; **Bridget Baker**
Holding the vision for 'Small is Beautiful'; 012 3742 93
Scientific & Medical Network, Fife Scotland; **David Lorimer**
Newsletter & meetings; 013 3334 0492
Scottish Enterprise, Scotland
Contact point for business help, sometimes holistic;
014 1248 2700
Scottish Enterprise Foundation, Stirling Scotland; **Frank Martin**
Holistic Business Training at Stirling University; 017 8646 7347
Scottish Telecottage Association, Scotland; **Roy Guthrie**
Advice for teleworkers; 013 2466 4164
Searle, London UK; **Joanne Searle**
Work, money and psychotherapy
m.shelley@virgin.net; 020 8802 0281
Self-Esteem Company, London UK; **Patricia Cleghorn**
Value yourself; 020 8579 0435
Self-Esteem Network, London UK; **Titus Alexander**
Self-esteem activists group
titus.alexander@MCRI.poptel.org.uk; 020 8521 6977
Shakespeare Workshop, London UK; **Tony Butler**
Human awareness - the reality of imagination; 020 8444 5132
Skyros/Atsitsa, London UK; **Yannis Andricopoulos**
Holidays: "2 week celebration of life"
skyros@easynet.co.uk; 020 7267 4424
Social Venture Network Europe, London UK; **Administrator**
Network of socially/green responsible businesses
svneurope@freedom2surf.co.uk; 020 7881 9007
Social Venture Network Europe, Amsterdam ZO Netherlands
Dina Buelow
Business transformation in Europe; 0031 206 971129
Society for Effective Affective Learning, UK; **Robert Gillan**
Supports self-empowering learning
seal@soceal.demon.co.uk; 012 2546 624
Sonairte: National Ecology Centre, CoMeath Ireland; **Anna Doran**
Ecology in action, ideas for sustainable living
00353 (0)41 27572
Spectrum, London UK; Psychotherapeutic Centre; 020 8341 2277
Spice UK, Manchester UK; **Dave Smith**
High spirited adventure; www.spiceuk.com; 016 1872 2213

Spirit in Action, NSW Australia, **Patrick Bradbery**
Spirituality, Leadership & Management Conference
sjoyce@csu.edu.au; 0061 2 6338 4254
Spiritual Vision at Work, Suffolk UK; **Ansal Trafford**
Business Mentor & Creative Adviser; 014 7372 1286
Springboard, Glos UK; **Jenny Daisley**
International personal development programme
www.springboardconsultancy.com; 014 5387 8540
Springfield Centre, East Sussex UK; **Jen Popkin**
Business with spirit; 014 2442 8470
St Katherines Health Club, London UK
Health Club; mahbohc@dircon.co.uk; 020 7264 5298
St Luke's, London UK
Futuristic Promotional Agency; 020 7380 8888
Stuart Brown & Associates, London UK; **Dominic Stuart**
Ethical Financial Advisors; helmbob@aol.com; 020 7372 5000
Telecottage Association, Warks UK; **Alan Denby**
Teleworking information
Training & Enterprise Councils UK
Contact point for training etc, sometimes holistic
011 4259 4776
Triodos Bank, Bristol UK; **Glen Saunders**
Socially responsible banking; www.triodos.co.uk; 011 7973 9339
Turning Point 2000, Oxon UK; **James Robertson**
Central focus point for new thinking
robertson@tp2000.demon.co.uk; 014 9165 2346
University of Bath School of Management, UK; **Robert Craven**
The manager as jazzman; 012 2582 6902
University of Life, London UK; **Teresa Turner**
Holistic training; 020 8671 7644
URBED Urban/Economic Devel Group, London UK; **Nicholas Falk**
Urban Regeneration/Economic Development
urbed@urbed.co.uk; 020 7436 8050
Vegi Ventures, Norfolk UK; **Nigel Walker**
Holidays UK & Overseas; 017 6075 5888
Venture Capital Report, Oxon UK
Guide to private finance; 018 6578 4411
Visioform, Germany; **Dr Ulla Sebastian**
Giving form to your vision
ulla@visioform.com; 0049 23 07 73545
Waterstones, UK; Booksellers: National Network
Watkins Books, London UK; Booksellers; 020 7836 6700
Win Win Group, New Zealand; **Hilary Jackson**
Trading Insights; 0064 9 307 0888

Wisborough, West Sussex UK; **Chrissie McGinn**
Work, life & relationships; 019 0374 2731
Women in Enterprise, Yorks UK; Staying a woman in business
Womens Enterprise Network, London UK; **Barbara Petersen**
Staying a woman in business; 020 7792 2607
Womens Environmental Network, London UK; **Diana Cripps**
Sustainable Lifestyle pioneering; 020 7354 8823
Working Vision, Hants UK; **Alan Heeks**
Natural growth
working_vision@compuserve.com; 019 6285 2900
World Business Academy, USA; Big companies trying to change
wba@together.org; 001 202 783 3213
World of Difference, London UK; **Eniko Kortvelyessy**
The Ecology Shop; 020 7387 2363
Wrekin Trust, Surrey UK; **Janice Dolley**
Education in relation to spiritual evolution
dolley@cwcom.net; 017 3777 9386

Resource Index: Books & Publications
Author, Title & Publisher

Arewa, Caroline: Opening to Spirit
The chakras explained, Thorson
Bach, Richard: Illusions
Adventures of a Reluctant Messiah, Pan
Bach, Richard: Jonathan Livingstone Seagull
Fable of LifeShift, Pan
Berne, Eric: Games People Play
Changed *my* l ife!, Penguin
Blanchard, Kenneth& Spencer Johnson: The One Minute Manager
Person-centred management, Fontana
Bloom, William: First Steps
Introduction to Spiritual Practice, Findhorn Press
Bloom, William: Meditation in a Changing World
Recommended guide, Gothic Image
Boldt, Lawrence: How to Find the Work You Love, Arkana
Button, John & William Bloom (Editors): The Seeker's Guide
New Age Resource Book, Aquarian
Caddy, Eileen: Flight into Freedom
Autobiography of a Visionary, Element
Caddy, Eileen: Opening Doors Within
Daily reminder to listen, Findhorn Publications

Ferguson, Marilyn: The Aquarian Conspiracy
Proof business leaders know this stuff, Paladin
Ferrucci, Piero: What We May Be
Visions and Techniques of Psychosynthesis, Turnstone Press
Fynn: Mister God, This Is Anna
Out of the mouths, Fountain/Harper Collins
Gibran, Kahlil: The Prophet
70 year old prose poem of ineffable beauty, Heinemann
Goyder, Mark: Living Tomorrowa Company
Shaping big business, Gower
Handy, Charles: Future of Work
Where we're headed, Blackwell
Handy, Charles: The Age of Unreason
More on the changing corporate world, Hutchinson
Handy, Charles: The Empty Raincoat
Encouragement to be personally present, Arrow
Harland, Maddie: Healthy Business
Holistic enterprise manual (also permaculture), Hyden House Ltd
Hawken, Paul: The Ecology of Commerce
The US scene, Phoenix
Heider, John: The Tao of Leadership
Brilliant melding of ancient and modern, Humanics
Heller, Joseph: Catch 22
Organisational mayhem, Vintage
Hingston, Peter: The Greatest Little Business Book
Nitty gritty aspects of small business, Hingston
Jackson, Tom: The Perfect CV
Excellent guide to defining your career, Piatkus
Jampolsky, Gerry: Love Is Letting Go of Fear
Change your mindset, Celestial Arts
Jeffers, Susan: Feel The Fear and Do It Anyway
Taking risks, Arrow
Jones, Judy & Polly Ghazi: Getting a Life (Downshifting)
LifeShift with money, Hodder & Stoughton
Jung, CG: Memories, Dreams, Reflections
Introducing the master, Flamingo
Krystal, Phyllis: Cutting The Ties That Bind Us
Freedom from the past, Samuel Weiser
Leadbetter, CW: The Chakras
1929 guide to spiritual realities, Theosophical Publishing House
Lievegoed, Bernard: Phases
Spiritual Rhythms of Adult Life, Rudolf Steiner Press
Lulic, Margaret: Who We Could Be At Work
Case stories, Butterworth-Heinemann

Russell, Peter: The White Hole in Time
Quantum Shift Time, Aquarian
Saint Exupery, Antoine De: The Little Prince
Fable appreciating what we have, Mammothl Heinemann
Sale, Charles: The Specialist
The first marketing book, Putnam
Satir, Virginia: The New Peoplemaking
Daily Temperature Reading: source, Science & Behaviour Books
Schumacher, Christian: To Live and Work
Personal & organisational redesign, WSL
Semler, Ricardo: Maverick
The story of a brave experiment, Arrow/Warner books
Settelen, Peter: Just Talk To Me
Presentation as Self-Development, Harper Collins
Shaffer, Carolyn & K Anundsen: Creating Community Anywhere
Beyond all the agonising - just do it! Inspiring, Tarcher/Perigee
Sheehy, Gail: Pathfinders
Source book on the journey through life, Bantam
Skynner, Robin & John Cleese: Life and How to Survive it
Personal reappraisal of life's purpose, Vermilion
Sleigh, Julian: 13 to 19 - Discovering The Light
Starting young, Floris
Spezzano, Chuck: The Enlightenment Book
Psychology of Vision, Rider
Steiner, Rudolf: How to Know Higher Worlds
See Chapter 8, Anthroposophic Press
Toffler, Alvin: Future Shock & The Third Wave
Saw it coming, Pan
Townsend, Robert: Up The Organisation
The best book on management, Coronet
Walker, Alex (Editor): The Kingdom Within
Understanding the inner life, Findhorn Publications
Wildman, Paul & Keith Banks: Creating Small Business Achievement – Holistic small business, Prosperity Press
Williams, Margery: The Velveteen Rabbit
Fable of reviewing values, Mammoth
Williams, Nick: The Work We Were Born To Do
Self-help: vision finding, Element Books